T0357460

UNDISRUPTED

UNDISRUPTED

BONUS INSIDE:
Find Your **Future**
Readiness Score

LEADERSHIP ESSENTIALS
ON BUSINESS TRANSFORMATION,
PROFITABILITY, AND FUTURE READINESS

IAN KHAN

WILEY

For general information on our other products and services or for technical support, please contact our Customer Care Department within the United States at (800) 762-2974, outside the United States at (317) 572-3993 or fax (317) 572-4002.

Wiley also publishes its books in a variety of electronic formats. Some content that appears in print may not be available in electronic formats. For more information about Wiley products, visit our web site at www.wiley.com.

Library of Congress Cataloging-in-Publication Data is available:

ISBN: 9781394215829 (cloth)
ISBN: 9781394215843 (ePub)
ISBN: 9781394215850 (ePDF)

Cover Design: Wiley
Cover Image: © flyalone/Adobe Stock, © juliiapanukoffa/Adobe Stock

SKY10093730_121824

To

My Parents, wife and kids for inspiring me to be the best

Contents

Introduction

Welcome to a journey that's as much yours as it is mine. Over the past twenty years, my fascination with future readiness has blossomed, fueled by countless hours spent across various industries and domains. Through these experiences, I've noticed a troubling trend: technology hype often dictates organizational decisions. Ten years ago, it was big data; then came analytics, blockchain, and now we find ourselves in the era of artificial intelligence. This unrelenting hype, driven by tech companies, has left many businesses struggling to grasp what true future readiness means.

Let's be clear—relying solely on technology as the solution to your organization's challenges is a misguided approach. Success is about much more than just the latest tech. It's about people, governance, leadership, and a myriad of other factors. For decades, futurists have crafted methodologies such as the Delphi method, horizon scanning, road maps, and backcasting to help foresee and shape the future. These tools are incredible for those of us who seek to steer our organizations in the right direction.

But here's the challenge: we lack a simple, universal metric to gauge future readiness. Think about the Net Promoter Score (NPS) and how it effortlessly measures customer satisfaction. This simplicity inspired me to question why we don't have a similar metric for future readiness.

This curiosity led me to develop the Future Readiness Score. It's a tool designed to help you envision and prepare your organization for the future without becoming overly narrow through the lens of technology, dismissing other crucial disciplines. Over the past few years, my team and I have dived deep into research, examining various business areas, metrics, case studies, and strategies that drive success. We consulted with foresight experts and collaborated with cohorts from esteemed institutions such as the University of Alberta and Arizona State University to refine this concept.

Creating the algorithm for the Future Readiness Score was challenging, especially in determining the parameters that would define the score. Today, this score serves as a key performance indicator (KPI) that you can use to assess your organization's trajectory across seven critical business areas. While there are other methodologies and scores out there, the Future Readiness Score offers a unique, comprehensive assessment.

As we embark on this book, think of it as the starting point of your journey toward understanding and enhancing your organization's growth and future. The criteria for measuring future readiness will inevitably evolve as the world changes. That's why it's crucial to reassess your Future Readiness Score annually, ensuring you stay aligned with shifting dynamics and remain future-ready.

As someone deeply invested in future readiness, I am humbled and inspired by the boundless potential organizations have to drive positive change. Whether you're in technology, manufacturing, sustainability, entertainment, health care, public services, or any other sector, pursuing future readiness should be a paramount goal.

Together, let's explore this fascinating landscape. Let's equip ourselves with the knowledge, tools, and mindset needed to thrive in an ever-changing world. Welcome to the journey of becoming future-ready.

Let's embark on this journey together, transforming challenges into opportunities and future readiness into a reality.

PART

How Future Ready Are You?

Now you can find out your level of future readiness through the Future Readiness Score (FRS). Whether you are an individual or an organization, the metric will provide you with guidance on

Your Current Level of Future Readiness based on 47 Data Points

Recommendations on How to Improve Your Ratings

Take the Future Readiness Score assessment by visiting

www.iankhan.com/frs

or scan the QR Code

1

Becoming Undisrupted

Undisrupted people and organizations are not surprised or shocked when the world around them changes. They expect change, they have prepared for it, and they know what else is coming. Disruption happens to those who least expect change. You must choose being the Undisrupted.

—Ian Khan

AT THE VERY core of every human lies a primal instinct: the need to survive. This deeply embedded urge, coded in our DNA, has fueled both the evolution and the disruption of human civilization throughout history. The drive to survive is more than just a biological imperative; it's a force that molds societies, technologies, economies, and cultures. It propels human innovation while also igniting conflict, pushing humanity toward both remarkable progress and chaotic turmoil. We know this by many names including *resilience, grit,* or, in this book, *Undisrupted.*

From the moment our ancestors picked up the first stone tool, the need to survive has driven technological innovation. Imagine early humans discovering fire—a game-changer that provided warmth, protection, and a way to cook food. Yuval Noah Harari, in his groundbreaking book *Sapiens,* describes this as the cognitive revolution—a leap that allowed *Homo sapiens* to not only survive but dominate.[1] Fast-forward to the Agricultural Revolution, a period that turned nomadic tribes into settled communities, birthing complex societies and bustling trade networks. This shift wasn't just about growing crops; it was a monumental disruption that led to the rise of cities and empires.

Yet, the survival instinct has a darker side. The quest for resources has sparked countless conflicts. Wars, colonization, and exploitation are all fueled by the desire to control food, land, and power. Jared Diamond, in *Guns, Germs, and Steel*, illustrates how competition for resources and territorial expansion often leads to societal collapse.[2] Fear and the urge for dominance have driven humanity into cycles of conquest and resistance, forever altering the fabric of societies.

The Industrial Revolution was another leap driven by the need to improve survival odds through efficiency and growth. It transformed societies but also disrupted them, leading to urbanization, environmental degradation, and significant social upheaval. The Digital Revolution, society's latest chapter, has reshaped our lives in unimaginable ways, offering connectivity and knowledge while challenging our privacy, security, and mental well-being. As Stephen Hawking once noted, "We are all now connected by the Internet, like neurons in a giant brain," highlighting the profound but disruptive impact of digital technologies.[3]

On a global scale, the survival instinct is at the heart of our response to climate change. This crisis, born from industrial growth, threatens our very existence. Yet, it is this same survival drive that fuels innovations in renewable energy and global efforts such as the Paris Accord. Humanity's fight against climate change is a testament to our instinct to endure and adapt.

Survival instincts shape our daily lives, influencing everything from career choices to social interactions. They drive us toward security and prosperity, spurring educational achievements and economic development. However, they also breed consumerism, inequality, and social isolation. Culturally, survival has crafted our traditions and identities, but globalization threatens to homogenize these rich tapestries, leading to a loss of cultural diversity.

Understanding the role of the survival instinct is crucial for navigating today's disruptions. By recognizing both its positive and negative impacts, we can strive for a balance that fosters progress while mitigating conflict and ensuring sustainable survival. Our journey as a species has always been about adapting and evolving, and our future will be shaped by how well we harness this primal drive for the greater good.

This book can be used by a business of any size, or an organization engaged in any activity, to understand the rules, laws, and phenomena that govern the state of being undisrupted. A lot is happening in our world on a daily basis, and it is hard to keep track of everything. Organizations of all sizes are inundated with different types of data and our minds with distractions such as digital content, noise, visuals, and information we may not necessarily be seeking. This is taking a toll on our preparedness for the future.

This book opens with the idea that to understand how to stay *undisrupted*, you must know more about disruption, from the early days of human developments and inventions that shaped our society, culture, and progress to current-day technological advances. The idea of future readiness and becoming *undisrupted* is at the core of our identities as humans. That is what defines us and sets us apart from other living organisms, including other mammals, trees, and bacteria. Humans are programmed to fight for survival, to communicate, to build, and to thrive.

This book is not just the story of how earlier generations innovated but how to succeed and thrive using the Undisrupted mindset, future readiness as a strategy, and the Future Readiness Score as a tool. We are beginning with the end in mind, for you to think of yourself as an undisruptable entity. Let us then trace our steps back to where and how to begin.

Take the Future Readiness Score at www.iankhan.com/frs or scan the QR Code

2

Early Human Disruptions

Eureka!

—Archimedes

What ARE the origins of disruption and what is the relation between disruption, innovation, and progress? To embrace the final idea of being "Undisrupted," I strongly believe we need to understand what change, disruption, and adaptation mean. In this chapter, we look at some of the early breakthroughs in human history that changed the fate of humanity forever.

The Archimedes Screw: An Ingenious Leap

The Archimedes screw, a device traditionally attributed to the ancient Greek mathematician and inventor Archimedes of Syracuse, stands as a testament to human ingenuity and its enduring impact on civilization. Though its exact origins remain a subject of historical debate, with suggestions that it may have been used in Babylon before Archimedes's time, the device is most commonly associated with Archimedes who lived in the third century BCE. This inspired invention, conceived to lift water, has not only facilitated irrigation and drainage for millennia but has also played a pivotal role in the development of technology and engineering throughout human history.

The Archimedes screw is believed to have been developed during Archimedes's visit to Egypt, where the need for efficient water irrigation was a constant challenge. The device consists of a screw contained within a hollow cylinder. When the screw is turned, water is drawn up from a lower elevation to a higher one. This simple yet effective mechanism was revolutionary, enabling the transfer of water against gravity with minimal effort and without the need for complex pumping systems.

The immediate impact of the Archimedes screw was most profoundly felt in agriculture. In regions such as the Nile Delta, where water management was crucial for the sustenance of crops, the device provided a reliable method for irrigating fields. It allowed communities to extend their agricultural activities into areas that would have otherwise remained arid and unproductive. By facilitating the expansion of arable land, the Archimedes screw contributed to the stabilization and growth of food supplies, which in turn supported population growth and the development of more complex societies.

Beyond agriculture, the Archimedes screw had significant implications for urban development and civil engineering. Ancient cities, particularly those in arid or flood-prone regions, faced considerable challenges in managing water resources for drinking, sanitation, and flood control. The Archimedes screw was employed to drain marshy lands and remove water from mines and ship bilges, showcasing its versatility. Its application in these areas not only improved public health and safety but also enabled the construction of more elaborate urban infrastructures, laying the groundwork for the advanced civilizations of the ancient world.

The invention of the Archimedes screw marked a significant milestone in the history of technology and mechanical engineering. It exemplified the application of the principles of physics to solve practical problems, an approach that would define the field of engineering. The device's simplicity, requiring no complex parts or materials, made it easily replicable and adaptable for various uses throughout history. Its design principles have inspired countless other inventions and mechanical devices, contributing to the evolution of engineering and technology.

Remarkably, the Archimedes screw has maintained its relevance into the modern era. It has been adapted for contemporary uses, including in wastewater treatment plants, where it serves as an efficient method for moving large volumes of water or sludge. The device's principle has also been reversed to serve as a hydroelectric power generator, demonstrating its versatility and the timeless nature of its design. Such applications underscore the Archimedes screw's enduring legacy as a sustainable and eco-friendly technology.

Beyond its practical applications, the Archimedes screw has left a lasting imprint on culture and education. It stands as a symbol of innovation and human curiosity, often featured in educational curricula to illustrate basic principles of physics and engineering. The story of Archimedes and his inventions, including the legendary moment of "eureka," continues to inspire generations to explore the realms of science, mathematics, and technology.

The Archimedes screw is more than just an ancient device for water lifting; it is a symbol of human ingenuity and its capacity to shape the environment and society. Through its impact on agriculture, urbanization, technology, and education, the Archimedes screw has played a crucial role in the advancement of civilization. Its simplicity, efficiency, and adaptability have allowed it to endure through millennia, serving as a reminder of the lasting value of innovative thinking and problem-solving. As we continue to face global challenges related to water management and sustainable energy, the principles embodied by the Archimedes screw remain as relevant as ever, guiding us toward solutions that are both ingenious and sustainable.

The Pulley: A Cornerstone of Mechanical Advantage

The pulley, a simple yet profoundly effective machine, stands as one of humanity's earliest and most significant technological innovations. Its basic principle—the use of a wheel on an axle or shaft designed to support movement and change the direction of a taut cable or belt—has been a cornerstone in the development of engineering and mechanics. The history of the pulley is intertwined with the evolution of human ingenuity, demonstrating our ancestors' understanding of mechanical advantage and their relentless pursuit to manipulate the physical world for their benefit.

The origins of the pulley system can be traced back to ancient civilizations, where the earliest examples were used to lift water, hoist flags, and build monumental structures. Evidence suggests that the Mesopotamians and Egyptians employed pulley systems as early as 1500 BCE.[1] The pulley's design and functionality were later enhanced by the Greeks, notably by the polymath Archimedes, who is often credited with formalizing its principles and introducing the compound pulley to multiply force.

The introduction of the pulley system marked a pivotal moment in human history, revolutionizing the way heavy loads were lifted and moved. Its impact was immediate and far-reaching, facilitating the construction of some of the most iconic architectural wonders of the ancient world, such as the pyramids of Egypt and the temples of Greece. By significantly reducing the amount of force required to move objects, the pulley system allowed for the construction of larger and more complex structures than ever before possible.

The pulley's significance extended well beyond the ancient world. During the Middle Ages and the Renaissance, pulley systems played a critical role in the construction of cathedrals, castles, and fortifications. They enabled builders to achieve greater heights and span wider spaces, contributing to the period's architectural innovations and the spread of Gothic and Renaissance architectural styles.

In the realm of engineering, the pulley became an indispensable tool in the development of machinery and transportation systems. From the hoists used in mining operations to the rigging on sailing ships that navigated the globe, the pulley system was central to advancements in various industries. Its principles were further applied in the development of cranes, elevators, and cable cars, transforming urban landscapes and enhancing human mobility.

The pulley system's impact on technological innovation cannot be overstated. It served as a fundamental concept in the study of physics, especially mechanics, influencing the work of renowned scientists and inventors such as Galileo, Leonardo da Vinci, and Isaac Newton. Their understanding and application of the pulley's principles contributed to significant scientific discoveries and the development of new technologies, laying the groundwork for the Industrial Revolution and the modern technological era.

Beyond its monumental contributions to construction and engineering, the pulley system found its way into everyday life, simplifying tasks and enhancing efficiency. From the well pulley used to draw water to the systems used in agricultural equipment, the pulley became a ubiquitous tool, integral to the functioning of society. Its simplicity, adaptability, and effectiveness in multiplying human effort made it a staple in workshops, farms, and households throughout history.

The pulley's enduring legacy is also reflected in education, where it continues to serve as a fundamental example of simple machines and mechanical advantage. Its study in physics and engineering courses not only demonstrates the principles of force and motion but also inspires students to appreciate the ingenuity of ancient inventors and the cumulative nature of technological progress.

The pulley system, with its origins shrouded in the mists of prehistory, emerged as a transformative tool that significantly influenced the course of human civilization. Its development marked a leap forward in our ancestors' ability to manipulate their environment, enabling the construction of monumental structures, the advancement of engineering and technology, and the simplification of everyday tasks. The pulley exemplifies the profound impact that simple innovations can have on the world, reminding us that progress often hinges on the clever application of basic principles. As we continue to push the boundaries of what is possible, the pulley system stands as a testament to human creativity and the enduring quest for efficiency and mastery over the physical world.

The Wheel: A Revolution in Motion

The wheel, undoubtedly one of the most pivotal inventions in human history, stands as a symbol of innovation and progress. Its invention is a hallmark of human ingenuity, transforming not just the way we transport ourselves and goods but fundamentally altering the trajectory of human civilization. This simple yet transformative technology has its roots in ancient times, and its impact spans across various aspects of life throughout history.

By large it is agreed upon that the wheel was invented around 3500 BCE, first emerging in ancient Mesopotamia, the cradle of civilization.[2] Early wheels were not used for transportation initially but were developed as potter's wheels, revolutionizing the production of pottery—a vital element in the storage and transportation of goods and resources. It wasn't long before the transformative potential of the wheel was realized for transportation. The first wheeled vehicles, carts and chariots, were developed, significantly enhancing trade, warfare, and the expansion of territories.

The introduction of the wheel into transportation is perhaps its most profound contribution to civilization. The efficiency of moving goods and people increased exponentially. Distance and time, which were once major barriers to trade and interaction among distant communities, were drastically reduced. This facilitated not just the exchange of goods but also ideas and cultures, promoting a level of interconnectedness among civilizations that had previously been unattainable.

Wheeled vehicles enabled societies to engage in trade over greater distances, fostering economic growth and the distribution of resources. This economic impact cannot be overstated; it laid the foundations for market economies and urban development. Cities and civilizations flourished along trade routes, and the wheel was central to these developments.

The military applications of the wheel further demonstrate its impact on civilization. Chariots and wheeled transport were crucial in ancient warfare, providing significant advantages in mobility and logistics. The wheel's utility in engineering projects—from the construction of monumental architecture to irrigation systems—further exemplified its importance. It facilitated the movement of heavy materials and the operation of complex machinery, enabling ambitious projects that would shape the landscapes of civilizations.

Beyond its practical applications, the wheel has been a powerful cultural symbol of progress and innovation. It has influenced art, religion, and mythology in various cultures, symbolizing cycles, change, and advancement. The social implications of the wheel were equally significant; it altered settlement patterns, enabling nomadic cultures to transition to sedentary agricultural lifestyles, which in turn led to the development of more complex societal structures.

The evolution of the wheel did not stop in ancient times; it continued to inspire innovations well into the modern era. The industrial revolution saw the wheel playing a crucial role in machinery, from the steam engine to textile mills. The advent of the rubber tire in the nineteenth century revolutionized transportation yet again, leading to the development of bicycles and automobiles, further shrinking the world and accelerating the pace of life.

In the twentieth and twenty-first centuries, the wheel's significance remains undiminished, integral to virtually every form of transportation, from cars and bikes to airplanes and spacecraft. Its applications have expanded into robotics, renewable energy (wind turbines), and even in the digital world, where the concept of the wheel informs user interface designs and navigation.

The wheel's widespread adoption and its role in facilitating industrialization and modern transportation have also contributed to environmental challenges, including pollution and habitat destruction. This underscores the dual nature of technological progress, where advancements come with both benefits and costs to the environment and society.

The wheel's journey from a pottery tool to a cornerstone of modern civilization encapsulates the essence of human innovation. Its invention was not merely a moment of genius but a catalyst for a series of developments that would redefine human existence. The wheel has not only propelled humanity forward but has become deeply embedded in the fabric of society, influencing economic systems, warfare, urbanization, and culture. Its story is a testament to the transformative power of technology and a reminder of the ongoing impact of ancient inventions on contemporary life. As we continue to innovate and tackle the challenges of the future, the wheel stands as a symbol of our capacity to reshape the world for the better.

Gunpowder: The Catalyst of Conflict and Conquest

Gunpowder, also known as black powder, is a substance that has dramatically altered the course of human history through its applications in warfare, engineering, and entertainment. Originating in ancient China, the discovery and evolution of gunpowder have had profound impacts on civilizations worldwide, reshaping military strategies, societal structures, and global power dynamics.

Gunpowder's invention is attributed to Chinese alchemists in the ninth century, who were initially seeking an elixir for immortality. Comprising saltpeter (potassium nitrate), charcoal, and sulfur, this serendipitous discovery would instead become an instrument of war and transformation. Early uses were primarily for fireworks and signals, but its potential for propulsion and destruction was quickly realized. By the tenth century, the Chinese were using gunpowder in bombs, grenades, and eventually, firearms, marking the beginning of a new era in military technology.

The knowledge of gunpowder spread from China to the Islamic world and then to Europe between the twelfth and thirteenth centuries, largely through the Silk Road and the Mongol invasions. Each civilization adapted and innovated on the technology, developing their own versions of gunpowder weapons. In Europe, the development of cannons and guns had a significant impact on warfare, leading to the decline of fortified castles and the traditional armored knight. Gunpowder leveled the playing field in warfare, as it required less physical strength to operate a gun or a cannon than to wield a sword or lance, democratizing the means of combat to some extent.

The advent of gunpowder weaponry fundamentally changed the art of war. The massive destructive power of cannons and firearms led to the development of new military tactics, fortifications, and the rise of standing armies. This shift had profound implications for the state's role and the nature of power, as those who controlled the gunpowder could wield significant influence and control over territories. The necessity to finance these innovations and standing armies also led to the centralization of state power and the emergence of the modern nation-state.

Gunpowder also indirectly influenced the social and political landscape by diminishing the role of the feudal military aristocracy. As warfare became more dependent on technology and less on individual valor, the importance of the knight and feudal lord waned, paving the way for more centralized forms of governance.

Gunpowder played a crucial role in the Age of Exploration and the subsequent colonial expansion by European powers. Armed with gunpowder weapons, European explorers and conquistadors had a devastating advantage over the indigenous populations of the Americas, Africa, and Asia. This military superiority enabled small European forces to conquer vast territories, subjugate native populations, and establish colonial empires that would dominate global politics and economics for centuries.

The gunpowder industry itself became a significant sector of the economy in many countries, driving advances in chemistry, metallurgy, and mechanical engineering. The demand for saltpeter, one of gunpowder's key ingredients, influenced global trade networks, including the establishment of plantations in the colonies to produce the substance.

Culturally, gunpowder has left its mark in literature, art, and language, often symbolizing power, destruction, and technological advancement. Festivities and celebrations around the world, notably fireworks displays, owe their spectacle to gunpowder, showcasing its dual capacity for beauty and violence.

Although supplanted by smokeless powder and more advanced explosives in the nineteenth and twentieth centuries, gunpowder's legacy is undeniable. It laid the groundwork for modern warfare and firearms, influenced the rise and fall of empires, and contributed to significant scientific and technological developments. Gunpowder has also raised ethical and moral questions about the use of technology in warfare, a debate that continues with today's advanced weaponry.

Gunpowder's invention is a pivotal moment in human history, a catalyst for change with far-reaching implications across centuries. Its story is one of innovation and adaptation, demonstrating humanity's capacity to transform accidental discoveries into tools that reshape the world. From altering the landscape of warfare to influencing global politics and cultural practices, gunpowder's impact on human civilization is profound, serving as a reminder of the dual-edged nature of technological progress.

Lenses and Telescopes: Unveiling the Cosmos

The invention of lenses and telescopes stands as a monumental disruption in human history, profoundly altering our understanding of the universe and our place within it. These technologies have not only expanded the frontiers of science but have also reshaped navigational methods, military strategies, and cultural perspectives, unveiling realms beyond the reach of the naked eye.

The history of lenses traces back to ancient civilizations, with the use of simple glass and crystal lenses to magnify objects. However, the transformative leap occurred in the late sixteenth and early seventeenth centuries with the advent of the telescope. Historically attributed to Hans Lippershey, a Dutch spectacle maker, in 1608, the telescope's invention quickly spread across Europe, with Galileo Galilei significantly improving its design and turning it toward the heavens in 1609.

Galileo's enhancements to the telescope allowed him to make unprecedented astronomical observations, including the moons of Jupiter, the phases of Venus, and the craters of the Moon. These discoveries challenged the prevailing geocentric models of the universe, which held Earth as the center of all celestial bodies, a view endorsed by the powerful Catholic Church. Galileo's support for the heliocentric model, which posited the Sun at the center of the solar system, led to a conflict with the Church, culminating in his house arrest. Despite this, his work laid the foundation for modern astronomy and marked a significant shift in how humanity perceived the cosmos.

The telescope's ability to magnify distant objects revolutionized not just astronomy but also navigation. Mariners could now use telescopic sights to accurately determine their position at sea by observing celestial bodies, greatly improving the safety and efficiency of sea travel. This had profound implications for global exploration, trade, and the Age of Discovery, enabling European powers to navigate the world's oceans with unprecedented precision, expanding their empires and influencing global geopolitics.

The telescope became a symbol of the Enlightenment, embodying the quest for knowledge through observation and reason. It disrupted centuries of speculative astronomy, replacing it with empirical evidence and observation. This shift encouraged a more skeptical and inquiry-based approach to understanding the natural world, contributing to the scientific revolution and the development of the scientific method.

In the centuries that followed, improvements in lens-making and telescope design allowed astronomers such as Johannes Kepler, Isaac Newton, and later, Edwin Hubble, to further push the boundaries of space exploration. These advancements led to groundbreaking discoveries, such as the laws of planetary motion, the nature of light and color, and the expanding universe theory. Telescopes enabled humanity to explore the vastness of space, leading to the identification of galaxies, nebulae, and black holes, fundamentally altering our understanding of the universe's size, structure, and history.

The telescope also had significant societal and cultural impacts. By revealing the vastness of the cosmos, it challenged human conceit and the notion of our central place in the universe, prompting philosophical and theological debates about humanity's role and the existence of extraterrestrial life. The technology democratized access to the heavens, previously the domain of the philosophical elite, inspiring wonder and curiosity across societal strata.

In the modern era, the Hubble Space Telescope and more recently the James Webb Space Telescope (JWST) have exemplified the telescope's disruptive legacy, orbiting Earth and providing images of unprecedented clarity. Launched in 1990 and 2021, respectively, Hubble and JWST have deepened our understanding of cosmic phenomena, contributing to significant scientific discoveries, such as the rate of the universe's expansion and the presence of exoplanets, potentially capable of supporting life.

The invention of lenses and telescopes represents a pivotal disruption in human history, expanding our knowledge and challenging our perceptions. From Galileo's celestial observations to the deep-space images captured by Hubble and JWST, these technologies have not only unraveled the mysteries of the universe but have also reshaped navigation, warfare, and our cultural and philosophical understanding of existence. The lens and telescope stand as testaments to human curiosity and our relentless pursuit of knowledge, reminding us of the power of technology to illuminate the unknown and transform our place in the cosmos.

The Steam Engine: Powering Progress

The steam engine, a cornerstone of the Industrial Revolution, stands as one of the most disruptive inventions in human history. Its development catalyzed an unprecedented era of economic, social, and technological transformation, reshaping the landscape of human civilization in ways that continue to echo into the modern era.

The history of the steam engine dates back to the first century CE, with the aeolipile, or "wind ball," described by Heron of Alexandria, but it wasn't until the seventeenth and eighteenth centuries that the foundations for the modern steam engine were laid. Thomas Savery and Thomas Newcomen developed early versions in the late 1600s and early 1700s, primarily for pumping water out of mines. However, these early machines were inefficient and limited in application.

The real disruption began with James Watt, a Scottish inventor who, in the mid-eighteenth century, made pivotal improvements to Newcomen's design, significantly enhancing efficiency by introducing a separate condenser. This innovation marked the birth of the modern steam engine, setting the stage for the Industrial Revolution and fundamentally altering the course of human development.

The steam engine's impact on the Industrial Revolution cannot be overstated. It provided a reliable and powerful source of energy that was not limited by the location of water streams or the vagaries of weather, unlike waterwheels. Steam power was essential in driving the machinery of textile mills, reducing reliance on human or animal labor, and massively increasing production capabilities. This shift not only revolutionized the manufacturing industry but also had profound effects on the global economy, facilitating the growth of industries such as mining, transportation, and manufacturing on scales previously unimaginable.

Perhaps one of the most visible impacts of the steam engine was on transportation. The development of the steam locomotive by George Stephenson and others in the early nineteenth century revolutionized land travel. Railways could now connect distant cities, dramatically reducing travel times and reshaping the social and economic landscape. The steamship similarly transformed sea travel and trade, enabling more reliable and faster passage across oceans. These advancements made global markets more accessible, fostering trade and cultural exchange and laying the groundwork for globalization.

The steam engine's influence extended far beyond the factories and transportation. It was a key driver in urbanization, as people moved from rural areas to cities in search of work in the burgeoning factories. This migration led to significant demographic shifts, the growth of new urban centers, and the development of new social classes, notably the industrial working class and the industrial capitalists.

The availability of cheap goods produced in factories powered by steam engines lowered prices and improved the standard of living for many, even as it introduced new challenges, including labor exploitation and environmental degradation. The steam engine also played a critical role in the expansion of empires, as European powers used steam-powered military technology and transportation to colonize and control large parts of Africa and Asia.

The widespread adoption of steam power marked the beginning of humanity's significant impact on the environment, contributing to deforestation and the acceleration of coal mining to meet fuel needs. The resulting air pollution and environmental degradation were among the first signs of the industrial activity's ecological footprint, issues that remain central to contemporary environmental challenges.

Culturally, the steam engine symbolized human progress and ingenuity, inspiring literature, art, and philosophy of the era. It represented the triumph of the Industrial Age, embodying the potential of technology to reshape the world. However, it also sparked debates about the ethical implications of industrialization, the dignity of labor, and the equitable distribution of technological benefits.

The steam engine was a disruptive force that marked the dawn of a new era in human history. Its development catalyzed the Industrial Revolution, transforming economic structures, social relations, and the global balance of power. By powering factories, revolutionizing transportation, and driving urbanization, the steam engine played a pivotal role in shaping the modern world. Its legacy is a testament to the profound impact of technological innovation on human civilization, offering lessons on the potentials and pitfalls of industrial progress that are still relevant today.

The Sextant: Guiding the Age of Exploration

The sextant, a precision navigational tool, represents a significant disruption in the annals of maritime exploration and navigation. Its invention in the early eighteenth century revolutionized the way mariners determined their longitude and latitude at sea, profoundly enhancing global trade, exploration, and the mapping of the world. This device not only enhanced the safety and efficiency of sea travel but also played a pivotal role in the expansion of empires and the development of global trade networks.

The sextant's origins can be traced back to the increasing need for accurate navigational instruments in the Age of Exploration. While the astrolabe and the cross-staff were used prior to the sextant, they were less accurate and more difficult to use, especially on a swaying ship. The invention of the sextant around the 1730s, primarily attributed to English mathematician John Hadley and independently to American inventor Thomas Godfrey, offered a more reliable and precise means of measuring celestial objects relative to the horizon.

The sextant's innovative design allowed navigators to measure the angle between any two visible objects, such as the sun and the horizon, with remarkable accuracy. Its key advancement was the incorporation of a double-reflecting system using mirrors, which enabled the user to simultaneously view the horizon and a celestial body, making precise measurements possible even in challenging sea conditions. This was a substantial improvement over earlier instruments, fundamentally changing the practice of celestial navigation.

The sextant directly contributed to the golden age of maritime exploration. It enabled sailors to navigate more accurately and confidently across open oceans, reaching previously inaccessible parts of the world. This instrument was essential in the voyages of legendary explorers such as Captain James Cook, who used it to chart the Pacific Ocean, including New Zealand and the Great Barrier Reef, with unprecedented precision. The sextant thus played a crucial role in expanding the geographical knowledge of the time, facilitating the discovery of new lands and sea routes.

The enhanced navigational capabilities provided by the sextant had a profound impact on global trade. By allowing ships to travel more safely and efficiently, it contributed to the intensification of international trade and the establishment of new trade routes. European powers, in particular, used their navigational advantages to expand their empires, colonizing vast territories in Asia, Africa, and the Americas. The sextant was, therefore, a tool of both exploration and imperialism, underpinning the economic and political dominance of maritime powers.

The sextant also significantly influenced the fields of astronomy, cartography, and oceanography. By facilitating precise measurements of the stars and planets, it contributed to advancements in astronomical knowledge and the development of more accurate celestial charts. Cartographers were able to create more detailed and reliable maps of the world, transforming navigation, trade, and military strategy. Furthermore, the sextant's use in measuring ocean currents and tides advanced the understanding of oceanographic phenomena, contributing to the safety of sea travel.

Beyond its practical applications, the sextant influenced the cultural and societal dimensions of the age. It symbolized human ingenuity and the quest for knowledge, embodying the Enlightenment ideals of reason and scientific progress. The ability to navigate the vast oceans also had profound implications for society, bringing distant cultures into contact and exchange, albeit sometimes violently through colonization and trade.

While technological advancements have introduced more sophisticated navigational tools, such as GPS, the sextant remains a symbol of the art of navigation and is still used as a reliable backup by mariners. Its legacy endures in the maritime tradition, navigation education, and the collective imagination as a symbol of exploration and adventure.

The sextant's invention was a disruptive milestone in maritime history, enabling unprecedented precision in celestial navigation and profoundly influencing global exploration, trade, and the mapping of the world. By enhancing the safety and efficiency of sea travel, it facilitated the expansion of empires, the exchange of goods and ideas, and the advancement of scientific knowledge. Its impact on human civilization is a testament to the transformative power of technological innovation, illustrating how a single tool can alter the course of history.

Final Words

Human history is full of innovative breakthroughs, whether it was the pure need that drove our ancestors to find solutions to problems they faced or unknowingly being able to observe a phenomenon and disrupt. Our past shows that we have always been innovative, creative, and incredible at changing the status quo. We have been great at solving problems with the tools we possessed. As we head into the next chapters of this book, we will see how this innovative mindset is now addressing problems of a larger nature and how at the foundation of every solution is our will to disrupt.

Resources

Check out the following resources that can help shed light on early disruptive technologies and breakthroughs.

Books

- *How the Wheel Changed History* by Melissa Higgins, 2015
- *From Apes to Cyborgs: New Perspectives on Human Evolution* by Claudio Tuniz and Patrizia Tiberi Vipraio, 2020
- *The Archimedes Codex: Revealing the Secrets of the World's Greatest Palimpsest* by Reviel Netz and William Noel, 2007

Watch List

- *Engineering an Empire: The Byzantines*, History Channel
- *Ancient Impossible: War Machines*, History Channel
- *The Hubble Space Telescope: Seeing Is Believing*, NASA
- *Revealing the Cosmos: A Startling New View from the James Webb Space Telescope*, World Science Festival

Take the Future Readiness Score at www.iankhan.com/frs or scan the QR Code

3

Financial System Disruptors

Money is a terrible master but an excellent servant.

—*P.T. Barnum*

THIS CHAPTER IS about money. Money is a foundational pillar on which our world stands. For centuries, money has been a driver of economies, a measure of wealth, and a proof of progress. Today, however, money is changing the way it is represented, exchanged, stored, and utilized. This chapter is about some of the major disruptive changes emerging in money. Big shifts in the global financial industry are happening at many fronts, from the actual mechanism of how money is created to exchange, distribution, and management. The digital age is powering much of this, and more advanced technologies such as cryptography, blockchain, and cloud computing are making things easier and faster. Let us take a look into how this revolution is emerging and creating new disruptors.

Blockchain Technology at the Core

Imagine a world where every transaction, every piece of data, every bit of information is recorded securely, transparently, and indelibly. This is the promise of blockchain technology—a decentralized ledger system that ensures data integrity through cryptographic proof. The genius of blockchain lies in its ability to operate without a central authority, making it a revolutionary force in numerous industries.

The concept of blockchain was introduced in 2008 by an unknown person or group of people using the pseudonym Satoshi Nakamoto. Nakamoto's white paper, "Bitcoin: A Peer-to-Peer Electronic Cash System," proposed a decentralized currency that would operate independently of any government or financial institution. The blockchain was the underlying technology that made Bitcoin possible, serving as a public ledger for all transactions conducted on the Bitcoin network.

Initially, blockchain was synonymous with Bitcoin. However, it didn't take long for innovators to realize the technology's potential beyond cryptocurrencies. The second major milestone came with the creation of Ethereum by Vitalik Buterin in 2015. Ethereum introduced the concept of smart contracts—self-executing contracts where the terms are directly written into code. This innovation expanded blockchain's applicability, enabling decentralized applications (dApps) and spawning a vibrant ecosystem of decentralized finance (DeFi), NFTs (non-fungible tokens), and more. For a simple and concise definition of an NFT, consider Wikipedia's page on non-fungible tokens, which defines them as.

"A **non-fungible token (NFT)** is a unique digital identifier that is recorded on a blockchain and is used to certify ownership and authenticity. It cannot be copied, substituted, or subdivided.[1] The ownership of an NFT is recorded in the blockchain and can be transferred by the owner, allowing NFTs to be sold and traded. Initially pitched as a new class of investment asset, by September 2023, one report claimed that over 95% of NFT collections had zero monetary value."

For more detailed information visit en.wikipedia.com/wiki/Non-fungible_token.

Blockchain technology has since evolved to address issues such as scalability, interoperability, and energy efficiency. Projects such as Polkadot, Cardano, and Solana represent the new wave of blockchain innovations aiming to overcome the limitations of their predecessors.

The future of blockchain is brimming with possibilities. Here are some potential impacts:

- **DeFi:** By removing intermediaries, DeFi can democratize access to financial services, making them more inclusive and efficient. As the technology matures, we can expect more sophisticated financial products and services to emerge.
- **Supply chain management:** Blockchain can enhance transparency and traceability in supply chains, reducing fraud, improving efficiency, and ensuring product authenticity. Companies such as IBM and Walmart are already leveraging blockchain for these purposes.

- **Digital identity:** Blockchain can provide individuals with control over their digital identities, enhancing privacy and security. This could revolutionize how we manage personal data and conduct transactions online.
- **Health care:** Blockchain can secure patient data, streamline health care records, and ensure the integrity of medical supply chains. This could lead to improved patient outcomes and more efficient health care systems.
- **Governance:** Decentralized autonomous organizations (DAOs) enabled by blockchain can facilitate more transparent, democratic, and efficient governance structures for both public and private organizations.

The Global Monetary System: Revolutionizing Finance

The global monetary system, a complex web of currencies, financial institutions, and regulatory frameworks, underpins the world economy. In recent years, this system has encountered several disruptive ideas that challenge traditional financial paradigms, promising to reshape how we think about money, value, and economic sovereignty. These disruptions are driven by technological advancements, shifts in global power, and a reevaluation of the principles that have governed financial transactions for decades.

Cryptocurrencies

Perhaps the most significant disruption in the global monetary system is the advent of digital currencies, notably cryptocurrencies such as Bitcoin and Ethereum. Unlike traditional currencies, these digital assets are not controlled by any central authority, offering a decentralized alternative to state-backed money. This fundamental shift challenges the monopoly of national governments over currency issuance and monetary policy, proposing a new model where trust is built on cryptographic proof rather than central bank authority.

Cryptocurrencies have introduced the concept of blockchain technology to the mainstream, providing a secure, transparent, and immutable ledger for transactions. This innovation not only underpins digital currencies but also offers potential applications in securing and streamlining financial transactions, supply chain management, and even voting systems.

Nassim Taleb, author of *The Black Swan*, says that "Bitcoin is the beginning of something great: a currency without government, something necessary and imperative." I personally could not agree more.

Cryptocurrencies disrupt the financial landscape by challenging the monopoly of traditional fiat currencies and the central banking system. Their decentralized nature eliminates the need for intermediaries in transactions, thereby democratizing access to financial services, especially for the unbanked or underbanked populations worldwide. Furthermore, the inherent features of blockchain technology, such as transparency, security, and immutability, introduce a new paradigm for trust in financial transactions.

Central Bank Digital Currencies Can Change Banking Forever

In response to the rise of cryptocurrencies and the digitization of the economy, several central banks are exploring or have already implemented their own digital currencies, known as *central bank digital currencies* (CBDCs). CBDCs represent a digital form of a nation's fiat currency, combining the efficiency and security of digital technology with the regulatory oversight and stability of central banking. By adopting CBDCs, central banks aim to modernize financial infrastructure, improve payment efficiencies, and maintain control over monetary policy in an increasingly digital world. Experts, including Christine Lagarde, president of the European Central Bank, believe that future central banks will need to manage both cash as well as digital currency to "ensure financial stability and inclusion."

CBDCs aim to combine the efficiency and innovation of digital currency with the stability and regulatory oversight of traditional banking. Unlike cryptocurrencies, CBDCs are centralized and regulated, offering a digital complement to fiat money that could enhance payment systems' efficiency and promote financial inclusion.

CBDCs represent a disruptive idea by potentially reshaping monetary policy implementation and the functioning of the global financial system. They offer central banks a new tool in their arsenal to directly influence the economy, bypass traditional banking systems, and reach end users more effectively. Moreover, CBDCs could significantly alter the competitive landscape of the financial sector, pushing commercial banks to innovate or risk obsolescence.

Another disruptive trend is the gradual shift away from the US dollar's dominance in international trade and finance, a movement known as *de-dollarization*. Countries such as China and Russia are actively promoting the use of their currencies for bilateral trade agreements, seeking to reduce their dependence on the dollar. This shift is facilitated by the development of alternative payment systems and trade mechanisms that bypass traditional dollar-based infrastructure, potentially leading to a more multipolar currency landscape.

Peer-to-Peer Lending and Crowdfunding Could Become Big

The rise of peer-to-peer (P2P) lending platforms and crowdfunding represents a disruption to traditional banking and investment models. These platforms allow individuals and businesses to lend and borrow directly from each other or raise funds from a large number of people, often bypassing traditional financial intermediaries. This democratization of finance can lead to more inclusive financial systems but also poses regulatory challenges and risks related to borrower default and market stability.

The Emergence of Decentralized Finance

DeFi takes the concept of blockchain and cryptocurrencies further by creating a comprehensive ecosystem of financial services, including lending, borrowing, and trading, that operates independently of traditional financial institutions. DeFi platforms offer users control over their assets through smart contracts, promising greater transparency, accessibility, and efficiency. However, the nascent DeFi sector faces challenges related to security, scalability, and regulatory compliance.

Through smart contracts on blockchain platforms such as Ethereum, DeFi enables the creation of dApps that replicate traditional financial services, such as lending, borrowing, and trading, without the need for centralized institutions.

Respected critical thinker Naval Ravikant has been heard saying, "DeFi is the most innovative financial technology since the advent of the Internet." DeFi challenges the centralized financial system by offering permissionless, transparent, and inclusive financial services. It disrupts the traditional gatekeepers of finance, allowing anyone with an Internet connection to access a global financial system. Furthermore, DeFi introduces innovative financial products and services that offer higher yields than traditional banking products, albeit with higher risks.

Sustainability-Linked Financial Instruments

Amid growing awareness of climate change and social inequality, there has been a surge in interest in sustainability-linked financial instruments. Green bonds, social bonds, and sustainability-linked loans tie the cost of capital to environmental, social, and governance (ESG) outcomes, incentivizing companies to pursue sustainable practices. This shift reflects a broader reevaluation of what constitutes value and success in the global economy, integrating social and environmental considerations into financial decision-making.

According to Larry Fink, CEO of BlackRock, "Sustainable investing is about doing the right thing for the planet and achieving strong financial returns."

The disruptive ideas transforming the global monetary system reflect broader societal shifts toward decentralization, digitalization, and sustainability. These innovations challenge the traditional roles of money, financial intermediaries, and regulatory bodies, offering opportunities to create a more inclusive, efficient, and resilient global financial system. However, they also present challenges related to security, inequality, and the potential erosion of national monetary sovereignty. Navigating these disruptions requires careful consideration of their implications for global economic stability, regulatory frameworks, and the equitable distribution of financial benefits. As we advance into an increasingly digital and interconnected world, the evolution of the global monetary system will undoubtedly continue to reflect the dynamic interplay between technological innovation, economic policy, and societal values.

Foresight on Money

Global and decentralized cryptocurrencies, CBDCs, and DeFi collectively have the potential to revolutionize how individuals and businesses transact, invest, and manage wealth. They offer solutions to longstanding issues such as financial inclusion, remittance costs, and the efficiency of cross-border transactions. For instance, cryptocurrencies such as Bitcoin and Ethereum have enabled global transactions without the need for currency conversion or hefty fees, while DeFi platforms such as MakerDAO and Compound are offering decentralized lending and borrowing services with competitive interest rates.

Looking ahead, these innovations could further democratize finance, making it more accessible, efficient, and tailored to individual needs. CBDCs, in particular, could play a crucial role in modernizing financial infrastructures, enhancing monetary policy effectiveness, and fostering economic growth. However, the realization of their full potential hinges on addressing challenges related to scalability, regulation, security, and user education.

Final Words

The emergence of cryptocurrency, CBDCs, and DeFi as disruptive ideas in the global monetary system signifies a pivotal shift toward a more inclusive, efficient, and transparent financial future. While each carries its unique challenges and risks, their collective potential to reshape the financial landscape is undeniable. As these innovations continue to evolve, they hold the promise of empowering individuals and businesses with more control over their financial destinies, heralding a new era of financial democracy and innovation.

Resources

Check out the following resources to go deeper into the future of the global financial industry.

Books

- *The Bitcoin Standard: The Decentralized Alternative to Central Banking* by Saifedean Ammous
- *Cryptocurrency All-in-One For Dummies* by Kiana Danial, Tiana Laurence, Peter Kent
- *Cryptocurrency QuickStart Guide: The Simplified Beginner's Guide to Digital Currencies, Bitcoin, and the Future of Decentralized Finance* by Jonathan Reichental

Watch List

- *Blockchain City* (2019) by Ian Khan (Amazon Prime, Tubi, YouTube)
- *The Bitcoin Dilemma* (2021) by Ian Khan (YouTube)
- *Banking on Bitcoin* (2016), directed by Christopher Cannucciari (Amazon Prime, Netflix, and YouTube)
- *The Rise and Rise of Bitcoin* (2014), directed by Nicholas Mross (Amazon Prime)
- *Magic Money: The Bitcoin Revolution* (2017), directed by Tim Delmastro (Amazon Prime, YouTube, and Google Play)

Take the Future Readiness Score at www.iankhan.com/frs or scan the QR Code

4

Health Care Industry Disruptions

One sometimes finds what one is not looking for.

—*Alexander Fleming*

IN THIS CHAPTER, we will explore the groundbreaking changes revolutionizing drug discovery and health care. From the serendipitous discovery of penicillin to the precision of genomics and AI-driven innovations, we delve into how these advancements are transforming patient care. We'll also cover the impact of robotic surgery and the promise of CRISPR technology. Join us as we navigate the future of health care, where technology and human ingenuity converge to redefine what's possible.

Drug Discovery

Drug discovery, once a painstakingly slow process, has become a hotbed of innovation, evolving into a more efficient and precise endeavor. This shift is pivotal in addressing global health care needs, from battling new diseases to managing chronic conditions. The journey of drug discovery is a testament to human ingenuity, transitioning from serendipitous discoveries to a technology-driven approach that harnesses the latest advancements in science and engineering, ensuring new treatments reach patients faster and more safely.

Drug discovery has its roots in identifying active ingredients in ancient remedies. The dawn of modern pharmaceuticals began in the early nineteenth century with the isolation of compounds such as morphine from opium. This era was marked by trial and error, with many breakthroughs coming from unexpected places. Take, for instance, the discovery of penicillin by Alexander Fleming in 1928—a happy accident that revolutionized medicine and earned Fleming the Nobel Prize.

The late twentieth century saw the introduction of high-throughput screening (HTS), a game changer in drug discovery. HTS is a powerful method used in drug discovery and biological research to quickly evaluate the biological or biochemical activity of a large number of compounds. By using automation, miniaturized assays, and sophisticated data analysis, HTS allows scientists to screen thousands to millions of samples in a relatively short period. This process helps identify active compounds, antibodies, or genes that modulate a particular biomolecular pathway. HTS has revolutionized the early stages of drug development by significantly speeding up the identification of potential drug candidates and facilitating a more efficient and targeted approach to discovering new therapeutics.

HTS allowed researchers to quickly evaluate thousands to millions of compounds for biological activity, significantly speeding up the identification of potential drug candidates. This shift from sequential to parallel processing in drug screening marked a leap in efficiency and productivity.

HTS revolutionized the early stages of drug discovery by enabling a broader exploration of chemical space and the rapid identification of hits that could be optimized into viable drug candidates. It also paved the way for automation and informatics in drug discovery, laying the foundation for advanced technologies to follow. Bill Gates once said, "We always overestimate the change that will occur in the next two years and underestimate the change that will occur in the next ten."[1] HTS exemplifies this, as its impact has grown exponentially over time.

The sequencing of the human genome at the turn of the twenty-first century ushered in an era of genomics and precision medicine, fundamentally changing drug discovery. Understanding the genetic basis of diseases has enabled the development of targeted therapies designed to modulate specific molecular pathways or genetic mutations.

AI and, in particular, machine learning (ML) are the latest disruptors in drug discovery. These technologies can analyze vast datasets, predict compound efficacy and safety, and even suggest new targets for drug development. DeepMind's AI system, AlphaFold, has made headlines by accurately predicting protein structures—a critical factor in understanding disease mechanisms and designing effective drugs. As Andrew Ng, a pioneer in AI, said, "AI is the new electricity," and its potential in drug discovery is just beginning to be realized.[2]

The Promise of CRISPR and Gene Editing

Gene editing technologies such as CRISPR-Cas9 are opening new frontiers in drug discovery. By allowing precise modifications to DNA, CRISPR offers the potential for curative therapies for a wide range of genetic disorders. Jennifer Doudna, one of the discoverers of CRISPR, likened its potential to "editing the source code of life."[3] Companies such as CRISPR Therapeutics are pioneering treatments for conditions including sickle cell disease and beta-thalassemia, directly targeting the underlying genetic causes.

Digital health technologies and wearables are also playing a role in drug discovery by providing real-world data on patient health and treatment outcomes. This data can inform the development of more effective, patient-centered therapies and enable personalized treatment approaches. The Apple Heart Study, which utilized data from Apple Watch users, is a pioneering effort to leverage wearable technology in large-scale health research.

How These Innovations Aid People Today and in the Future

The disruptive innovations in drug discovery hold immense promise for improving patient care and health outcomes. By making the drug discovery process faster, more efficient, and more targeted, these technologies can lead to treatments that are more effective, have fewer side effects, and can be tailored to individual patient needs. As Dr. Eric Topol, a leading voice in digital medicine, stated, "The future of medicine is about making healthcare more precise, predictive, and personalized."[4]

The disruptive ideas shaping drug discovery today are redefining the boundaries of what is possible in medicine. From HTS and precision medicine to AI, ML, and CRISPR technology, these innovations are accelerating pharmaceutical research and bringing new hope to patients worldwide. As we look to the future, the continued convergence of technology and biology promises even greater breakthroughs, making this an exciting time in the quest to conquer disease. As Paulo Coelho wrote in *The Alchemist*, "When you want something, all the universe conspires in helping you to achieve it."[5] The relentless pursuit of better health care embodies this spirit, pushing the boundaries of what we can achieve in drug discovery.

Robotic Surgery: A Breakthrough

Robotic surgery stands as one of the most significant technological advancements in medicine, disrupting traditional surgical practices and setting new standards for precision in complex procedures. By integrating robotics with advanced surgical techniques, robotic surgery enhances the capabilities of surgeons and offers patients safer options with potentially better outcomes and shorter recovery times.

The journey of robotic surgery began in the late twentieth century, with early systems designed to enhance surgical precision. The PUMA 560, used in 1985 for a neurosurgical biopsy, marked a pivotal moment in the integration of technology and medicine. However, it was the introduction of the da Vinci Surgical System in 2000 that truly revolutionized the field, offering a platform for performing complex surgeries with enhanced vision, precision, and control.

Robotic surgery transcends the limitations of human hands and eyesight, providing surgeons with high-definition, 3D views of surgical sites and translating hand movements into smaller, precise movements of tiny instruments inside the patient's body. This precision is particularly advantageous for intricate procedures performed in confined spaces. The minimally invasive nature of robotic surgery, enabled by smaller incisions, results in reduced pain, quicker recovery times, and lower infection risk, representing a significant shift from traditional open surgery.

Robotic surgery is now employed across various specialties, including urology, gynecology, and cardiothoracic surgery. The da Vinci Surgical System has been used in millions of procedures worldwide, from prostatectomies to heart valve repairs. Its precision and flexibility allow for surgeries with a level of detail previously unattainable. Beyond the da Vinci, systems such as the Mako Robotic-Arm Assisted Surgery system specialize in orthopedic surgeries, enabling precise joint replacements. The Versius Surgical Robotic System, with its small, versatile arms, aims to make robotic surgery more accessible and cost-effective.

Today, robotic surgery offers profound benefits, including less invasive procedures, reduced pain and scarring, and faster recovery. For health care systems, robotic surgery can reduce hospital stays and improve surgical efficiency, potentially leading to cost savings.

Looking forward, the integration of AI with robotic surgery promises even greater advancements. AI could enhance precision through real-time data analysis and decision support, reducing complications and improving outcomes. Tele-surgery capabilities, where surgeries can be performed remotely, could extend expert surgical care to underserved regions, democratizing access to high-quality health care.

Despite its advantages, robotic surgery raises ethical considerations and challenges, including the need for specialized training, concerns about patient safety in case of malfunctions, and high costs. Addressing these challenges requires ongoing research, investment in training, and discussions about equitable integration into health care systems.

Robotic surgery exemplifies the incredible potential of technological innovation to improve human health. By enhancing the precision, safety, and efficiency of surgical procedures, it represents a disruptive force in medicine. As this field evolves, driven by advancements in robotics, AI, and telemedicine, the future of surgery promises even greater breakthroughs, offering hope for better patient outcomes worldwide. The journey of robotic surgery illustrates how embracing innovation can lead to transformative improvements in health care, highlighting the importance of pushing the boundaries in the quest for better health.

Final Words

In this chapter, we delved into the transformative innovations revolutionizing the health care industry. From the precision of drug discovery with HTS and genomics to the groundbreaking potential of CRISPR gene editing, these advancements are reshaping patient care. AI and digital health technologies are making health care more predictive and personalized, while robotic surgery enhances surgical precision and recovery outcomes.

As we look forward, the integration of these technologies promises even greater breakthroughs in medicine. Dr. Eric Topol aptly highlights this future, emphasizing the importance of precision, prediction, and personalization in health care. These innovations embody the relentless pursuit of better health outcomes, pushing the boundaries of what is possible in medicine.

Resources

Check out the following resources for more information on health care breakthroughs.

Books

- *The Patient Will See You Now* by Eric Topol

Watch List

- "How CRISPS Works in Nature," *Nova | PBS*, https://www.pbs.org/wgbh/nova/video/how-crispr-works/

Take the Future Readiness Score at www.iankhan.com/frs or scan the QR Code

5

Manufacturing Industry Disruptions

You cannot connect the dots looking forward; you can only connect them looking backwards. So you have to trust that the dots will somehow connect in your future. You have to trust in something—your gut, destiny, life, karma, whatever. Because believing that the dots will connect down the road will give you the confidence to follow your heart even when it leads you off the well-worn path; and that will make all the difference.

—Steve Jobs[1]

THIS CHAPTER COVERS some key aspects of the manufacturing industry. Today the world we live in is a result of the progress manufacturing processes have gone through. Think about all the different aspects of this industry that make our world possible. From satellites to thumb pins everything is a result of an idea, a process, and planning.

Mass Industrial Manufacturing

Mass industrial manufacturing, once synonymous with assembly lines, economies of scale, and manual labor, is undergoing a seismic shift. Modern disruptions, fueled by technological advancements and evolving global economic patterns, are reshaping how products are made and redefining the essence of industrial manufacturing. This new era promises enhanced efficiency, customization, and sustainability, signaling profound changes in global trade, labor markets, and environmental practices.

The Advent of Industry 4.0

At the heart of modern disruption in mass industrial manufacturing is the Fourth Industrial Revolution, or Industry 4.0. This movement is characterized by the integration of physical production with smart digital technologies, machine learning, and big data, creating a more connected and efficient manufacturing ecosystem. Industry 4.0 introduces smart factories, where cyber-physical systems monitor physical processes and make decentralized decisions. The implementation of Internet of Things (IoT) devices, artificial intelligence (AI), and real-time data analytics brings unprecedented productivity and flexibility to manufacturing.

"In the coming decades, the technologies driving the fourth industrial revolution will fundamentally transform the entire structure of the world economy, our communities and human identities," says Klaus Schwab, founder and executive chairman of the World Economic Forum and author of *The Fourth Industrial Revolution*.[2]

The impact of these innovations on mass industrial manufacturing is profound. Automated systems and smart technologies operate around the clock, eliminating downtime and significantly reducing human error. Digitization and smart manufacturing introduce unparalleled flexibility, allowing manufacturers to switch product lines and customize products with minimal effort and cost, meeting the growing consumer demand for personalized goods.

Industry 4.0 technologies also enhance sustainability. Advanced analytics and IoT devices optimize energy use and reduce waste, contributing to environmentally friendly practices. Digitized supply chains improve transparency and traceability, ensuring responsible and sustainable resource sourcing.

The Role of Robotics and Automation

Robotics and automation, once revolutionary, are now integral to mass industrial manufacturing. Modern robots are adaptable, intelligent, and capable of performing complex tasks with high precision. Collaborative robots (cobots) work alongside humans to enhance productivity and ensure safety, bridging the gap between fully automated systems and human-operated processes. Automation extends beyond the factory floor, revolutionizing inventory management, quality control, and after-sales services, creating a seamless flow of operations from production to customer delivery.

Elon Musk's Tesla factories exemplify this integration, with robots and humans working in tandem to produce electric vehicles efficiently and sustainably.

Additive Manufacturing: A Game Changer

Additive manufacturing, or 3D printing, once limited to prototyping, is now central to mass production. This technology allows for the on-demand production of parts with complex geometries, impossible with traditional methods. It significantly reduces material waste and production time, offering a more sustainable alternative. Companies such as GE Aviation and Adidas leverage additive manufacturing for end-use parts and products, signaling a shift toward more flexible and sustainable manufacturing models.

As Jeff Immelt, former CEO of GE, noted, "The ability to innovate, adapt, and adopt new technologies is crucial for industrial manufacturing to thrive."

What Is the Future of Mass Industrial Manufacturing?

The future of mass industrial manufacturing is poised to be more interconnected, efficient, and sustainable. The integration of AI into data-driven manufacturing processes will likely lead to greater automation and predictive maintenance, minimizing downtime and extending machinery life span. Additive manufacturing promises a shift toward localized production models, reducing the need for extensive global supply chains and mitigating the carbon footprint associated with transportation.

Moreover, the digitization of manufacturing opens possibilities for circular economy models. Advanced recycling technologies and IoT-enabled product tracking could facilitate the reuse and refurbishment of parts and materials, moving the industry from a linear "take-make-dispose" model to a more sustainable, circular approach.

Despite these promising developments, the transition to a fully digitized, sustainable manufacturing model faces challenges. Job displacement due to automation, the need for significant investment in new technologies, and the threat of cyberattacks on connected manufacturing systems are major concerns. Addressing these challenges requires industry leaders, policymakers, and educational institutions to collaborate on upskilling the workforce, prioritizing cybersecurity, and ensuring the benefits of disruptive technologies are equitably distributed.

As Satya Nadella, CEO of Microsoft, stated, "Our industry does not respect tradition—it only respects innovation."[3]

The disruption in mass industrial manufacturing marks a pivotal moment in the evolution of production. As manufacturers integrate new technologies into their operations, the potential for creating more resilient, sustainable, and personalized manufacturing processes has never been greater. Embracing these changes will ensure businesses' competitiveness in the global market and contribute to a more sustainable and innovative manufacturing landscape for future generations.

How Important Are Microprocessors?

The microprocessor, often hailed as the brain of modern electronics, has been a cornerstone of technological progress since the early 1970s. This tiny silicon chip, capable of performing complex calculations at astonishing speeds, has evolved dramatically, fueling advancements in computing, telecommunications, and numerous other fields. Today, the disruption initiated by microprocessors continues unabated, with emerging technologies pushing the boundaries of what these silicon marvels can achieve.

The journey of the microprocessor began with the Intel 4004, released in 1971. This first commercially available microprocessor laid the groundwork for the digital revolution, enabling the development of personal computers, digital watches, and later, smartphones and tablets. The relentless pace of innovation, often encapsulated by Moore's law—the prediction that the number of transistors on a microchip doubles approximately every two years—has seen microprocessors become exponentially more powerful and energy-efficient.

As Gordon Moore, cofounder of Intel, famously said, "What can be done in a lab today can be done in a garage tomorrow."

The microprocessor has revolutionized industries and transformed daily life. It has made computing devices more powerful and portable, leading to the proliferation of personal computers, laptops, and mobile devices. In telecommunications, microprocessors have enabled the development of smartphones, bringing the world's collective knowledge to our fingertips. In automation and robotics, they have facilitated more sophisticated and autonomous systems, from manufacturing robots to self-driving cars.

Microprocessors have democratized access to technology, fostering innovation and creativity globally. They are the foundation on which start-ups and tech giants build new products and services, driving economic growth and creating new markets. Steve Jobs aptly summarized this revolution: "The people who are crazy enough to think they can change the world are the ones who do."

Key Elements of Modern-Day Disruption

Today's disruption in microprocessors is characterized by several key trends:

- **Quantum computing:** Quantum processors, leveraging the principles of quantum mechanics, represent a significant departure from traditional microprocessor technology. Quantum computers, such as those being developed by Google and IBM, promise to solve complex problems currently beyond classical computers' reach, potentially revolutionizing fields such as cryptography, materials science, and drug discovery.
- **AI chips:** Specialized AI microprocessors designed to efficiently handle AI workloads, such as neural network processing, are becoming increasingly important as machine learning and other AI applications proliferate. Companies such as NVIDIA and Intel are developing chips tailored for tasks including deep learning, enabling faster and more energy-efficient AI computations.
- **Edge computing:** The rise of IoT devices has spurred interest in microprocessors optimized for edge computing. These processors process data locally, at the network's edge, reducing latency and bandwidth use in applications ranging from smart homes to autonomous vehicles.

The future of microprocessors lies in continued miniaturization, increased energy efficiency, and integrating emerging technologies such as photonics and neuromorphic computing. Photonics, which uses light rather than electricity to transmit data, promises to dramatically increase speed and reduce microprocessors' energy consumption. Neuromorphic computing, inspired by the human brain's architecture, aims to create more efficient and adaptive computing systems.

Flexible and wearable microprocessors represent another promising area. These devices could be integrated into clothing or directly onto the human body, opening new possibilities in health monitoring and wearable technology.

Foresight

As microprocessors evolve, they face challenges, including physical limitations to further miniaturization and the increasing complexity and cost of chip fabrication. Additionally, the environmental impact of producing and disposing of electronic devices containing microprocessors is a growing concern.

Addressing these challenges requires innovation in materials science, manufacturing techniques, and sustainable design. It also calls for a global effort to manage electronic waste and promote recycling and reuse of electronic components.

For nearly half a century, the microprocessor has driven technological progress, continually disrupting and reshaping industries and societies. Its evolution, marked by increasing power, efficiency, and specialization, highlights the incredible potential of human ingenuity to push the boundaries of what is possible. As we stand on the brink of new breakthroughs in quantum computing, AI, and beyond, the microprocessor remains at the heart of the digital age, promising to unlock new horizons of innovation and discovery.

How E-Commerce Changed Trade

E-commerce, the buying and selling of goods and services over the Internet, has revolutionized retail, reshaping consumer behavior, transforming business models, and redefining the global marketplace. Since its emergence in the 1990s, e-commerce has grown exponentially, fueled by technological advancements, changing consumer preferences, and the globalization of trade. This modern-day disruption has significant implications for retailers, consumers, and economies worldwide, signaling a shift toward a more digital and interconnected commercial ecosystem.

The genesis of e-commerce can be traced back to the World Wide Web's introduction in the early 1990s, which opened new avenues for electronic transactions. Pioneers such as Amazon and eBay leveraged the Internet to offer goods directly to consumers, bypassing traditional retail channels. This democratization of retail allowed for a vast selection, competitive pricing, and convenience, factors contributing to e-commerce's explosive growth.

As Jeff Bezos, founder of Amazon, famously said, "We see our customers as invited guests to a party, and we are the hosts. It's our job every day to make every important aspect of the customer experience a little bit better."

E-commerce has profoundly revolutionized retail by introducing convenience and customization previously unavailable. Consumers can now shop for anything, anytime, anywhere, with products delivered directly to their doorstep. This shift has led to increased competition among retailers, forcing traditional brick-and-mortar stores to adapt by developing their online presence or adopting omnichannel strategies that integrate online and offline shopping experiences.

E-commerce has facilitated the rise of consumer-centric business models, where data analytics and customer feedback directly influence product development, marketing, and customer service. This shift toward a more customer-focused approach has improved satisfaction and loyalty, driving further growth in online sales.

The Globalization of Trade Is Inevitable

E-commerce has played a pivotal role in the globalization of trade, enabling small and medium-sized enterprises (SMEs) to access international markets with relative ease. Platforms such as Alibaba and Etsy provide SMEs with the tools and visibility to reach customers worldwide, breaking down geographical and logistical barriers that once favored large multinational corporations. This democratization of international trade has spurred economic growth, created jobs, and facilitated cultural exchange, contributing to a more interconnected global economy.

Looking ahead, the future of e-commerce is poised for continued innovation and expansion. Emerging technologies such as augmented reality (AR) and virtual reality (VR) are expected to offer immersive shopping experiences, allowing consumers to visualize products in their own space or navigate virtual stores. Blockchain technology promises to enhance payment security, streamline supply chains, and improve transparency, addressing current limitations and challenges in e-commerce.

The growing emphasis on sustainability and ethical consumerism is likely to shape the future of e-commerce. Consumers are increasingly conscious of the environmental and social impact of their purchases, prompting e-commerce businesses to adopt more sustainable practices, from reducing packaging waste to ensuring fair labor conditions in their supply chains.

Foresight

Despite its numerous benefits, e-commerce also presents challenges, including data privacy and security concerns, the digital divide limiting access for certain populations, and the environmental impact of increased packaging and shipping. Addressing these challenges requires businesses, governments, and consumers to promote responsible e-commerce practices that prioritize security, inclusivity, and sustainability.

E-commerce has undeniably disrupted the traditional retail industry, ushering in an era of digital commerce that offers unprecedented convenience, choice, and global reach. As it continues to evolve, driven by technological innovations and changing consumer expectations, e-commerce holds the promise of further transforming the way we shop, conduct business, and interact in the global marketplace. Navigating its future successfully will hinge on balancing growth and innovation with ethical and sustainable practices, ensuring that the benefits of e-commerce are shared broadly across society.

Proximity Manufacturing

Proximity manufacturing, characterized by localizing or regionalizing production processes, is a modern disruptor in the global manufacturing landscape. This shift from the widely adopted model of globalized production and long supply chains emphasizes manufacturing goods closer to their end users. This approach, powered by technological advancements, changing consumer demands, and the need for resilient supply chains, is reshaping the industry and offering a glimpse into a future where local manufacturing could redefine economic, environmental, and social paradigms.

The Emergence of Proximity Manufacturing

The trend toward proximity manufacturing has been catalyzed by several factors, including the vulnerabilities of global supply chains exposed by crises such as the COVID-19 pandemic, trade tensions, and growing concerns over carbon footprints. Advancements in technologies such as 3D printing, robotics, and AI have made local manufacturing more viable and cost-effective, even for complex products.

The significance of proximity manufacturing lies in its potential to transform the global manufacturing and supply chain ecosystem:

- **Supply chain resilience:** Shortening supply chains reduces vulnerability to global disruptions, from pandemics to geopolitical tensions. Proximity manufacturing allows for greater flexibility and agility, ensuring a more stable supply of goods.
- **Economic benefits:** Localized manufacturing can stimulate job creation and economic growth within communities, reducing dependency on imports. It supports SMEs by lowering entry barriers to manufacturing and fostering innovation and entrepreneurship.

- **Environmental sustainability:** Shorter supply chains mean reduced transportation distances for goods, leading to lower carbon emissions and a smaller environmental footprint. Proximity manufacturing often leverages technologies that are more sustainable, such as additive manufacturing, which minimizes waste.
- **Customization and speed to market:** Being closer to the end consumer allows manufacturers to respond more quickly to market trends and demands. This agility enables higher levels of customization and faster delivery times, enhancing customer satisfaction and competitiveness.

Adidas's "Speedfactory" is a notable example of proximity manufacturing. Using automated technology and 3D printing, it produces sneakers on-demand, significantly reducing the lead time from design to retail and allowing for unprecedented levels of product customization.

The Future of Proximity Manufacturing

The future of proximity manufacturing is intrinsically linked to the continued evolution of manufacturing technologies and shifts in global economic and environmental policies. Key trends shaping its trajectory include:

- **Advancements in manufacturing technologies:** Continuous improvements in 3D printing, robotics, and AI will further reduce the costs and complexities of localized production, making it accessible to a wider range of products and industries.
- **Sustainable and circular economy models:** The push toward sustainability will drive the adoption of proximity manufacturing as part of broader circular economy strategies. This includes using renewable materials, designing products for disassembly and recycling, and integrating production processes that regenerate natural systems.
- **Digitization and the IoT:** The digitization of manufacturing and the use of IoT devices will enhance the efficiency and transparency of localized production, enabling real-time monitoring, predictive maintenance, and seamless integration of production systems.
- **Policy and regulatory support:** Government policies and incentives promoting domestic manufacturing, research and development in advanced manufacturing technologies, and sustainability could significantly influence the adoption of proximity manufacturing models.

Despite its potential, the shift toward proximity manufacturing faces challenges. Initial high investment costs in technology, the need for a skilled workforce to operate advanced systems, and regulatory hurdles can impede adoption. The transition to localized production models also requires rethinking global trade structures and relationships, with implications for international cooperation and development.

Proximity manufacturing represents a disruptive shift toward more resilient, sustainable, and consumer-responsive production models. By leveraging advancements in technology and aligning with broader economic and environmental goals, proximity manufacturing has the potential to transform the manufacturing sector, contributing to a more localized, efficient, and sustainable global economy. As this trend continues to evolve, the future of manufacturing appears increasingly localized, promising benefits extending well beyond the factory floor to encompass broader societal and environmental well-being.

For more information, check out the book *Proximity* by Robert C. Wolcott and Kaihan Krippendorff to understand this concept better.[4]

Final Words

The advent of Industry 4.0 marks a pivotal moment, integrating smart technologies and data analytics to create highly efficient and flexible manufacturing ecosystems. The role of robotics and automation has moved from revolutionary to essential, enhancing productivity and safety. Additive manufacturing is a game changer, enabling on-demand production with minimal waste and greater customization. The journey through these disruptions underscores a broader narrative: the manufacturing industry is at the cusp of a profound transformation. Embracing these changes will ensure competitiveness in the global market and contribute to a more innovative and sustainable future.

Resources

Check out the following resources for more information on manufacturing breakthroughs.

Books

- *The Fourth Industrial Revolution* by Klaus Schwab
- *Proximity* by Robert C. Wolcott and Kaihan Krippendorff
- *Industry 4.0: The Industrial Internet of Things* by Alasdair Gilchrist

Videos

- "How AI Could Empower Any Business," TED Talk by Andrew Ng

Take the Future Readiness Score at www.iankhan.com/frs or scan the QR Code

6

Innovation at the Speed of Light

Innovation is the ability to see change as an opportunity, not a threat.
—*Steve Jobs*

IN TODAY'S RAPIDLY evolving landscape, disruption in ideation and innovation has become a driving force, reshaping industries, advancing societal progress, and transforming how we tackle complex problems. This shift moves away from linear, incremental innovation to more dynamic, interdisciplinary approaches leveraging technology, collaboration, and a deep understanding of human needs and behaviors. The impact is profound, opening new pathways to tackle global challenges, enhance quality of life, and foster sustainable growth.

How Are Ideation and Innovation Transforming Our World?

Traditionally, innovation followed a top-down approach, where ideas trickled down from research labs to the market, often siloed within specific industries. The digital age and the democratization of information and technology have fundamentally altered this dynamic. Today, ideation and innovation are increasingly collaborative and user-centered, drawing insights from diverse fields and stakeholders to create inclusive, accessible, and effective solutions.

Steve Jobs famously said, "Innovation distinguishes between a leader and a follower," emphasizing the importance of staying ahead through continuous creativity and improvement.[1]

Disruption in ideation and innovation has led to groundbreaking technologies and services addressing real-world problems. Fintech innovations such as mobile payments and peer-to-peer lending platforms have revolutionized banking, providing financial services to millions of unbanked or underbanked individuals. Similarly, advancements in renewable energy technologies, such as solar panels and wind turbines, are critical in transitioning toward a sustainable global energy system.

One significant aspect of modern ideation is the embrace of crowdsourcing and open innovation models. Platforms such as Kickstarter and Indiegogo allow entrepreneurs to present their ideas to the public, garnering support and funding from a global community. Initiatives such as OpenIDEO challenge solvers worldwide to tackle pressing social and environmental issues, fostering a culture of collaboration and shared purpose.

Bill Gates once remarked, "Do not let complexity stop you," capturing the spirit of open innovation that encourages diverse perspectives and collective problem-solving.[2]

Technology is central to the disruption of ideation and innovation, providing tools and platforms that enable collaboration, rapid prototyping, and scalability. Social media and digital collaboration tools facilitate idea exchange across geographies, while AI, big data, and blockchain offer new ways to analyze trends, predict outcomes, and secure intellectual property. Rapid prototyping technologies, such as 3D printing, allow innovators to test and refine ideas quickly, reducing development time and cost.

The modern approach to ideation and innovation has yielded solutions with significant societal impact. Telemedicine and wearable health technologies have made medical care more accessible, especially in remote areas. Online learning platforms and educational apps have democratized education, offering new learning opportunities regardless of location or resources. The focus on sustainable innovation has led to products and services that reduce waste, conserve resources, and mitigate climate change impacts.

The Future of Ideation and Innovation?

The future of ideation and innovation will intertwine with global trends such as urbanization, climate change, and demographic shifts. Innovators will need to navigate these complexities, leveraging emerging technologies and interdisciplinary approaches to create solutions that are technologically advanced, socially responsible, and environmentally sustainable.

One promising area is the convergence of biotechnology and materials science, potentially leading to bio-based materials and energy sources, revolutionizing industries from manufacturing to construction. The potential for AI and in particular machine learning (ML) to unlock new insights into human behavior and societal trends will drive innovation in public policy to consumer products.

Despite its potential, the disruption in ideation and innovation poses challenges, including ethical considerations around data privacy, the digital divide, and the risk of exacerbating inequality. Addressing these issues requires a thoughtful approach that prioritizes inclusivity, equity, and long-term societal impacts.

"The best way to predict the future is to create it," said Peter Drucker, underscoring the proactive role of innovators in shaping a better world.[3]

Future Insights

Disruption in ideation and innovation is a powerful catalyst for positive change, offering new tools and methodologies to address the world's most pressing challenges. By embracing collaboration, leveraging technology, and focusing on sustainable and inclusive solutions, innovators can drive progress and shape a future that benefits all. As ideation and innovation processes evolve, they will play a crucial role in determining the trajectory of human development in the twenty-first century and beyond.

Artificial Intelligence

Artificial intelligence (AI) stands as one of the most transformative forces of modern disruption, influencing nearly every industry and aspect of our lives. From altering business models to reshaping societal norms, AI's impact is vast and multifaceted. Its rapid advancement presents unparalleled opportunities and significant challenges, necessitating a nuanced exploration of its impact, significance, and future trajectory.

AI's journey began in the mid-twentieth century with the quest to understand if machines could think. This led to the development of algorithms mimicking human intelligence aspects such as learning, problem-solving, and perception. Today, AI encompasses a broad range of technologies, including ML, natural language processing (NLP), and computer vision, each contributing to AI's growing capabilities and applications.

Why Is the AI Disruption Significant?

AI's disruption is evident across several domains:

- **Health care:** AI revolutionizes health care through early disease detection, personalized medicine, and robotic surgeries. Systems such as IBM Watson analyze medical data at unprecedented speeds, offering diagnostics and treatment options based on vast datasets.
- **Transportation:** Autonomous vehicles powered by AI promise to transform transportation by reducing accidents caused by human error, optimizing traffic flow, and decreasing carbon emissions. Companies such as Tesla and Waymo are leading the development of these technologies.
- **Finance:** AI enhances fraud detection, risk management, and customer service. AI algorithms efficiently identify patterns indicative of fraudulent activity, enhancing security in digital transactions.
- **Environmental conservation:** AI aids in environmental conservation through predictive analytics in climate modeling, monitoring wildlife and biodiversity, and optimizing energy consumption in smart grids.

AI contributes extensively to society. Beyond industry-specific impacts, AI fosters innovation, drives economic growth, and enhances the quality of life. AI-driven personal assistants and smart home devices simplify daily tasks, while AI in education personalizes learning experiences, accommodating individual styles and pacing.

During the COVID-19 pandemic, AI tools tracked virus spread, analyzed public health data, and accelerated vaccine research, demonstrating AI's potential in crisis response.

The future of AI is promising yet fraught with ethical considerations. As AI systems become more advanced, achieving greater autonomy, innovations will emerge that are currently unimaginable. The development of general AI (also called AGI), systems performing any intellectual task a human can, remains a long-term goal with the potential to redefine science, art, and human cognition.

However, concerns include job displacement, privacy issues with surveillance technologies, and ethical AI use in decision-making. Steering AI development to maximize benefits while mitigating risks and ensuring equitable access is essential.

Addressing AI's challenges requires collaboration among policymakers, technologists, and civil society to establish guidelines and regulations promoting responsible AI development and use. This includes tackling bias in AI algorithms, safeguarding against malicious AI uses, and ensuring advancements benefit society without exacerbating inequality.

Education and workforce development are crucial, requiring training in technical skills and understanding AI's ethical, social, and cultural implications.

Future Insights

AI, with its profound capability to disrupt and transform, stands at the forefront of modern technological evolution. Its impact spans from enhancing efficiency and creating new opportunities in various sectors to posing challenges requiring careful consideration and management. As we navigate the AI-driven era, focus must be on harnessing its potential to foster innovation, address global challenges, and improve the human condition, while safeguarding against its risks. The future of AI, shaped by today's human choices and actions, holds the promise of a more intelligent, efficient, and connected world.

Brain Implants

Brain implants, or neural implants, represent a frontier at the convergence of neuroscience and technology, offering unprecedented possibilities for treating neurological disorders, enhancing human capabilities, and exploring human cognition. This emerging field, though still in its nascent stages, has the potential to radically transform medical treatment, rehabilitation, and our understanding of the brain.

The concept of brain implants dates back several decades when early versions were used primarily for deep brain stimulation (DBS) to treat chronic pain, tremors, and Parkinson's disease. Advances in microtechnology, computing, and neuroimaging have expanded neural implants' potential applications, from cochlear implants restoring hearing to sophisticated systems offering direct brain-computer interfaces (BCIs).

"The brain is the last and grandest biological frontier," remarked James Watson, codiscoverer of the DNA structure, emphasizing the significance of neural research.[4]

The impact of brain implants on medicine and society is profound:

- **Treating neurological disorders:** Brain implants provide relief to patients with Parkinson's disease, essential tremor, and epilepsy, improving quality of life and offering control over debilitating conditions.
- **Restoring sensory and motor functions:** Advances in neural implants restore sensory and motor functions in individuals with spinal cord injuries or neurodegenerative diseases. Projects such as BrainGate enable paralyzed individuals to control external devices with their thoughts, offering newfound independence.
- **Enhancing human capabilities:** Beyond medical applications, there's interest in enhancing cognitive functions including memory and concentration. These possibilities raise ethical, philosophical, and security considerations about human enhancement.

Brain implants offer substantial societal benefits, particularly in health care and rehabilitation. For individuals with severe disabilities, these devices can dramatically improve daily functioning and well-being. The ability to bypass damaged neural pathways and restore communication between the brain and limbs promises to revolutionize physical rehabilitation and assistive technologies.

From a broader perspective, brain implant research advances our understanding of the human brain, potentially leading to breakthroughs in treating mental health disorders, enhancing learning, and mitigating brain aging effects.

Brain implants, or neural implants, represent a frontier at the convergence of neuroscience and technology, offering unprecedented possibilities for treating neurological disorders, enhancing human capabilities, and exploring human cognition. This emerging field, though still in its nascent stages, has the potential to radically transform medical treatment, rehabilitation, and our understanding of the brain.

The Future of Brain Implants?

The future of brain implants will be shaped by advancements in materials science, miniaturization, and AI. Developing more biocompatible materials and wireless technologies could reduce implantation surgery risks and improve devices' longevity and functionality. AI can analyze complex neural data, offering personalized and effective stimulation therapies, adapting in real time to user needs.

Emerging applications, such as integrating artificial sensory inputs or facilitating direct brain-to-brain communication, present fascinating exploration avenues. The intersection of BCIs with virtual reality could open new realms of experience, blurring physical and digital reality lines.

Brain implants raise significant ethical, privacy, and security issues. The prospect of enhancing or altering human cognition invites debate over identity, agency, and potential inequality between those with access to such technologies and those without. Privacy concerns are paramount, as brain implants could theoretically access or manipulate an individual's thoughts.

The regulatory landscape for brain implants is evolving, requiring careful oversight to ensure patient safety, informed consent, and equitable access. Addressing these challenges requires a multidisciplinary approach, involving ethicists, policymakers, technologists, and the public in ongoing dialogue.

"The question of whether a computer can think is no more interesting than the question of whether a submarine can swim," said renowned computer scientist Edsger Dijkstra, underscoring the philosophical depths of technology's role in human augmentation.[5]

Future Insights

Brain implants stand at the intersection of technological innovation and human aspiration, offering profound possibilities for healing, enhancement, and exploration. Navigating the complexities of integrating these devices into our bodies and societies requires focusing on harnessing their potential for the greater good while safeguarding individual rights and dignity. The future of brain implants promises to redefine human capability and understanding, marking a new chapter in human progress.

Strategy Development

In today's fast-paced, complex global landscape, strategy development is undergoing significant disruption. This transformation is driven by the need to adapt to rapid technological advancements, changing consumer preferences, and the volatile global economy. Traditional strategic planning models, often linear and based on predictable conditions, are being challenged by dynamic, flexible, and innovative approaches. This disruption reshapes how organizations envision their future, make decisions, and position themselves for long-term success.

What Is the Shift in Strategy Development?

Historically, strategy development involved long-term planning cycles, often spanning 5–10 years, focusing on stability and gradual growth. This approach relied heavily on historical data and assumed relatively stable market conditions. The digital revolution, globalization, and disruptive technologies have rendered these methods less effective.

Modern strategy development emphasizes agility, adaptability, and continuous innovation. Organizations adopt frameworks allowing them to respond swiftly to market changes, technological innovations, and shifts in consumer behavior. Agile strategy involves shorter planning cycles, real-time data analysis, and a willingness to pivot based on emerging trends.

Disruption in strategy development has profound implications:

- **Enhanced competitiveness:** Agile planning enables organizations to stay competitive by adapting quickly to changes and seizing new opportunities.
- **Increased innovation:** This new paradigm fosters a culture of innovation, leading to groundbreaking products, services, and business models.
- **Risk management:** Modern planning incorporates scenario planning and continuous monitoring, allowing organizations to anticipate and mitigate risks effectively.
- **Customer-centricity:** Modern strategies emphasize understanding and meeting customer needs, leveraging data analytics to deliver superior value and enhance loyalty.

The disruption in strategy development helps organizations in various ways:

- **Agility in uncertain times:** Flexible planning allows organizations to navigate challenges and capitalize on opportunities in an uncertain era.
- **Alignment with digital transformation:** Agile strategy ensures organizations effectively integrate new technologies and digital business models.
- **Sustainability and social responsibility:** Modern planning increasingly incorporates sustainability and social responsibility, ensuring long-term growth while contributing positively to society and the environment.

The future of strategy development will be characterized by:

- **Integration of AI:** ML and other areas of AI will play significant roles, offering predictive insights, automating data analysis, and facilitating decision-making.
- **Emphasis on ecosystems:** Organizations will increasingly collaborate within ecosystems, creating shared value with partners, competitors, and stakeholders.
- **Continuous learning and adaptation:** The "learning organization" concept will become integral, with continuous learning, experimentation, and adaptation at the core.
- **Greater focus on purpose and values:** Strategies will align with organizational purpose and values, meeting consumer and employee expectations and achieving broader societal objectives.

The disruption in strategy development reflects broader transformations in business, driven by the need for agility, innovation, and resilience. The ability to develop and execute dynamic strategies will be crucial for achieving sustainable success. Integration of technology, focus on ecosystems, and commitment to continuous learning and purpose will define the next horizon of strategic planning. Organizations that adapt their strategic approaches to embrace change and uncertainty will thrive.

"In preparing for battle, I have always found that plans are useless, but planning is indispensable," said Dwight D. Eisenhower, emphasizing the importance of flexibility in strategy.[6]

Final Words

In today's rapidly evolving landscape, innovation and ideation have become transformative forces, reshaping industries and advancing societal progress. This shift moves away from linear, incremental innovation to dynamic, interdisciplinary approaches leveraging technology, collaboration, and a deep understanding of human needs and behaviors.

The modern approach to innovation has led to groundbreaking technologies and services. Fintech innovations such as mobile payments and peer-to-peer lending have revolutionized banking, while advancements in renewable energy technologies are critical in transitioning toward a sustainable global energy system. Crowdsourcing and open innovation models, such as those facilitated by platforms including Kickstarter and OpenIDEO, have democratized the innovation process, allowing for greater collaboration and shared purpose.

Technology plays a central role in this disruption, providing tools and platforms that enable collaboration, rapid prototyping, and scalability. Social media and digital collaboration tools facilitate idea exchange, while AI, big data, and blockchain offer new ways to analyze trends, predict outcomes, and secure intellectual property. Innovations such as telemedicine and online learning platforms have made significant societal impacts, improving access to health care and education.

Looking ahead, the future of ideation and innovation will intertwine with global trends such as urbanization, climate change, and demographic shifts. Innovators will need to navigate these complexities, leveraging emerging technologies and interdisciplinary approaches to create solutions that are technologically advanced, socially responsible, and environmentally sustainable. Ethical considerations, such as data privacy and the digital divide, will also be crucial to address to ensure that innovation benefits all segments of society.

As Steve Jobs aptly put it, "Innovation is the ability to see change as an opportunity, not a threat." Embracing this mindset will be key to driving progress and shaping a better future for all.

Resources

To further explore these topics and prepare for future disruptions, consider the following resources.

Books and Journals

- *The Innovator's Dilemma* by Clayton Christensen
- *Exponential Organizations* by Salim Ismail
- *The Lean Startup* by Eric Ries
- Journals including *Harvard Business Review* and *MIT Technology Review*

TED Talks

- TED Talks on innovation and technology

Online Courses

■ Online courses on AI and machine learning (Coursera, edX)

Watch List

■ *The Social Dilemma* (film, 2020)
■ *Ex Machina* (film, 2015)
■ *The Matrix* (film, 1999)

Take the Future Readiness Score at www.iankhan.com/frs or scan the QR Code

7

Disruptive Mobility and Transportation

The future belongs to those who prepare for it today.

—*Malcolm X*

ELECTRIC VEHICLES (EVs), autonomous transport, vertical takeoff and landing (VTOL): these are some of the innovative areas within the global transportation industry. In this chapter we look at some of the breakthroughs currently under way in the global mobility and transportation sector. This includes autonomous transportation, EVs, and air transport.

Emergence of Autonomous Transportation

The advent of autonomous transportation signifies a paradigm shift in how people and goods move, promising to redefine mobility with profound implications for society, the economy, and the environment. This modern-day disruption, driven by advancements in artificial intelligence (AI), robotics, and sensor technology, envisions a future where vehicles navigate the world with little to no human intervention. As we stand on the cusp of this transformative era, exploring the impact, significance, and future of autonomous transportation offers insights into a journey toward safer, more efficient, and sustainable mobility.

Autonomous transportation, encompassing self-driving cars, drones, and autonomous shipping, has roots in decades of research and development.

From early experiments in automated guided vehicles to today's sophisticated prototypes equipped with AI, LiDAR (light detection and ranging), and computer vision technologies, the journey of autonomous transportation has been marked by significant milestones. Companies such as Tesla, Waymo, and Uber, alongside automotive giants such as Ford and General Motors, are leading efforts to bring autonomous vehicles (AVs) to public roads, while start-ups and tech giants explore drone delivery and autonomous shipping solutions.

- Autonomous transportation represents one of the most significant disruptions in the mobility sector, with the potential to make transportation safer, more efficient, and more accessible. As this technology transitions from prototype to public roads, it challenges existing paradigms and invites us to reimagine the future of mobility. While the road ahead is fraught with challenges, the collaborative efforts of technologists, policy-makers, and society at large can steer this disruption toward a future where autonomous transportation is an integral, beneficial part of daily life, transforming not just how we travel but how we live, work, and interact with our cities and each other.

Self-Driving Vehicle Stats

It is still early days for autonomous vehicles but the data proves the need. Here are some key statistics that can help to understand the bigger picture.

- The global autonomous vehicle market is expected to reach $60 billion by 2030, driven by advancements in AI, especially machine learning, and sensor technologies.
- Autonomous vehicles could potentially reduce traffic accidents by up to 90%, saving thousands of lives annually, as human error accounts for the majority of road accidents.
- Autonomous electric vehicles (EVs) can significantly cut greenhouse gas emissions, contributing to the reduction of urban air pollution and promoting sustainable urban living.
- The rise of autonomous vehicles is expected to disrupt traditional automotive jobs but create new opportunities in tech development, fleet management, and AI systems.
- Cities might repurpose up to 30% of their current parking spaces for other uses, such as parks and public spaces, as autonomous ride-sharing reduces the need for personal car ownership.

The Rise of Electric Vehicles

The rise of EVs marks a pivotal disruption in the automotive industry, steering it toward a more sustainable and innovative future. Once viewed as niche or futuristic, EVs are now at the forefront of a global shift, driven by advancements in battery technology, regulatory pressures for reduced emissions, and growing consumer consciousness about environmental issues. This transformation is reshaping the landscape of personal and public transportation, with profound implications for energy consumption, urban planning, and the global economy.

The modern EV revolution began in earnest in the early twenty-first century, catalyzed by technological advancements and a renewed focus on sustainability. Pioneers such as Tesla have been instrumental in bringing EVs into the mainstream, demonstrating that electric cars can compete with, and even outperform, their gasoline-powered counterparts in terms of performance, safety, and desirability. Meanwhile, traditional automotive giants and new entrants alike are expanding their EV offerings, signaling a broad industry shift toward electrification.

Future Insights

Despite the optimistic outlook, the shift to electric vehicles faces challenges, including raw material sourcing, battery recycling and disposal, and the social and economic impacts on industries reliant on the traditional automotive and oil sectors. Addressing these challenges requires a coordinated approach involving industry, government, and society to ensure that the transition to electric vehicles is sustainable, equitable, and beneficial for all.

The disruption brought about by electric vehicles is transforming transportation, energy, and society in profound ways. As technology continues to advance and societal attitudes shift, the future of mobility looks increasingly electric. Embracing this change offers the promise of a cleaner, healthier, and more sustainable world, underscoring the power of innovation to drive positive environmental and social outcomes.

Drone Transportation

The advent of drone technology for delivery services represents a significant disruption in the logistics and delivery industry, offering a glimpse into a future where goods are transported with unprecedented speed and efficiency. As we navigate the twenty-first century, the emergence of drone deliveries stands out as a testament to human ingenuity and the relentless pursuit of innovation to overcome logistical challenges, particularly in the last mile of delivery. This section explores the impacts, significance, and future prospects of drone delivery systems.

How Are Delivery Services Being Transformed by Drones?

Drone delivery systems promise to revolutionize the way goods are transported, particularly for short distances or in hard-to-reach areas. By taking to the skies, drones bypass traditional ground transportation challenges such as traffic congestion and poor road infrastructure, offering a faster, more reliable way to deliver packages. Companies such as Amazon, with its Prime Air service, and UPS Flight Forward, are pioneering this space, conducting trials and securing regulatory approvals to integrate drones into their delivery fleets.

How Is Last-Mile Delivery Evolving?

Modern-day logistics and e-commerce are undergoing significant transformation, driven by the disruption in "last-mile delivery." This crucial segment of the delivery chain, referring to the final step of the process where goods are transported from a transportation hub to the final destination, has traditionally been the most expensive, least efficient, and most problematic aspect of the shipping process. However, innovations in technology, business models, and consumer expectations are reshaping last-mile delivery, promising to enhance efficiency, reduce costs, and improve customer satisfaction.

The surge in e-commerce, fueled by digital platforms and changing consumer behaviors, particularly in the wake of the COVID-19 pandemic, has put unprecedented pressure on last-mile delivery systems. Consumers now expect faster, more flexible, and more reliable delivery services, often at no additional cost. This demand, coupled with the need for sustainability and efficiency, has spurred a wave of innovation aimed at disrupting traditional last-mile delivery practices.

Technologies Driving Last-Mile Delivery

Several key technological advancements are at the forefront of disrupting last-mile delivery:

- **AVs and drones:** Companies such as Amazon and UPS are experimenting with drones and self-driving vehicles to automate deliveries, promising to reduce delivery times and costs while addressing driver shortages.

- **EVs:** The adoption of EVs for delivery fleets is on the rise, driven by the dual goals of reducing operational costs and minimizing environmental impact.
- **Advanced routing algorithms:** Machine learning (ML) and other areas of AI are being used to optimize delivery routes in real-time, improving efficiency and reducing the time drivers spend on the road.
- **Crowdsourced delivery models:** Platforms such as Postmates and Uber Eats leverage a network of independent couriers to offer flexible, on-demand delivery services, catering to the growing expectation for same-day or even same-hour delivery.

Future Insights

Looking ahead, the future of last-mile delivery will likely be shaped by continued technological innovation, regulatory changes, and evolving consumer preferences:

- **Expansion of autonomous and drone deliveries:** As technology advances and regulatory hurdles are overcome, autonomous vehicles and drones could become commonplace in last-mile delivery, especially in urban areas.
- **Integration with smart city infrastructure:** Last-mile delivery operations may increasingly be integrated with smart city technologies, such as IoT devices for traffic management and smart lockers for secure, unattended deliveries.
- **Increased focus on sustainability:** With growing awareness of environmental issues, sustainable delivery options, including zero-emissions vehicles and package consolidation, will become more prominent.
- **Customization and personalization:** Technology will enable more personalized delivery experiences, with consumers having greater control over delivery times, locations, and preferences.

The disruption in last-mile delivery encapsulates the challenges and opportunities of adapting to a rapidly changing e-commerce landscape. By leveraging technology, rethinking business models, and prioritizing sustainability and customer satisfaction, last-mile delivery can transcend its traditional limitations, offering a glimpse into a future where logistics are more efficient, environmentally friendly, and aligned with consumer demands. As this sector continues to evolve, balancing innovation with ethical and practical considerations will be key to realizing its full potential.

How Will Urban Air Mobility (UAM) Transform Cities?

Urban air mobility (UAM) involves the use of small, electric or hybrid-electric vertical takeoff and landing (eVTOL) aircraft to transport passengers and cargo within urban areas. This concept, driven by advancements in electric propulsion, autonomous flight, and aerospace technology, promises to offer a faster and more flexible mode of transportation, particularly in congested urban centers.

UAM envisions a future where air taxis, drones, and other aerial vehicles provide a viable alternative to traditional ground transportation, easing congestion, reducing travel times, and reshaping urban environments.

What Are the Potential Benefits of Urban Air Mobility?

The introduction of UAM systems could bring several significant benefits:

- **Reduced congestion:** By moving transportation to the skies, UAM can alleviate road traffic congestion, reducing the strain on existing infrastructure.
- **Faster commutes:** eVTOL aircraft can provide direct routes between locations, bypassing the delays associated with ground traffic, leading to shorter travel times.
- **Environmental benefits:** UAM vehicles are often designed to be electric, reducing emissions compared to traditional gasoline-powered vehicles. This supports urban sustainability goals and improves air quality.
- **Economic opportunities:** The development and deployment of UAM systems can create new jobs in manufacturing, operations, maintenance, and air traffic management.
- **Enhanced connectivity:** UAM can improve accessibility in urban areas, connecting remote or underserved regions more efficiently.

What Is the Future of Urban Air Mobility?

The future of UAM looks promising, with several key developments on the horizon:

- **Pilot programs and trials:** Cities around the world are initiating pilot programs to test UAM solutions. These trials will provide valuable insights into operational feasibility and public response.

- **Integration with existing transit systems:** The success of UAM depends on its integration with existing transportation networks, creating seamless, multimodal transit solutions.
- **Advanced air traffic management:** Developing sophisticated air traffic management systems to safely coordinate a high volume of UAM vehicles in urban airspace is essential.
- **Commercialization and scaling:** As technology matures and regulations solidify, UAM services will scale, becoming a common feature in urban transportation landscapes.

Future Insights

Urban Air Mobility represents a bold vision for the future of urban transportation, promising to transform how we navigate cities. By addressing the technological, regulatory, and societal challenges, UAM can unlock a new era of efficient, sustainable, and connected urban mobility.

Hydrogen as a Fuel

Hydrogen fuel cell technology is emerging as a promising alternative to conventional fossil fuels and electric batteries in the quest for sustainable transportation. By converting hydrogen gas into electricity, fuel cells produce only water and heat as byproducts, offering a clean and efficient energy source for various transportation modes, from cars and buses to trains and ships.

Hydrogen fuel cells generate electricity through a chemical reaction between hydrogen and oxygen. The process involves an anode, a cathode, and an electrolyte membrane. Hydrogen gas flows into the anode, where it is split into protons and electrons. The protons pass through the electrolyte membrane to the cathode, while the electrons flow through an external circuit, creating an electric current. At the cathode, the protons, electrons, and oxygen combine to form water, the only emission from the fuel cell.

What Are the Advantages of Hydrogen Fuel Cells?

The cost of producing hydrogen from renewable electricity could fall by 30% by 2030, making it a more viable option for widespread use. However, green hydrogen, produced via electrolysis using renewable energy, currently remains expensive compared to traditional methods involving fossil fuels.[1]

Hydrogen fuel cells offer several notable benefits:

- **Zero emissions:** The only byproduct of hydrogen fuel cells is water, making them an environmentally friendly alternative to fossil fuels.
- **High efficiency:** Fuel cells are more efficient than ICEs and can achieve higher energy conversion rates.
- **Fast refueling:** Hydrogen vehicles can be refueled quickly, similar to gasoline vehicles, providing a significant advantage over battery EVs, which require longer charging times.
- **Energy security:** Hydrogen can be produced from various domestic resources, including natural gas, water, and biomass, enhancing energy security and reducing dependence on imported oil.
- **Versatility:** Hydrogen fuel cells can power a wide range of applications, from passenger vehicles and buses to industrial equipment and stationary power systems.

What Does the Future Hold for Hydrogen Fuel Cells?

The future of hydrogen fuel cells looks promising, with several key developments on the horizon:

- **Investment and innovation:** Increased investment in research and development is driving advancements in hydrogen production, storage, and fuel cell technologies.
- **Policy support:** Governments worldwide are implementing policies and incentives to promote hydrogen fuel cell adoption, including funding for infrastructure projects and emissions regulations.
- **Sector integration:** Hydrogen fuel cells are being integrated into various sectors, including transportation, industry, and power generation, expanding their applications and driving economies of scale.
- **Collaborations and partnerships:** Public-private partnerships and international collaborations are essential for accelerating the development and deployment of hydrogen fuel cell technologies.

Future Insights

Hydrogen fuel cells represent a crucial component of the future transportation landscape, offering a clean, efficient, and versatile energy solution. By overcoming the current challenges and leveraging the advantages of hydrogen technology, we can pave the way for a sustainable and secure energy future.

What Are the Implications of 3D Printing for Transportation?

Three-dimensional, or 3D, printing, also known as additive manufacturing, is poised to revolutionize the transportation industry by enabling the production of complex, lightweight, and customized components. This technology has the potential to streamline manufacturing processes, reduce material waste, and enhance the design and functionality of vehicles, revolutionizing everything from automotive and aerospace to maritime and rail transport.

This manufacturing process involves creating three-dimensional objects by adding material layer by layer based on digital models. This allows for the precise and efficient production of complex geometries that would be difficult or impossible to achieve with traditional manufacturing methods. Common materials used in 3D printing include plastics, metals, and composites.

What Are the Benefits of 3D Printing in Transportation?

The adoption of 3D printing in the transportation sector offers several key advantages:

- **Design flexibility:** 3D printing allows for the creation of intricate and customized designs, enabling innovation in vehicle components and structures.
- **Lightweight components:** The ability to produce lightweight parts can improve vehicle performance and fuel efficiency and reduce emissions.
- **Reduced material waste:** Additive manufacturing minimizes waste by using only the necessary amount of material, contributing to more sustainable production processes.
- **Rapid prototyping:** 3D printing accelerates the development of prototypes, reducing the time and cost associated with traditional manufacturing and testing.
- **On-demand production:** The capability to produce parts on-demand reduces inventory costs and enhances supply chain efficiency.

Future Insights

Three-dimensional, or 3D, printing is set to transform the transportation industry by offering innovative solutions for design, manufacturing, and supply chain management. By embracing this technology and addressing its challenges, the transportation sector can achieve greater efficiency, sustainability, and innovation.

How Will Smart Transportation Systems Improve Urban Mobility?

Smart transportation systems are revolutionizing urban mobility by integrating advanced technologies such as the Internet of Things (IoT), AI, and big data analytics. These systems aim to enhance the efficiency, safety, and sustainability of transportation networks, addressing the growing challenges of urbanization and increasing mobility demands.

What Are Smart Transportation Systems?

Smart transportation systems encompass a wide range of technologies and solutions designed to optimize the movement of people and goods within urban environments. Key components include:

- **Connected vehicles:** Vehicles equipped with sensors and communication technologies that enable them to interact with each other and with infrastructure.
- **Intelligent traffic management:** Systems that use real-time data to monitor and manage traffic flow, reduce congestion, and enhance road safety.
- **Smart public transit:** Enhanced public transportation systems that leverage data analytics and mobile apps to improve service efficiency, reliability, and user experience.
- **Mobility-as-a-service (MaaS):** Platforms that integrate various transportation modes into a single accessible service, offering users seamless travel planning and payment options.

Future Insights

Smart transportation systems have the potential to transform urban mobility by making transportation networks more efficient, safe, and sustainable. By addressing the challenges and leveraging the benefits of these systems, cities can enhance the quality of life for their residents and create more resilient and adaptable urban environments.

How Are Artificial Intelligence and Machine Learning Revolutionizing Transportation?

ML and other forms of AI are at the forefront of technological advancements, revolutionizing the transportation sector by enhancing the efficiency, safety, and convenience of mobility systems. These technologies are driving innovations across various transportation modes, from AVs and predictive maintenance to smart traffic management and personalized travel experiences.

What Role Does AI Play in Autonomous Vehicles?

AI is the cornerstone of AV technology, enabling vehicles to perceive their environment, make decisions, and navigate safely without human intervention. Key components include:

- **Computer vision:** AI-powered cameras and sensors provide real-time data on the vehicle's surroundings, identifying objects, obstacles, and road conditions.
- **Path planning:** ML algorithms process data from sensors to determine the optimal path, ensuring safe and efficient navigation.
- **Decision-making:** AI systems analyze vast amounts of data to make split-second decisions, such as when to stop, accelerate, or change lanes.
- **Vehicle-to-everything (V2X) communication:** AI enables vehicles to communicate with each other and with infrastructure, enhancing safety and traffic flow.

What Are the Benefits of Artificial Intelligence and Machine Learning in Transportation?

The integration of ML and other forms of AI in transportation offers numerous benefits:

- **Enhanced safety:** AI systems improve safety by reducing human error, detecting hazards, and preventing accidents.
- **Increased efficiency:** AI optimizes routing, traffic management, and resource allocation, leading to more efficient transportation systems.
- **Cost savings:** Predictive maintenance and optimized operations reduce costs for transportation providers and users.
- **Personalized travel:** AI-driven platforms offer personalized travel recommendations, enhancing the user experience.
- **Environmental impact:** AI optimizes vehicle performance and traffic flow, reducing fuel consumption and emissions.

Future Insights

The future of AI in transportation is promising, with several key trends and innovations to watch for:

- **Advancements in autonomous vehicles:** Continued improvements in different areas of AI will enhance the capabilities and safety of autonomous vehicles, bringing them closer to widespread adoption.
- **Integration with smart infrastructure:** AI systems will be integrated with smart infrastructure, creating cohesive and adaptive urban transportation networks.
- **Expansion of predictive maintenance:** AI-driven predictive maintenance will become standard practice, enhancing the reliability and life span of transportation assets.
- **Personalized mobility solutions:** AI platforms will offer increasingly personalized and seamless mobility solutions, tailored to individual preferences and needs.
- **Collaborative ecosystems:** Collaboration among technology providers, transportation operators, and regulators will drive the development and deployment of AI in transportation.

ML and other forms of AI are revolutionizing the transportation sector, offering transformative solutions that enhance safety, efficiency, and user experience. By addressing the challenges and leveraging the benefits of these technologies, we can create smarter, more resilient, and more sustainable transportation systems.

How Are Electric Aviation Technologies Shaping the Future of Air Travel?

Electric aviation technologies are set to transform the aviation industry by offering cleaner, quieter, and more efficient alternatives to traditional aircraft. With advancements in battery technology, electric propulsion, and aerodynamics, electric aviation promises to reduce the environmental impact of air travel and revolutionize short-haul and regional flights.

What Are Electric Aviation Technologies?

Electric aviation involves the use of electric-powered aircraft for various flight applications. Key technologies include:

- **Electric propulsion systems:** These systems use electric motors to drive propellers or fans, reducing or eliminating the need for conventional jet engines.
- **Advanced batteries:** High-energy-density batteries provide the necessary power for electric aircraft, enabling longer flight ranges and faster charging times.
- **Hybrid-electric systems:** Combining electric propulsion with traditional fuel-based engines, hybrid systems enhance efficiency and reduce emissions.
- **Lightweight materials:** Advanced composite materials reduce the weight of aircraft, improving performance and efficiency.

What Does the Future Hold for Electric Aviation?

The future of electric aviation is promising, with several key trends and innovations to watch for:

- **Short-haul and regional flights:** Electric aircraft are expected to become viable for short-haul and regional flights, providing sustainable alternatives for routes up to 500 miles.
- **UAM:** eVTOL aircraft will enable UAM solutions, offering efficient transportation within cities and metropolitan areas.
- **Advancements in battery technology:** Ongoing research will lead to higher energy-density batteries, extending the range and capabilities of electric aircraft.
- **Collaborative development:** Partnerships between aerospace companies, technology providers, and regulatory bodies will drive the development and deployment of electric aviation.
- **Sustainability initiatives:** Increased focus on sustainability will accelerate the adoption of electric aviation, aligning with global efforts to reduce carbon emissions and combat climate change.

Future Insights

Electric aviation technologies are poised to revolutionize the aviation industry by offering sustainable, efficient, and innovative solutions for air travel. By addressing the challenges and leveraging the benefits of electric propulsion, we can create a cleaner, quieter, and more efficient future for aviation.

Final Words

This chapter delves into the transformative innovations reshaping global mobility and transportation, highlighting EVs, autonomous transport, and vertical takeoff and landing (VTOL) aircraft. These advancements are redefining how people and goods move, promising significant impacts on society, the economy, and the environment.

Autonomous transportation, led by AI-driven companies such as Tesla, Waymo, and Uber, is poised to enhance safety, increase efficiency, and reduce congestion. However, it also brings societal challenges, such as job displacement and the need for new ethical and legal frameworks. Achieving full autonomy will require further technological advancements, regulatory development, and infrastructure adaptation, alongside building public trust.

These disruptive technologies collectively point to a future where mobility is safer, more efficient, and more sustainable. As they transition from prototypes to mainstream solutions, the collaborative efforts of technologists, policymakers, and society will be crucial in navigating the challenges and fully realizing the potential of these innovations. The future of transportation promises to not only transform how we travel but also how we live, work, and interact with our surroundings.

A few years ago, I was part of an exercise with the Regional Transportation Authority of the United Arab Emirates. At this specific occasion they had their top brass engaged in a workshop to plan future scenarios of transportation in the UAE up to the year 2071. We are headed toward an incredible future. Undoubtedly technology will change the world, but what powers the change is leadership and commitment. Take a look at countries such as the United Arab Emirates where thinking big is the normal thing to do. They are also a country where many firsts are being developed and launched. From the UAE to Singapore and now Saudi Arabia and others, there is no absence of impeccable leadership that will change the future. Ask yourself, what interests you from the future of the mobility and transportation industry and how do you see playing a part in it?

Resources

Books

- *Autonomous Driving: How the Driverless Revolution Will Change the World* by Andreas Herrmann, Walter Brenner, and Rupert Stadler
- *The Second Machine Age: Work, Progress, and Prosperity in a Time of Brilliant Technologies* by Erik Brynjolfsson and Andrew McAfee
- *Smart Cities: Big Data, Civic Hackers, and the Quest for a New Utopia* by Anthony M. Townsend

Take the Future Readiness Score at www.iankhan.com/frs or scan the QR Code

8

Public-Sector Future Readiness

The care of human life and happiness, and not their destruction, is the first and only object of good government.

—Thomas Jefferson

THIS CHAPTER COVERS transformation and evolution within the public sector. Governments form a critical part of our lives, and as such their role is pivotal in ensuring that people have access to services, amenities, and convenience when and where needed.

The Evolution of the Government Experience

In recent years, the concept of the "government experience" has undergone profound transformation, driven by technological innovations, evolving citizen expectations, and the increasing demand for transparency and efficiency in governance. This disruption signifies a shift toward a more citizen-centric approach, leveraging digital technologies to enhance service delivery, engagement, and trust between the public sector and its constituents. This evolution reflects broader societal shifts toward digitization and personalization, changing how governments operate and interact with the public.

The digital revolution has been a critical driver of change in the government experience. With the widespread adoption of the Internet, mobile technology, and social media, citizens now expect the same level of convenience, accessibility, and responsiveness from government services that they experience in the private sector. This expectation has propelled governments worldwide to embark on digital transformation initiatives, aiming to streamline processes, improve service delivery, and foster greater citizen engagement through digital platforms.

What Is the Significance of Digital Governance?

The disruption in the government experience has several significant implications:

- **Enhanced service delivery:** Digital platforms and e-government services, from online tax filing to digital health records, make accessing government services more convenient for citizens. This not only improves satisfaction but also increases compliance and participation in government programs.
- **Increased transparency and accountability:** Digital tools enable governments to share information more openly and interactively, promoting transparency and allowing citizens to hold public officials accountable. Open data initiatives and online platforms for public consultation and feedback are examples of how technology fosters a more transparent governance model.
- **Greater citizen engagement:** By leveraging social media, mobile apps, and online forums, governments can engage with citizens in real time, gathering insights, addressing concerns, and co-creating solutions. This participatory approach to governance strengthens democracy and ensures that policies and services are aligned with public needs and expectations.
- **Empowering citizens:** Digital governance tools empower citizens by providing them with easy access to information, services, and channels for participation. This empowerment can lead to a more informed and engaged citizenry, crucial for the functioning of democratic societies.
- **Improving efficiency and reducing costs:** Digital processes can streamline administrative tasks, reduce paperwork, and eliminate redundancies, leading to significant cost savings and more efficient use of public resources.
- **Enhancing policy outcomes:** Data analytics and digital feedback mechanisms can provide governments with real-time insights into policy impacts, enabling more agile and evidence-based policy-making.

■ **Fostering innovation:** The disruption in the government experience encourages innovation within the public sector, as governments explore new technologies and approaches to meet evolving citizen needs. This can lead to the development of novel solutions to public challenges, from smart city technologies to digital health initiatives.

What Do Future Governments Look Like?

Looking forward, the future of the government experience is likely to be shaped by several emerging trends:

■ **Artificial intelligence (AI) and automation:** AI and automation are set to play a larger role in government services, from chatbots for customer service to AI-driven analytics for policy development. These technologies can further enhance efficiency and personalize the government experience for citizens.

■ **Blockchain for transparency and security:** Blockchain technology has the potential to revolutionize government record-keeping, providing a secure, transparent, and tamper-proof system for everything from voting records to land registries.

■ **Integrated service delivery:** Future government services may be delivered through integrated digital platforms that provide a seamless, one-stop-shop experience for citizens, consolidating access to various services in one interface.

■ **Focus on digital inclusion:** As governments move more services online, ensuring digital inclusion will become increasingly important. This involves addressing the digital divide and ensuring that all citizens have the skills and access needed to benefit from digital government services.

While the shift toward a more digital and citizen-centric government experience holds promise, it also presents challenges. Issues of data privacy, cybersecurity, and digital equity must be addressed to ensure that the benefits of digital governance are realized without compromising citizen rights or exacerbating inequalities. Moreover, the success of these initiatives depends on cultural and organizational changes within governments, as well as the development of digital literacy and engagement among the public.

The disruption in the government experience marks a pivotal shift toward more accessible, efficient, and responsive governance. By embracing digital technologies and placing citizens at the heart of government services, public sector organizations can enhance public trust, improve policy outcomes, and meet the evolving needs of society. As this trend continues, the future of governance looks set to be more inclusive, transparent, and connected, reshaping the relationship between governments and the governed in the digital age.

The Evolution of Social Credits and Scores

The concept of social credits and scoring systems represents a significant disruption in how societal behavior is monitored, evaluated, and influenced. Originating most notably from China, where the government is implementing a social credit system aimed at assessing the trustworthiness of individuals and businesses, this concept has sparked a global debate on its implications for privacy, governance, and social norms.

Basically, social credit systems use data analytics to assess individuals' and businesses' behavior against a set of desired criteria, ranging from financial reliability to social behavior and legal compliance. Scores or ratings are then used to incentivize certain behaviors, with higher scores granting privileges such as easier access to loans, faster service at government agencies, and more favorable terms from partners, while lower scores can lead to restrictions and penalties.

What Is the Significance of Social Credits and Scores?

The primary impact of social credits and scoring systems lies in their potential to significantly alter societal behavior. By rewarding conformity to certain standards and penalizing deviations, these systems can drive a more orderly and compliant society. However, this impact is not without controversy:

- **Enhanced governance and compliance:** Proponents argue that social credit systems can streamline governance, reduce crime and corruption, and encourage responsible behavior, contributing to societal harmony and trust.
- **Privacy and surveillance concerns:** Critics raise alarms about the invasive nature of these systems, highlighting the risks of surveillance, data privacy breaches, and the potential for abuse by authorities or other actors.
- **Social segmentation and discrimination:** There is also concern that such systems could exacerbate social divisions, discriminating against individuals or groups by codifying biases into the scoring criteria and algorithms.

Despite the controversies, there are scenarios where social credits and scoring can offer benefits:

- **Financial inclusion:** In the financial sector, alternative credit scoring using non-traditional data (such as utility bill payments or social media activity) can help individuals without extensive credit histories access loans and other financial services.
- **Public service enhancement:** In public services, a form of social scoring could prioritize services for citizens based on their social contributions or needs, potentially making public service delivery more efficient and targeted.
- **Corporate accountability:** For businesses, social scoring can promote corporate social responsibility, encouraging companies to adopt sustainable and ethical practices to maintain high scores and public trust.

Future Insights

Social credits and scoring systems represent a modern-day disruption with the power to reshape societal norms, governance structures, and individual behavior. While offering potential benefits in terms of financial inclusion, governance, and corporate accountability, they also pose significant challenges related to privacy, surveillance, and social equity. Navigating this disruption requires a balanced approach that leverages technological advancements to enhance societal well-being while vigilantly safeguarding individual rights and fostering a just and inclusive society. The future of social credits and scoring will hinge on our collective ability to harness these tools responsibly, ensuring they contribute to the public good without compromising fundamental values and freedoms.

Future Thinking for Governments

In an era marked by rapid technological advancements and global interconnectedness, "future thinking" has emerged as a crucial discipline. It transcends traditional forecasting, inviting individuals and organizations to envision and shape the future proactively. It leverages interdisciplinary insights, drawing from science, technology, sociology, and economics, to anticipate changes and prepare for various future outcomes. This modern-day disruption in thought and strategic planning encourages a shift from reactive strategies to a more anticipatory, flexible approach to the challenges and opportunities of tomorrow.

What Is the Significance of Future Thinking?

The impact of future thinking is profound and wide-reaching:

- **Innovation and creativity:** By embracing uncertainty and considering multiple future scenarios, organizations can foster a culture of innovation and creativity. This mindset is crucial for developing new products, services, and business models that address emerging needs and trends.
- **Resilience and adaptability:** Future thinking equips organizations and societies with the tools to build resilience and adaptability, allowing them to respond more effectively to shocks and disruptions. This preparedness is essential in an age where change is the only constant.
- **Informed decision-making:** By analyzing trends and potential future developments, future thinking supports more informed, strategic decision-making. This foresight can guide investments, policy-making, and strategic planning, aligning short-term actions with long-term visions.
- **Societal impact:** Beyond organizational benefits, future thinking has the potential to address global challenges, from climate change and technological disruption to social inequality. By envisioning preferable futures, societies can mobilize collective action toward sustainable, equitable outcomes.

How Can Future Thinking Help Governments?

Future thinking can help in various contexts:

- **Business strategy:** In the business world, future thinking can identify emerging market opportunities and technological trends, guiding innovation and strategic investments. Companies such as Google and Apple invest heavily in future-oriented research and development to maintain their competitive edge.
- **Public policy and governance:** For governments and public institutions, future thinking can inform policy development and urban planning, ensuring that initiatives are robust against future uncertainties. Singapore's Centre for Strategic Futures is a prime example, applying foresight to enhance the nation's resilience and strategic readiness.

- **Education and workforce development:** In education, integrating future thinking into curricula can prepare students for future job markets and societal changes, fostering skills such as adaptability, critical thinking, and innovation.
- **Environmental sustainability:** Future thinking is critical for addressing environmental sustainability, allowing for the anticipation of ecological shifts and the development of strategies to mitigate climate change impacts.

As we look toward the future, several trends are likely to shape the evolution of future thinking:

- **Greater integration of AI and big data:** The use of AI and big data analytics will enhance the ability to model complex future scenarios, providing deeper insights and more accurate forecasts.
- **Widespread adoption across sectors:** Future thinking will become increasingly mainstream, adopted by a broader range of sectors beyond technology and business, including education, health care, and nonprofit organizations.
- **Emphasis on inclusivity and diversity:** Recognizing that diverse perspectives enrich future scenarios, there will be a stronger emphasis on inclusivity in future thinking processes. This approach will ensure that a wider range of voices, including those from marginalized communities, is considered in envisioning future possibilities.
- **Collaborative and cross-border efforts:** Global challenges require global solutions. Future thinking will likely involve more collaborative and cross-border efforts, bringing together different countries, industries, and disciplines to tackle issues such as climate change, global health, and digital ethics.

While future thinking offers numerous benefits, it also faces challenges. These include the risk of bias in scenario planning, the difficulty of predicting black swan events, and the potential for future anxiety among individuals and organizations. Addressing these challenges requires a careful balance between openness to diverse possibilities and grounded, evidence-based analysis.

Future thinking represents a significant disruption in how we approach planning, decision-making, and innovation. By enabling a proactive, anticipatory stance toward the future, it empowers individuals, organizations, and societies to navigate uncertainty with confidence and purpose. As this discipline continues to evolve, its integration into strategic planning and education will be critical for building a future that is not only imagined but actively shaped by today's decisions and actions.

Case Study: How Estonia Became a Leader of Innovation

Estonia's rise as a global leader in digital innovation and e-governance is a remarkable story of transformation. From the rubble of its Soviet past, this small Baltic nation has emerged as a pioneering digital society, often dubbed *e-Estonia*. This journey from post-Soviet reconstruction to technological forefront showcases the profound impact of strategic vision, societal resilience, and an unwavering commitment to innovation. Estonia's story serves as a compelling case study in harnessing digital technologies to enhance governance, economic development, and citizen welfare.

Estonia regained its independence from the Soviet Union in 1991. Facing the colossal task of building a new state infrastructure, Estonia's leaders made a strategic decision to invest in information and communication technologies. This was not merely a choice but a necessity, given the country's limited resources and the absence of legacy systems that might have hindered technological adoption. This forward-thinking approach laid the groundwork for what would become the world's most advanced digital society.

The cornerstone of Estonia's digital revolution was the establishment of a secure, universal digital identity for every citizen. Introduced in 2002, the digital ID card enables Estonians to access a wide array of services securely online, from voting to health care, from banking to business registration. This digital identity system, underpinned by robust cybersecurity measures and a transparent, blockchain technology called KSI, ensures trust, privacy, and ease of use.

Estonia's government has digitized virtually all its interactions with citizens, leading to unprecedented levels of efficiency and transparency in governance. Key initiatives include:

- **e-Residency:** Launched in 2014, e-Residency allows global citizens to start and manage an EU-based company online, making entrepreneurship accessible and borderless.
- **X-Road:** A decentralized digital data exchange layer that connects various public and private sector e-services databases, facilitating seamless and secure data transactions.
- **i-Voting:** Estonia became the first country to offer online voting in 2005, enhancing electoral participation and setting a global benchmark for electoral innovation.
- **e-Health:** A comprehensive digital health record system improves health care delivery and patient outcomes by providing physicians with instant access to medical histories.

Estonia's digital transformation has had profound implications for its economy, governance, and society:

- **Economic growth:** Digital innovation has spurred economic growth, attracting foreign investment and boosting the IT sector. Estonia is home to a vibrant start-up ecosystem, with more start-ups per capita than any other European country, including global success stories such as Skype and TransferWise.
- **Efficient governance:** The shift to digital governance has streamlined administrative processes, reduced bureaucracy, and saved significant time and resources. For example, the ease of doing business, including the ability to register a company online in just a few hours, has positioned Estonia as an attractive destination for entrepreneurs.
- **Enhanced citizen welfare:** Digital services have greatly enhanced the convenience and quality of citizen welfare services, from education to health care. The transparency and efficiency of digital systems have also bolstered trust in public institutions.

Looking forward, Estonia continues to innovate and push the boundaries of what is possible in a digital society. Emerging technologies such as AI, 5G, and quantum computing are being explored to further enhance e-services and cybersecurity. Estonia's ambition to remain at the forefront of digital innovation is encapsulated in initiatives such as the e-Estonia Briefing Centre, which shares Estonia's best practices with the world.

Estonia is also committed to sharing its expertise and experiences to support global digital transformation efforts. Through international collaborations and platforms such as the Digital 5 (D5) group of leading digital nations, Estonia advocates for the benefits of digital governance worldwide.

Despite its successes, Estonia's digital journey faces challenges, including cybersecurity threats, privacy concerns, and the need to continuously update technology and skills. Addressing these challenges is critical to sustaining trust and security in digital services. Furthermore, as a global leader in digital innovation, Estonia has a unique opportunity to influence international norms and policies on digital governance, cybersecurity, and technology ethics.

Estonia's story of innovation is not just about technology; it's about a bold vision for societal transformation. By prioritizing digital infrastructure, embracing change, and fostering a culture of innovation, Estonia has redefined what it means to be a digital nation. As the world grapples with the challenges and opportunities of the digital age, Estonia's journey offers valuable lessons in resilience, innovation, and the transformative power of technology. The future of e-Estonia, bright with possibilities, continues to inspire nations worldwide to embark on their digital transformation journeys.

Case Study: How the UAE Is Leading as a Digital Government Innovator

The United Arab Emirates (UAE) has emerged as a global leader in digital government innovation, setting benchmarks for smart governance and citizen-centric services. The country's visionary leadership has embraced digital transformation as a cornerstone of national development, fostering a dynamic ecosystem that integrates advanced technologies to enhance government operations and public services. This proactive approach has propelled the UAE to the forefront of digital governance, making it a model for other nations.

The UAE's journey toward digital governance began with strategic initiatives aimed at modernizing public services and enhancing government efficiency. In the early 2000s, the UAE government launched the eGovernment program, which laid the foundation for digital service delivery. This initiative focused on leveraging technology to streamline administrative processes, improve service accessibility, and enhance citizen engagement.

The vision for a digital UAE was further solidified with the launch of the UAE Vision 2021, which aimed to position the country as one of the best in the world by the 50th anniversary of its formation. This vision included a strong emphasis on smart governance and digital transformation as key drivers of national progress.

The UAE has implemented several key initiatives to advance its digital government agenda:

- **Smart Dubai:** Launched in 2014, Smart Dubai aims to make Dubai the happiest city on Earth through technology innovation. The initiative focuses on transforming Dubai into a smart city by integrating IoT, AI, and blockchain technologies to improve urban living, enhance public services, and foster sustainability.
- **UAE Pass:** UAE Pass is a national digital identity and signature solution that enables residents to access government services securely and conveniently. It allows users to sign documents digitally and verify their identity for various transactions, promoting seamless and paperless interactions with the government.

- **Blockchain Strategy 2021:** The UAE government has committed to using blockchain technology to enhance transparency, efficiency, and security in public services. The Blockchain Strategy 2021 aims to make the UAE a global leader in blockchain adoption, with applications across sectors such as finance, health care, and real estate.
- **Emirates Government Services Excellence Program (EGSEP):** This program aims to improve the quality of government services by implementing best practices, fostering innovation, and ensuring customer satisfaction. It includes the Mohammed bin Rashid Government Excellence Award, which recognizes outstanding government entities and initiatives.

The UAE's digital government initiatives have had a significant impact on various aspects of governance and public services:

- **Enhanced service delivery:** Digital platforms and e-services have made government interactions more convenient and efficient for citizens and businesses. Services such as online visa applications, digital health records, and smart city solutions have streamlined processes and reduced administrative burdens.
- **Increased transparency and trust:** By leveraging blockchain and other digital technologies, the UAE has enhanced transparency and accountability in government operations. This has fostered greater trust between the government and its constituents.
- **Economic growth and innovation:** The focus on digital transformation has spurred economic growth by attracting investments, fostering innovation, and creating new job opportunities. The UAE's vibrant start-up ecosystem and its position as a hub for technology and innovation are testament to the success of these initiatives.
- **Sustainability and efficiency:** Smart city initiatives and digital services have contributed to sustainability goals by optimizing resource use, reducing waste, and promoting energy efficiency. The integration of smart technologies in urban planning and infrastructure has made cities such as Dubai more resilient and sustainable.

The UAE continues to push the boundaries of digital governance with several forward-looking strategies and initiatives:

- **AI:** The UAE has appointed a Minister of State for Artificial Intelligence, Digital Economy, and Remote Work Applications and launched the UAE AI Strategy 2031, aiming to position the country as a global leader in AI. The strategy focuses on integrating AI across various sectors, including health care, education, and transportation, to improve efficiency and innovation.

- **5G and smart infrastructure:** The deployment of 5G technology and the development of smart infrastructure are key priorities for the UAE. These advancements will enable faster and more reliable connectivity, supporting the growth of smart cities and digital services.
- **Digital inclusion:** Ensuring that all segments of society can benefit from digital services is a critical focus for the UAE. Initiatives aimed at enhancing digital literacy and providing access to technology for underserved communities are essential for inclusive growth.
- **Global collaboration:** The UAE is actively engaging in global collaborations and partnerships to share its expertise and learn from other leading digital nations. This collaborative approach will help the UAE stay at the forefront of digital innovation and governance.

While the UAE's digital transformation has been highly successful, it also faces challenges that need to be addressed to sustain progress:

- **Cybersecurity:** As digital services expand, ensuring robust cybersecurity measures is crucial to protect sensitive data and maintain public trust. The UAE must continue to invest in advanced security technologies and practices to mitigate cyber threats.
- **Data privacy:** Balancing the benefits of data-driven governance with the need to protect individual privacy is a key consideration. The UAE must establish clear policies and regulations to ensure data privacy and compliance with international standards.
- **Technological adaptation:** Rapid technological advancements require continuous adaptation and skill development. The UAE needs to invest in education and training to equip its workforce with the skills needed to thrive in a digital economy.

The UAE's leadership in digital government innovation showcases the transformative power of technology in enhancing governance, service delivery, and citizen engagement. By embracing digital transformation and fostering a culture of innovation, the UAE has set a global benchmark for smart governance. As the country continues to advance its digital agenda, the future of governance in the UAE looks promising, characterized by greater efficiency, transparency, and inclusivity. The UAE's experience serves as an inspiring model for other nations seeking to leverage technology to drive national development and improve the quality of life for their citizens.

Global Digital Government Rankings

Global digital government rankings provide a comparative analysis of countries based on their adoption and implementation of digital governance practices. These rankings consider various factors, including the availability and quality of online services, infrastructure, human capital, and the use of emerging technologies. They offer insights into how well countries leverage digital tools to enhance public service delivery, transparency, and citizen engagement.

There are several different rankings.

United Nations E-Government Development Index

The United Nations E-Government Development Index (EGDI) is one of the most comprehensive and widely recognized rankings. It assesses the e-government development of UN member states based on three components:

- **Online Service Index (OSI):** Evaluates the scope and quality of online services provided by the government.
- **Telecommunication Infrastructure Index (TII):** Measures the development and availability of telecommunication infrastructure.
- **Human Capital Index (HCI):** Assesses the level of human capital development, including education and skills.

European Commission's Digital Economy and Society Index

The Digital Economy and Society Index (DESI) is used to monitor Europe's digital performance and track the progress of EU member states. It includes five main dimensions:

- **Connectivity:** The extent and quality of broadband infrastructure.
- **Human capital:** Digital skills of the population.
- **Use of Internet services:** The uptake of various online activities by individuals.
- **Integration of digital technology:** The digitalization of businesses and e-commerce.
- **Digital public services:** The availability and use of e-government services.

OECD Digital Government Index

The OECD Digital Government Index (DGI) evaluates the digital government maturity of OECD member countries. The index is based on six dimensions:

- **Digital by design:** Integrating digital technologies into public sector strategies and operations.
- **Data-driven public sector:** Using data to drive decision-making and service delivery.
- **Government as a platform:** Providing shared infrastructure and services to support digital innovation.
- **Open by default:** Ensuring transparency and accessibility of government data and information.
- **User-driven:** Designing services based on user needs and feedback.
- **Proactiveness:** Anticipating and addressing citizen needs proactively.

World Bank GovTech Maturity Index

The World Bank GovTech Maturity Index (GTMI) assesses the maturity of digital government transformation. The index includes four main components:

- **Core government systems:** The integration and effectiveness of digital systems supporting government operations.
- **Public service delivery:** The availability and quality of online public services.
- **Citizen engagement:** The mechanisms for engaging citizens in governance and decision-making.
- **Governance:** The policies, strategies, and institutional frameworks supporting digital transformation.

Leading Countries in Digital Government

According to the latest available data from these rankings, several countries consistently perform well in digital government:

- **Denmark:** Often ranks highly due to its advanced e-government services, strong digital infrastructure, and proactive digital policies.
- **Estonia:** Known for its comprehensive digital identity system, e-residency program, and innovative digital services.

- **South Korea:** Excels in online service delivery, digital infrastructure, and citizen engagement through technology.
- **Finland:** Noted for its robust digital infrastructure, high levels of digital skills, and user-centric digital services.
- **Singapore:** Recognized for its smart nation initiatives, integrated digital platforms, and emphasis on innovation.

Global digital government rankings play a crucial role in highlighting the progress and areas for improvement in digital governance across countries. They provide valuable insights for policymakers, researchers, and the public, driving efforts to enhance the efficiency, transparency, and inclusivity of government services. As digital transformation continues to evolve, these rankings will remain essential tools for measuring and guiding the development of digital government worldwide

Final Words

Governments need to adapt to a multitude of changes, in particular the changes brought about due to things not in their control. These include political instability in the world, climate change, refugee crisis, and global pandemics. Governments worldwide have been increasingly working on ensuring the best for citizens when it comes to service delivery. Other examples that have not been covered include those from Saudi Arabia, Singapore, India, Rwanda, and other countries. For governments to be at the cutting edge of service delivery, a public-private partnership is necessary. In addition, collaborating with other governments that have received results from their initiatives is key to success.

Resources

Books

- *Digital Government: Leveraging Innovation to Improve Public Sector Performance* by Darrell M. West
- *The Smart Enough City: Putting Technology in Its Place to Reclaim Our Urban Future* by Ben Green
- *E-Government: Information, Technology, and Transformation* edited by Hans J. Scholl
- *The Fourth Industrial Revolution* by Klaus Schwab
- *Digital Transformation at Scale: Why the Strategy Is Delivery* by Andrew Greenway, Ben Terrett, Mike Bracken, and Tom Loosemore

Watch List

- *GX Now - Full Documentary on Government Experience*, https://youtu.be/FmDijK3e37E
- *The Most Advanced Digital Government in the World*, https://youtu.be/nPJ7IVFNEhI?si=BuOg8TGYjEtpnYj2
- TED Talks on digital governance and smart cities
- The Digital Economy: The Digital Society, Coursera course
- *Smart City* (Netflix documentary series)

Take the Future Readiness Score at www.iankhan.com/frs or scan the QR Code

9

Exploring Space

The universe is a pretty big place. If it's just us, seems like an awful waste of space.

—Carl Sagan

SPACE TRAVEL IS not something that comes to mind on a daily basis for most of us. In fact there is a very small minority of humans who have ever gone into space. That is fast changing. This chapter explores space travel and its possibilities, creating disruption not just in the space tourism industry but also in many niche areas such as medicine, precious metals, and manufacturing, all in space.

How Will Space Tourism Transform Our Access to the Cosmos?

Space travel, once the exclusive domain of astronauts and cosmonauts, is transforming into a burgeoning industry, space tourism, signaling a disruptive shift in how humanity perceives and accesses the cosmos. This modern-day disruption is facilitated by pioneering companies and visionary entrepreneurs who are democratizing access to space, offering ordinary people an unprecedented opportunity to experience the final frontier.

Companies such as SpaceX, Blue Origin, and Virgin Galactic are at the forefront, developing spacecraft capable of carrying civilians beyond Earth's atmosphere. These endeavors represent a new era of commercial space exploration, marked by the transition from government-led space programs to a burgeoning space tourism industry.

Richard Branson, founder of Virgin Galactic, encapsulates this vision: "Space is Virgin territory. We are going to democratize space travel so that it's affordable and open to all."[1]

Elon Musk's SpaceX has been pivotal in reducing the cost of space travel with its reusable rockets. Musk famously stated, "I want to die on Mars, just not on impact," highlighting his long-term vision for human colonization of Mars and making space travel accessible to the general public.[2]

Jeff Bezos, through Blue Origin, has also been a significant player, aiming to build the infrastructure for millions of people to live and work in space. Bezos often speaks about his vision: "We need to go to space to save Earth."[3]

What Is the Significance of Space Tourism?

The rise of space tourism carries profound implications:

- **Technological innovation:** The challenge of making space travel safe and accessible for civilians is driving rapid advancements in aerospace technology, including reusable launch vehicles, advanced propulsion systems, and enhanced safety protocols. When SpaceX successfully landed its Falcon 9 rocket for the first time in 2015, it marked a monumental step toward making space travel more affordable and sustainable. Elon Musk remarked, "It's a critical step along the way towards being a multi-planet species."[4]

- **Economic opportunities:** Space tourism is catalyzing the growth of a new space economy, creating jobs, stimulating technological innovation, and opening up new markets. This industry has the potential to generate significant revenue, with estimates suggesting it could become a multibillion-dollar market in the coming decades. Jeff Bezos envisions Blue Origin enabling "a future where millions of people can live and work in space," creating a new economic sphere.[5]

- **Inspiring interest in STEM:** The excitement generated by space tourism is inspiring a new generation to pursue careers in science, technology, engineering, and mathematics (STEM), contributing to the development of a skilled workforce capable of addressing future challenges. A young student once asked astronaut Chris Hadfield during a live video call from the International Space Station, "What's it like to float in space?" His response not only described the physical sensation but ignited a spark of curiosity in thousands of young viewers around the world.

- **Expanding humanity's horizon:** By making space more accessible, space tourism expands humanity's horizon, offering a new perspective on our place in the universe and the fragile beauty of our planet Earth.

The Societal Benefits of Space Tourism?

Space tourism extends beyond the thrill of the experience, offering several benefits to society:

- **Global collaboration:** The international nature of the space tourism industry encourages collaboration between countries, companies, and individuals, fostering a sense of global community and shared purpose in the exploration of space. "The Earth is the cradle of humanity, but mankind cannot stay in the cradle forever," said Konstantin Tsiolkovsky.[6]
- **Environmental awareness:** Viewing Earth from space often enhances individuals' appreciation for its beauty and vulnerability, inspiring greater environmental stewardship and a commitment to sustainable living. Astronauts often speak of the "overview effect," a cognitive shift in awareness reported during spaceflight, often while viewing the Earth from orbit. Astronaut Edgar Mitchell described it as "a feeling of interconnectedness with everyone and everything."[7]
- **Scientific research:** Commercial space flights provide opportunities for scientific research in microgravity environments, contributing to advancements in medicine, materials science, and other fields.

What Does the Future of Space Tourism Look Like?

The future of space tourism is poised for significant growth, with several key trends shaping its trajectory:

- **Technological advancements:** Ongoing improvements in spacecraft technology, safety measures, and cost efficiency will make space tourism more accessible to a broader audience. What innovations will make space travel as routine as air travel? How far are we from that reality?
- **Regulatory frameworks:** Developing clear regulations and safety standards will be crucial for ensuring the safe and sustainable growth of the space tourism industry.
- **Environmental considerations:** Efforts to minimize the environmental impact of space tourism, such as developing greener propulsion systems, will be important for the industry's long-term sustainability.

Future Insights

Space tourism represents a significant disruption in how we engage with space, offering the potential to make space travel safer, more accessible, and more inspiring. As this industry grows, it challenges us to rethink our relationship with the cosmos and our responsibilities to our home planet. The collaborative efforts of technologists, policymakers, and society at large can steer this disruption toward a future where space tourism is a beneficial and integral part of our lives, transforming how we explore, understand, and protect our universe.

How Is the Vision of Living on Mars or the Moon Shaping Our Future?

The prospect of living on Mars, the Moon, or colonizing space represents a bold vision transitioning from science fiction to a tangible objective pursued by governments, private enterprises, and the scientific community. This modern-day disruption in our celestial ambitions reflects a growing understanding of space as not merely a frontier for exploration but as a potential habitat for human life. Driven by advancements in space travel, habitat technology, and a pressing need to address Earth's environmental and existential challenges, the aspiration to establish human settlements beyond our planet is reshaping our future in the cosmos.

What Are the Key Steps to Space Colonization?

The journey toward establishing human colonies on Mars, the Moon, or in space involves overcoming significant challenges across various domains:

- **Transportation:** Reusable rocket technology, exemplified by SpaceX's Starship and NASA's Artemis program, aims to reduce the cost of space travel, making it more feasible to transport humans and cargo to Mars or the Moon. "The important achievement of Apollo was demonstrating that humanity is not forever chained to this planet and our visions go rather further than that and our opportunities are unlimited," said Neil Armstrong.[8]
- **Habitat construction and life support:** Developing self-sustaining habitats that can support human life in the harsh conditions of space is a critical challenge. Innovations in closed-loop life support systems, in-situ resource utilization (ISRU), and habitat construction are

essential for long-term colonization. NASA's Mars Habitat Challenge invites teams to design and build sustainable shelters for Mars, showcasing innovations that could one day house the first Martian settlers.

- **Health and well-being:** Addressing the health impacts of long-duration space travel, including exposure to cosmic radiation and the effects of low gravity on the human body, is crucial for the success of space colonization efforts.
- **Economic viability:** Establishing the economic foundations for space colonization, including resource extraction, agriculture, and tourism, is vital for ensuring the sustainability of extraterrestrial settlements.

What Are the Promising Industries for Space?

The following industries will benefit from space exploration:

- **Space tourism:** Space tourism is already taking its first steps, with companies such as SpaceX, Blue Origin, and Virgin Galactic leading the way. This industry has the potential to become a multibillion-dollar market, offering suborbital and orbital trips, and eventually, stays in space hotels.
- **Mining and resource extraction:** The vast resources available on asteroids, the Moon, and other celestial bodies could be tapped for valuable minerals, including rare earth elements, platinum, and even water. Companies such as Planetary Resources and Deep Space Industries are exploring the feasibility of asteroid mining, which could provide materials crucial for both space and Earth-based industries.
- **Manufacturing and 3D printing:** The microgravity environment of space offers unique advantages for manufacturing, allowing for the production of high-quality materials and complex structures that are difficult or impossible to create on Earth. This includes advanced pharmaceuticals, fiber optics, and new materials. NASA and private companies have already demonstrated 3D printing in space, which could enable on-demand manufacturing of tools, equipment, and even habitats, reducing the need to launch supplies from Earth.
- **Space agriculture:** Developing sustainable agriculture in space is essential for long-term human habitation on Mars, the Moon, or space stations. Advances in hydroponics, aeroponics, and genetic engineering could enable the growth of food crops in space, supporting the nutrition needs of astronauts and future space colonists.

- **Space-based solar power:** Space-based solar power systems could collect solar energy in space, where it is more abundant and consistent, and transmit it back to Earth using microwave or laser technology. This could provide a clean, inexhaustible energy source for our planet, addressing the growing demand for renewable energy.
- **Pharmaceutical and medical research:** The microgravity environment of space offers unique conditions for medical research, including the study of protein crystal growth, which can lead to the development of new and more effective drugs. Space-based research can also provide insights into aging and various diseases, potentially leading to breakthroughs in medicine.
- **Satellite servicing and space debris removal:** With the increasing number of satellites in orbit, services that maintain, repair, and refuel satellites could become essential. Companies such as Northrop Grumman are already working on satellite servicing vehicles. Additionally, addressing the growing problem of space debris is critical for the safety of future space operations. Innovations in debris removal technologies could create a new industry focused on cleaning up space.
- **Entertainment and media:** Space offers a unique and captivating environment for entertainment and media. From filming movies and documentaries in space to live-streaming events from the International Space Station, the potential for creating immersive and inspiring content is vast. Space-themed experiences and virtual reality (VR) content could also become a significant market.
- **Biotechnology and life sciences:** The unique conditions of space can drive advancements in biotechnology and life sciences. Research on the effects of microgravity on biological organisms can lead to innovations in human health, agriculture, and biotechnology. Space agencies and private companies are investing in understanding how living organisms adapt to space environments, which can have profound implications for life on Earth and future space missions.
- **Space colonization infrastructure:** As the vision of living on Mars or the Moon becomes more tangible, the development of infrastructure to support space colonization will be crucial. This includes habitats, life support systems, transportation, communication networks, and energy systems. Companies such as SpaceX and Blue Origin are already working on technologies that could support human settlements on other planets.

While the potential for these industries is immense, several challenges must be addressed to realize their full potential:

- **Technical feasibility:** Developing and deploying the necessary technologies for space-based industries requires significant research and innovation.
- **Regulatory frameworks:** Establishing clear regulations and international agreements is essential to ensure the safe and sustainable growth of space industries.
- **Cost and accessibility:** Reducing the cost of space travel and making it accessible to more players is crucial for the development of space industries.
- **Environmental impact:** Ensuring that space activities do not harm the space environment or Earth's environment is critical for long-term sustainability.
- **Ethical and legal considerations:** Addressing the ethical and legal implications of space resource utilization, space colonization, and other activities is essential to ensure fair and responsible use of space.

Final Words

The modern-day disruption of pursuing life on Mars, the Moon, or space colonization embodies humanity's unyielding spirit of exploration and aspiration for progress. While the challenges ahead are daunting, the collective endeavor to extend human presence beyond Earth could redefine our future, sparking innovation, fostering global cooperation, and inspiring generations to come. As we stand on the brink of this new era, the journey toward space colonization not only promises to expand the horizons of human civilization but also reflects our responsibilities to our home planet and to each other.

As Carl Sagan wisely noted, "The cosmos is within us. We are made of star-stuff. We are a way for the universe to know itself."[9] Perhaps exploring the universe is not a bad thing after all if it leads to us having a better future.

Resources

Books

- *The Right Stuff* by Tom Wolfe
- *An Astronaut's Guide to Life on Earth* by Chris Hadfield
- *The Martian* by Andy Weir

- *Elon Musk: Tesla, SpaceX, and the Quest for a Fantastic Future* by Ashlee Vance
- *Space Chronicles: Facing the Ultimate Frontier* by Neil deGrasse Tyson

Watch List

- *Cosmos: A Spacetime Odyssey* (documentary Series)
- *For All Mankind* (Apple TV+)
- *The Mars Generation* (Netflix documentary)
- *SpaceX: The Road to Mars* (YouTube)
- *First Man* (film)

Take the Future Readiness Score at www.iankhan.com/frs or scan the QR Code

10

How Immersive Tech Drives
the Future

When we strive to become better than we are, everything around us becomes better too.

—*Paulo Coelho, The Alchemist*

IN RECENT YEARS the rise of immersive technologies has shifted the way we see the world around us. Virtual reality (VR), Extended reality, the Metaverse are all terms we are now familiar with. In fact, there are bigger investments being made into this area of technology than ever before. This chapter captures what the future looks like through the scope of such immersive tech.

How Is the VR/MR Metaverse Revolutionizing Communication?

The rise of the VR and mixed reality (MR) Metaverse is revolutionizing communication, marking a dramatic shift from traditional interaction to immersive digital realms. Powered by advanced VR and MR technologies, this transition is more than an evolution—it's a disruption. It offers new ways for individuals to connect, collaborate, and explore digital frontiers. The Metaverse, a collective virtual shared space, is emerging as a transformative concept, extending the boundaries of reality to enable experiences and interactions previously confined to the imagination.

What Is the Significance of the VR/MR Metaverse?

The VR/MR Metaverse disrupts conventional communication and interaction. Unlike traditional digital platforms that rely on screens and keyboards, the Metaverse uses VR and MR to create a sense of presence and immersion. "Metaverse is not a thing a company builds. It's the next chapter of the Internet overall," says Mark Zuckerberg, cofounder, chairman, and CEO of Meta Platforms.[1]

Users experience a digital world as if physically present, making interactions more natural, intuitive, and engaging. Furthermore, the Metaverse's ability to converge different aspects of digital life into a unified, immersive experience represents a paradigm shift in how people perceive and engage with digital content.

Imagine a classroom where students do not just read about the Roman Empire but actually walk through ancient Rome, exploring its streets, conversing with historical figures, and witnessing pivotal events firsthand. This is the potential of the VR/MR Metaverse in education, where immersive experiences can enhance comprehension and engagement. Students can explore historical sites, conduct scientific experiments, and visualize complex data in three-dimensional space, making learning an interactive adventure.

In entertainment, envision attending a concert where you are not just a spectator but part of the performance, interacting with the band and other attendees in a vibrant, shared virtual space. The Metaverse opens new dimensions for content creation and consumption. Users can attend virtual concerts, explore interactive narratives, and engage in gaming experiences that transcend physical space. This immersive approach enriches the user experience, offering unparalleled engagement and fostering a deep sense of community among participants.

The Good and the Bad

Today, the VR/MR Metaverse provides invaluable tools for remote work and collaboration. As the global workforce becomes increasingly decentralized, the Metaverse offers a platform where teams can interact in a shared virtual space, breaking down geographical barriers and enhancing productivity. Virtual workspaces can simulate the dynamics of physical offices, facilitating brainstorming sessions, meetings, and presentations in a more engaging and effective manner.

Looking to the future, the Metaverse has the potential to address broader societal challenges, such as accessibility and environmental sustainability. For individuals with mobility issues or those in remote locations, the

Metaverse provides access to experiences, services, and opportunities that would otherwise be out of reach. Moreover, by enabling virtual experiences that reduce the need for physical travel, the Metaverse can contribute to environmental sustainability efforts by lessening the carbon footprint associated with transportation.

While the prospects of the VR/MR Metaverse are promising, integrating it into society presents several challenges. Issues such as data privacy, cybersecurity, and the digital divide must be addressed to ensure the Metaverse is accessible, safe, and equitable for all users. Additionally, the psychological impacts of prolonged immersion in virtual environments require careful consideration and research to safeguard mental health and well-being.

Early Movers in the Virtual World

Several companies are at the forefront of the VR/MR Metaverse revolution, each with unique strategies and innovations that are driving success in this emerging field.

- **Facebook (Meta Platforms Inc.):** Under the leadership of Mark Zuckerberg, Meta has made significant investments in building the Metaverse. The rebranding of Facebook to Meta reflects its commitment to this new digital frontier. Meta's acquisition of Oculus has positioned it as a leader in VR hardware, while its Horizon Workrooms and Horizon Worlds platforms aim to provide immersive social and work environments. Despite controversies and challenges, Meta's focus on creating a connected virtual world highlights its ambition to shape the future of digital interaction.
- **Microsoft:** With its HoloLens and Azure cloud platform, Microsoft is pioneering MR applications for both enterprise and consumer markets. CEO Satya Nadella has emphasized the importance of MR in transforming industries such as health care, education, and manufacturing. Microsoft's success lies in its ability to integrate MR with existing enterprise solutions, providing practical, scalable applications that enhance productivity and innovation.
- **Sony:** Through its PlayStation VR (PSVR) ecosystem, Sony has achieved considerable success in the gaming segment of the Metaverse. By leveraging its extensive library of gaming IPs and focusing on immersive gaming experiences, Sony has captured a significant share of the VR market. CEO Kenichiro Yoshida's strategy of integrating VR into the broader PlayStation ecosystem has proven effective, driving both hardware and software sales.

- **Epic Games:** Known for its Unreal Engine, Epic Games has become a pivotal player in the development of the Metaverse. Tim Sweeney's vision for an open, interoperable Metaverse has guided Epic's efforts to create realistic virtual environments and tools that empower creators. Epic's collaborations with various industries, from entertainment to architecture, demonstrate the wide-ranging applications of its technology.

The adoption and impact of the VR/MR Metaverse vary across global markets and regions, influenced by technological infrastructure, economic conditions, and cultural factors.

- **North America:** The United States leads in VR/MR adoption, driven by major tech companies and a robust start-up ecosystem. Investments in VR/MR technology are substantial, with Silicon Valley being a hotbed for innovation. The education sector, in particular, is seeing significant adoption, with schools and universities integrating VR/MR into their curricula.
- **Europe:** Countries such as Germany, the UK, and France are witnessing growing interest in VR/MR, particularly in industrial applications. Germany's manufacturing sector is leveraging MR for training and maintenance, while the UK is focusing on VR for health care and education. European policies on data privacy and digital sovereignty also shape the adoption landscape.
- **Asia-Pacific:** China and South Korea are at the forefront of VR/MR innovation in Asia. China, driven by companies such as Tencent and Alibaba, is investing heavily in the Metaverse, with applications spanning gaming, social media, and e-commerce. South Korea's advanced digital infrastructure supports widespread VR/MR adoption, with significant government support for research and development.

Future Insights

The VR/MR Metaverse is a modern-day disruption in communication, offering a glimpse into a future where digital and physical realities coalesce. By enabling immersive experiences that transcend geographical and physical limitations, the Metaverse has the potential to revolutionize education, entertainment, work, and social interactions. As this technology continues to evolve, it presents opportunities to foster innovation, enhance connectivity, and address societal challenges. However, realizing the full potential of the Metaverse requires a collaborative effort to navigate its challenges, ensuring it serves as a force for positive change in the digital era.

How Is the Internet of Things Revolutionizing Our World?

The Internet of Things (IoT) is a powerful disruptor, weaving a network that blurs the lines between the physical and digital worlds. This revolution extends Internet connectivity beyond traditional devices to a vast array of objects and systems, embedding them with electronics, software, sensors, and actuators. From smart homes and wearables to industrial sensors and smart cities, IoT is redefining how we live, work, and interact with our environment, offering unprecedented levels of efficiency, convenience, and insight.

IoT's disruption stems from its ability to connect and digitize the physical world, offering control and analysis previously unimaginable. By generating vast amounts of data from everyday objects and environments, IoT provides insights that drive decision-making and innovation across sectors. "The IoT is not just a technology; it's a revolution," states Kevin Ashton, who coined the term "Internet of Things."[2] This network of connected devices represents a shift toward more intelligent systems that can predict, adapt, and respond to their surroundings, fundamentally changing the relationship between humans and technology.

How Is IoT Transforming Everyday Life, Industries, and Cities?

Consider Sarah, a busy professional who juggles work, family, and personal time. Her smart home, powered by IoT, makes her life significantly easier. Every morning, her home wakes up before she does: the thermostat adjusts to the perfect temperature, the coffee maker brews her favorite blend, and her virtual assistant reads out her schedule for the day. IoT devices automate tasks, enhance security, and conserve energy, providing comfort and peace of mind while promoting sustainability. Wearables track health metrics in real time, empowering individuals with data to make informed decisions about their health and lifestyle. This seamless integration of technology into daily routines exemplifies IoT's potential to enhance quality of life.

Beyond personal use, IoT is revolutionizing entire industries. In manufacturing, the Industrial Internet of Things (IIoT) optimizes production processes, reduces downtime, and improves safety. A case in point is GE Aviation, which uses IoT sensors to monitor jet engine performance in real time, predicting maintenance needs and avoiding costly downtime.[3] Agriculture benefits from precision farming techniques enabled by IoT, which allow for the monitoring of crop conditions and automation of irrigation systems, leading to increased yield and reduced resource use. The transportation sector is witnessing the advent of smart logistics and fleet management solutions, reducing operational costs and improving delivery times.

One of the most ambitious applications of IoT is in the development of smart cities. IoT technologies facilitate the monitoring and management of urban infrastructures such as traffic, public transportation, and energy systems, improving efficiency and reducing congestion and pollution. Barcelona, for instance, has implemented a range of IoT solutions to manage everything from waste collection to street lighting, resulting in significant cost savings and enhanced quality of life for its residents. Smart city initiatives also aim to enhance public safety through connected surveillance systems and emergency response mechanisms, showcasing IoT's ability to address complex urban challenges.

What Are the Benefits and Challenges?

Today, IoT is delivering tangible benefits. Enhanced efficiency, safety, and convenience are just the beginning; IoT also paves the way for new services and business models, creating economic opportunities and jobs. Looking to the future, IoT holds the promise of addressing pressing challenges, including climate change, health care, and urbanization. By enabling smarter resource management, personalized health care solutions, and sustainable urban development, IoT has the potential to significantly improve living standards and foster a more sustainable society.

The journey toward a fully connected IoT world is not without challenges. Concerns around privacy, security, and data ownership are paramount, as the proliferation of connected devices increases the risk of data breaches and cyberattacks. Additionally, the digital divide poses a barrier to IoT's benefits being universally accessible, highlighting the need for inclusive policies and infrastructure investments. Addressing these challenges requires a concerted effort from policymakers, industry leaders, and the public to ensure that IoT develops in a secure, equitable, and respectful manner.

Which Companies Are Leading the Charge?

Several companies are spearheading the IoT revolution, each contributing uniquely to its development and success. Some of these are the following:

- **Amazon:** Through its AWS IoT platform, Amazon provides a comprehensive suite of tools and services for IoT applications. CEO Andy Jassy has emphasized the importance of IoT in driving innovation and efficiency across industries. Amazon's Echo devices, powered by Alexa, have become synonymous with smart home technology, showcasing the company's dominance in the consumer IoT space.

- **Cisco Systems:** Known for its networking hardware, Cisco is leveraging its expertise to create secure and scalable IoT solutions. CEO Chuck Robbins has guided Cisco in developing IoT infrastructure that supports smart cities, industrial automation, and connected health care. Cisco's focus on security and interoperability has made it a trusted partner for enterprises adopting IoT technologies.
- **Siemens:** With its MindSphere IoT operating system, Siemens is transforming industries such as manufacturing, energy, and transportation. CEO Roland Busch has positioned Siemens as a leader in IIoT, emphasizing the importance of data analytics and digital twins in optimizing industrial processes and reducing downtime.
- **Samsung:** Samsung's SmartThings platform integrates a wide range of smart home devices, providing users with seamless control over their connected environments. CEO Kim Ki-nam's vision for a connected lifestyle has driven Samsung's innovation in consumer IoT, making smart homes more accessible and user-friendly.

Global Market Insights

The adoption and impact of IoT vary across global markets and regions, influenced by technological infrastructure, economic conditions, and cultural factors.

- **North America:** The United States leads in IoT adoption, driven by major tech companies and a robust start-up ecosystem. Investments in IoT technology are substantial, with Silicon Valley being a hotbed for innovation. The health care sector, in particular, is seeing significant adoption, with IoT-enabled medical devices improving patient outcomes and operational efficiency.
- **Europe:** Countries such as Germany, the UK, and France are witnessing growing interest in IoT, particularly in industrial applications. Germany's manufacturing sector is leveraging IIoT for predictive maintenance and process optimization, while the UK focuses on smart city initiatives and connected health care solutions. European regulations on data privacy and digital sovereignty also shape the adoption landscape.
- **Asia-Pacific:** China and India are at the forefront of IoT innovation in Asia. China, driven by companies such as Huawei and Xiaomi, is investing heavily in smart city projects and IIoT applications. India is seeing rapid IoT adoption in agriculture and health care, with start-ups developing solutions tailored to local needs. Government initiatives and investment in digital infrastructure are further accelerating IoT growth in the region.

Future Insights

The Internet of Things represents a paradigm shift in the interconnectivity of the physical and digital worlds, heralding a new era of efficiency, innovation, and intelligence. As IoT continues to evolve, it promises to revolutionize how we live, work, and interact with our environment, offering solutions to pressing challenges facing humanity. However, realizing the full potential of IoT demands careful navigation of its ethical, security, and societal implications, ensuring this disruption leads to a future that is more connected, sustainable, inclusive, and human-centric.

How Is a Connected World Shaping Our Future?

The concept of a "connected world" is not just an evolution of technology; it's a transformative disruption that redefines the boundaries of communication, business, and society. A connected world leverages the IoT, big data, cloud computing, and artificial intelligence (AI) to create a network where devices, systems, and people are interconnected in unprecedented ways. This interconnectedness offers vast opportunities for innovation and efficiency but also presents unique challenges and ethical considerations.

The connected world is built on decades of digital transformation, marked by the rise of the Internet and mobile technology. Recent advancements in IoT and AI have accelerated this transformation, embedding connectivity into everyday objects and industrial systems. Picture a farmer in a remote village using IoT-enabled sensors to monitor soil moisture levels and optimize irrigation, ensuring his crops receive just the right amount of water. From smart homes and wearables to autonomous vehicles and smart cities, the connected world encompasses a wide range of technologies and applications, all aimed at enhancing efficiency and quality of life.

What Are the Benefits and Challenges?

In business, the connected world has revolutionized operations, supply chains, and customer engagement. Real-time data collection and analysis enable businesses to optimize processes, reduce costs, and respond more swiftly to market demands. For instance, Coca-Cola uses IoT-enabled vending machines to track inventory and maintenance needs, ensuring timely restocking and reducing downtime. Furthermore, the connected world has spawned new business models and revenue streams, as data becomes a valuable asset and connectivity enables previously unimaginable services. This disruption extends beyond the tech industry; sectors from agriculture to health care harness connectivity to innovate and compete globally.

For individuals, the connected world offers numerous benefits that enhance daily life. Smart home devices provide convenience and security, wearable technology promotes health and wellness, and digital platforms facilitate communication and access to information. Moreover, the connected world can address larger societal issues, such as energy conservation through smart grids and improving access to education and health care via digital services. Consider the story of Raj, a student in a rural area who can now access world-class educational resources and attend virtual classrooms thanks to Internet connectivity and online learning platforms.

The connected world also drives social and cultural change, shaping how we interact, consume media, and perceive privacy and security. Social networks and digital platforms have transformed the way people connect, share, and mobilize, while also raising concerns about data privacy, misinformation, and the digital divide. "Connectivity is a human right," says Sundar Pichai, CEO of Google, highlighting the importance of ensuring equitable access to the benefits of the connected world.[4] As connectivity permeates more aspects of life, society must navigate these challenges, balancing the benefits of a connected world with the need to protect individual rights and promote digital literacy.

Despite its potential, the connected world faces significant challenges. Privacy and security concerns top the list, as the increasing volume of personal and sensitive data online becomes a target for cyber threats. Additionally, the risk of widening the digital divide looms large, as access to connected technologies remains uneven across regions and socioeconomic groups. Addressing these challenges requires a multi-stakeholder approach, involving policymakers, tech companies, and civil society in crafting regulations and standards that protect users while fostering innovation.

What Is the Future of Connectivity?

Looking forward, the connected world is poised to become even more integrated into our lives, with emerging technologies such as 5G, edge computing, and blockchain enhancing the speed, security, and reliability of connections. These advancements will enable more sophisticated applications of IoT and AI, further blurring the lines between the physical and digital worlds. Imagine a city where autonomous vehicles communicate with each other to prevent accidents and optimize traffic flow, or where blockchain ensures the integrity of financial transactions. However, as connectivity expands, so does the complexity of managing and securing vast networks of devices and data, underscoring the importance of robust cybersecurity measures and ethical guidelines.

Which Companies Are Leading the Charge?

Several companies are driving the transformation to a connected world, each with unique strategies and contributions.

- **Google:** Under Sundar Pichai's leadership, Google has been a pioneer in IoT and AI integration. Google's Nest products exemplify the smart home concept, providing users with seamless control over their environment. Google's focus on AI-driven services and cloud computing has also enhanced its IoT capabilities, positioning it as a key player in the connected world.
- **IBM:** IBM's Watson IoT platform leverages AI to analyze data from connected devices, providing actionable insights for businesses. CEO Arvind Krishna's emphasis on AI and hybrid cloud solutions has driven IBM's success in IIoT and smart city projects, helping organizations optimize operations and improve decision-making.
- **Huawei:** Despite facing geopolitical challenges, Huawei has made significant strides in IoT and 5G technology. CEO Ren Zhengfei's focus on innovation and R&D has enabled Huawei to develop advanced connectivity solutions that support smart cities, autonomous vehicles, and connected health care systems. Huawei's contributions to the global IoT landscape underscore its role as a major player in the connected world.

Final Words

The connected world is a modern-day disruption reshaping society, offering new opportunities for efficiency, innovation, and connectivity. As we navigate this interconnected landscape, the potential to enhance the quality of life, drive economic growth, and address global challenges is immense. However, realizing this potential demands careful consideration of the ethical, privacy, and security implications of an increasingly connected existence. By fostering collaboration and dialogue among all stakeholders, we can harness the benefits of a connected world while ensuring it serves the greater good, creating a future that is more connected, sustainable, equitable, and human-centric.

Resources

By staying informed, engaging with experts, exploring case studies, leveraging technology, collaborating internationally, investing in education, and focusing on sustainability, you can enhance your understanding and contribute to the future of communication and connectivity. The recommended readings, watch lists, and places to visit offer valuable resources to deepen your knowledge and inspire innovative approaches. Embrace these opportunities to stay ahead in the rapidly evolving landscape of the VR/MR Metaverse, IoT, and the connected world.

Books

- *The Fourth Industrial Revolution* by Klaus Schwab
- *The Age of Em* by Robin Hanson
- *Digital Transformation: Survive and Thrive in an Era of Mass Extinction* by Thomas M. Siebel
- *Hooked: How to Build Habit-Forming Products* by Nir Eyal
- *Life 3.0: Being Human in the Age of Artificial Intelligence* by Max Tegmark

Recommended Watching

- *Black Mirror* (Netflix series)
- *Ready Player One* (film)
- *The Social Dilemma* (Netflix documentary)
- *Connected: The Hidden Science of Everything* (Netflix series)
- *The Great Hack* (Netflix documentary)

Take the Future Readiness Score at www.iankhan.com/frs or scan the QR Code

11

The Rise of Cognitive Cities

The best way to predict the future is to invent it.

—*Alan Kay*

IT MAY NOT be in the distant future when we live in cognitive cities. These are cities and infrastructure development far more advanced than the concept of smart cities. Think about AI-driven systems, data collection at hundreds of millions of points within a city, and ensuring citizen services are anticipatory and well-thought-out. What if I told you these ideas are already under way?

What Are Cognitive Cities?

The concept of cognitive cities represents a profound evolution in urban living, blending the physical infrastructure of cities with digital intelligence and connectivity. This modern-day disruption goes beyond the smart city paradigm by integrating advanced technologies such as AI, the Internet of Things (IoT), and big data analytics to create urban environments that can think, learn, and adapt. Cognitive cities promise to revolutionize urban planning and management, enhancing sustainability, efficiency, and the quality of life for residents.

The roots of cognitive cities can be traced back to ancient civilizations, where urban planning first began to take shape. The Indus Valley Civilization, for instance, demonstrated advanced urban planning with its grid layouts and sophisticated drainage systems. Fast-forward to the twentieth century, the

Industrial Revolution brought about rapid urbanization, leading to the development of modern cities. In the late twentieth and early twenty-first centuries, the rise of the Internet and digital technologies paved the way for the concept of smart cities. Today, cognitive cities represent the next evolutionary step, integrating not just connectivity but also intelligent systems capable of making real-time decisions.

Cognitive cities build on the foundation laid by smart cities, leveraging extensive sensor networks and connectivity to gather data on every aspect of urban life. However, cognitive cities take this a step further by employing machine learning and other forms of AI to analyze this data, enabling the city to make informed decisions, predict future trends, and dynamically respond to changes and challenges. This level of intelligence and responsiveness marks a significant leap forward in how cities are managed and experienced.

In Singapore, for example, the government's Smart Nation initiative uses data and AI to manage urban issues such as traffic congestion and public safety. IBM's Watson IoT platform has transformed Dublin by improving traffic management and public safety through advanced data analytics. Under the leadership of CEO Arvind Krishna, IBM's focus on AI and IoT integration has been pivotal in this transformation.

A Global Transformation in Urban Living

According to the United Nations, by 2050, it is projected that 68% of the world's population will live in urban areas, up from 55% today.[1] This rapid urbanization underscores the need for innovative solutions such as cognitive cities to manage resources efficiently, ensure sustainable development, and improve the quality of life for millions of people.

The impact of cognitive cities on urban living is multifaceted. By analyzing real-time data, these cities can optimize traffic flow, reducing congestion and pollution and enhancing the efficiency of public transportation systems. Energy systems become more efficient as cognitive cities predict demand patterns and integrate renewable energy sources, reducing the carbon footprint. Furthermore, public safety and emergency services benefit from predictive analytics, allowing for quicker responses and potentially saving lives.

Imagine New York City on a typical busy weekday. Traffic congestion is a notorious issue, costing commuters time and increasing pollution. Now, envision a cognitive New York where AI analyzes traffic patterns in real time, optimizing traffic signals and rerouting vehicles to ease congestion. This is not just a dream—cities such as Singapore are already implementing such technologies, reducing congestion and improving air quality.

Enhancing Citizen Engagement

One of the most significant aspects of cognitive cities is their potential to foster a new level of engagement between the city administration and residents. Through mobile apps and interactive platforms, citizens can report issues, access services, and provide feedback, creating a two-way dialogue with the city. This participatory approach empowers residents, making urban governance more transparent, responsive, and inclusive.

Consider Barcelona's Smart Citizen platform, which allows residents to monitor air quality, noise levels, and traffic conditions. This platform not only informs citizens but also collects data to help the city make better decisions. It's a perfect example of how cognitive cities can transform citizen engagement.[2]

Revolutionizing Urban Planning and the Future of Sustainability

Cognitive cities have the potential to revolutionize urban planning by using predictive models and simulations to inform development and policy decisions. This data-driven approach allows for the anticipation of future challenges, such as population growth or climate change impacts, ensuring that cities can evolve sustainably. By optimizing resource use and promoting sustainable practices, cognitive cities play a crucial role in addressing global environmental challenges.

Imagine city planners in Tokyo using AI to model the effects of population growth over the next 50 years. By simulating various scenarios, they can design infrastructure that will accommodate future needs without overburdening the environment. This proactive approach is already being used in cities such as Amsterdam, where urban planners use AI to create more sustainable and resilient urban environments.

The Positive

In the present day, cognitive cities offer solutions to some of the most pressing urban challenges, including traffic congestion, pollution, and inefficient public services. By making cities more livable and efficient, they enhance the daily lives of residents. Looking to the future, cognitive cities hold the promise of creating more sustainable and resilient urban environments. They can adapt to changing conditions and demands, ensuring that cities remain vibrant and viable for generations to come.

The transition to cognitive cities is not without challenges. Privacy and security concerns arise from the extensive collection and analysis of data. Ensuring that citizens' data is protected and used ethically is paramount. Additionally, there is the risk of exacerbating social inequalities if technological benefits are not accessible to all segments of society. Addressing the digital divide and ensuring inclusive access to the benefits of cognitive cities is crucial for their success.

However, companies such as Siemens, under the leadership of CEO Roland Busch, are making strides in addressing these issues by developing secure, scalable smart infrastructure solutions. Siemens' work in cities such as London demonstrates the potential of cognitive technologies to improve urban living while maintaining high standards of data security and inclusivity.

Future Insights

Cognitive cities represent a significant disruption in urban living, offering a vision of the future where cities are not just smart but intelligent and adaptive. By harnessing the power of AI, IoT, and big data, cognitive cities can enhance sustainability, efficiency, and the quality of life, transforming the urban landscape. However, realizing this vision requires careful consideration of the ethical, privacy, and inclusivity challenges. As we move toward this future, the collaborative effort of governments, technology providers, and citizens will be key to creating cognitive cities that are not only intelligent but also equitable and human-centric.

Case Study: NEOM, Saudi Arabia

NEOM represents one of the most audacious and forward-thinking urban development projects in modern history, encapsulating the essence of disruption in urban living and sustainable development. Announced by Saudi Arabia, NEOM is envisioned as a new destination on the map, a megacity that promises to be a living laboratory for innovation, technology, and sustainability. Spanning over 26 500 km^2 in the northwest corner of Saudi Arabia, this $500 billion project aims to push the boundaries of what is possible in urban design, energy and water use, mobility, and human well-being, setting a new benchmark for future cities worldwide.

NEOM's vision is grounded in the ambition to create a "new future," one where the latest technologies and sustainable practices are integrated from the ground up. This involves leveraging renewable energy sources, primarily solar and wind, to power the entire city, ensuring it operates with a net-zero carbon footprint. The project aims to be at the forefront of innovation, from autonomous mobility solutions and urban air mobility to advanced health care systems and robotic services, aiming to enhance the quality of life for its residents and set new standards in sustainable living.

Redefining Urban Living   NEOM seeks to redefine urban living by creating an environment where nature and urbanism coexist harmoniously. Plans for the city include vast green spaces, AI-enabled infrastructure, and designs that minimize environmental impact while maximizing human wellness. The city's layout is expected to challenge conventional urban sprawl, promoting compact, efficient spaces that encourage walking, cycling, and the use of clean public transport, drastically reducing the reliance on fossil fuels commonly seen in today's urban centers.

Imagine a city where the streets are designed not for cars, but for people. NEOM envisions a pedestrian-friendly urban space, where autonomous electric vehicles and drones ensure mobility without congestion or pollution. This is a stark contrast to the car-centric cities we know today and represents a bold step toward sustainable urban living.

Innovation in Sustainability and Technology   At its core, NEOM is about pioneering in sustainability and technology. The project's commitment to being powered entirely by renewable energy is just the start. It also plans to revolutionize water desalination and waste management processes, making them more efficient and less harmful to the environment. NEOM's approach to technology extends beyond infrastructure; it aims to be a global hub for innovation, attracting tech companies and start-ups focused on AI, robotics, and the digital economy, fostering a dynamic ecosystem of creativity and technological advancement.

Alibaba's City Brain project in Hangzhou, which uses AI to manage urban infrastructure, provides a glimpse into the kind of technological ecosystem NEOM aims to foster. Under the leadership of CEO Daniel Zhang, Alibaba has showcased how AI can significantly improve urban management, from traffic control to emergency response.

Economic Diversification and Global Ambition   NEOM is a key part of Saudi Arabia's Vision 2030, a strategic framework to reduce the country's dependence on oil, diversify its economy, and develop public service sectors. By attracting international investment and talent, NEOM is positioned to become a global economic hub, contributing to the Kingdom's economic diversification while setting new precedents for global urban development projects. Its ambition is to not only transform the region but also to influence urban development practices worldwide, showcasing how cities can be built in harmony with nature while driving economic growth.

Challenges and Considerations   The path to realizing NEOM is fraught with challenges, from the logistical hurdles of building a megacity from scratch in a relatively remote and harsh environment to the socioeconomic impacts on local communities. Additionally, there are significant environmental concerns related to constructing such an ambitious project in a pristine natural landscape. Addressing these challenges requires careful planning, innovative solutions, and a commitment to ethical and sustainable development practices.

The experiences of companies such as Siemens in developing smart city technologies highlight the importance of addressing these challenges head-on. Under CEO Roland Busch, Siemens has navigated similar challenges in other cities, emphasizing the need for secure, inclusive, and sustainable development practices.

The Future Implications of NEOM   The implications of NEOM for the future are profound. If successful, it could serve as a model for new cities around the world, demonstrating how to integrate technology, sustainability, and urban design in ways that enhance human well-being and protect the planet. NEOM has the potential to catalyze a new era of urban development, where cities are not just places to live but ecosystems that support a high quality of life, economic opportunity, and environmental sustainability.

In conclusion, NEOM embodies the essence of modern-day disruption in urban living, challenging conventional notions of what cities can be and how they should function. With its ambitious goals and innovative vision, NEOM stands as a testament to human ingenuity and the relentless pursuit of progress. As the project unfolds, it will undoubtedly face numerous challenges, but its potential to redefine urban development and inspire future generations of cities makes it a landmark initiative in the quest for a more sustainable and technologically advanced world.

Future Living Scenarios

As humanity stands at the crossroads of technological advancement and environmental crisis, the concept of "future living scenarios for humanity" emerges as a critical focal point for exploration and innovation. This notion encompasses a broad spectrum of possibilities, from sustainable urban ecosystems and off-grid living to space colonization and digital existence. Each scenario presents a unique set of opportunities and challenges, reflecting our collective aspirations and concerns about the future.

Sustainable Urban Ecosystems

One of the most immediate future living scenarios involves the transformation of cities into sustainable ecosystems. Driven by the urgent need to address climate change and urbanization challenges, this scenario envisages cities that are powered by renewable energy, designed for zero waste, and built to encourage community living and biodiversity. Innovations in green architecture, vertical farming, and smart transportation systems play pivotal roles in this vision, aiming to create urban spaces that not only support human life but also thrive in harmony with the environment.

Consider Copenhagen, which has set an ambitious goal to become the world's first carbon-neutral capital by 2025. Through extensive investment in green infrastructure, renewable energy, and sustainable urban planning, Copenhagen is leading the way in creating a sustainable urban ecosystem.

Off-Grid Living and Self-Sufficiency

Amid growing disillusionment with consumerism and ecological degradation, an alternative scenario centers on off-grid living and self-sufficiency. This movement, gaining traction worldwide, advocates for a lifestyle that minimizes dependence on centralized utilities and promotes self-reliance. Advances in solar energy, rainwater harvesting, and permaculture design enable individuals and communities to sustain themselves, reducing their ecological footprint and fostering a deeper connection with nature.

In the mountains of Colorado, a growing number of families are embracing off-grid living, relying entirely on solar panels, wind turbines, and sustainable farming practices. This lifestyle, though challenging, offers a compelling model for self-sufficiency and environmental stewardship.

Space Colonization: A New Frontier for Humanity

The prospect of space colonization offers a radical departure from terrestrial living, presenting an opportunity to extend human presence beyond Earth. With projects such as Mars One and SpaceX's interplanetary travel plans, this scenario explores the viability of establishing human settlements on other planets or in space habitats. While fraught with technical and ethical challenges, space colonization embodies humanity's exploratory spirit and its quest for survival in the face of existential threats.

Elon Musk's vision for SpaceX includes the establishment of a human colony on Mars. Despite the enormous challenges, Musk's relentless pursuit of this goal underscores the potential for space colonization to become a reality within our lifetime.

Digital Existence and Virtual Realities

The rapid evolution of digital technologies has paved the way for a scenario where virtual realities become an integral part of human existence. In this future, augmented reality (AR), virtual reality (VR), and the Metaverse enable immersive experiences that blur the lines between the physical and digital worlds. People could work, socialize, and explore in virtual spaces, potentially reducing the environmental impact of physical infrastructure and offering new avenues for creativity and expression.

Companies such as Meta (formerly Facebook), under the leadership of Mark Zuckerberg, are investing heavily in the development of the Metaverse. Zuckerberg envisions a future where virtual and augmented realities become as commonplace as smartphones, transforming how we interact with the digital world.

Challenges and Ethical Considerations

Each future living scenario, while promising, raises significant challenges and ethical considerations. The transition to sustainable urban ecosystems requires systemic changes in policy, industry, and consumer behavior, alongside investments in green technologies. Off-grid living, although appealing for its sustainability, may not be feasible on a global scale without addressing issues of land availability and social inequality. Space colonization, meanwhile, confronts immense technical hurdles and ethical dilemmas about human impact on other celestial bodies. Finally, the embrace of digital existence necessitates careful navigation of privacy, mental health, and the digital divide.

The experiences of historical urban planning and technological adoption highlight the importance of addressing these challenges. For instance, the rise of smart cities has shown that technological benefits can sometimes exacerbate social inequalities if not carefully managed.

Integrating Humanity's Aspirations with Technological Innovation

The successful realization of these future living scenarios depends on our ability to integrate humanity's aspirations with technological innovation, ensuring that progress serves the well-being of people and the planet. Collaborative efforts across governments, industries, and communities are essential to drive forward sustainable solutions and equitable access to technology. Moreover, fostering a culture of innovation and resilience can empower individuals to actively shape their futures, whether through grassroots initiatives or participation in global projects.

In conclusion, the exploration of "future living scenarios for humanity" opens up a landscape of possibilities for how we might live, work, and thrive in the coming decades. Each scenario reflects a different facet of our collective hopes and fears, challenging us to reimagine our relationship with technology, the environment, and each other. As we navigate these possibilities, the choices we make today will determine the legacy we leave for future generations. Embracing this moment of disruption as an opportunity for positive transformation can lead us toward a future where humanity flourishes in harmony with the natural world and the vast expanses beyond.

Case Study: Masdar City: A Vision of Sustainability, United Arab Emirates

Major Developments:

- **Renewable energy:** Masdar City is designed to rely heavily on solar energy and other renewable sources. It hosts one of the largest solar plants in the Middle East.
- **Green building standards:** The city is built to high environmental standards, with buildings designed to reduce energy and water consumption.
- **Innovation hub:** Masdar Institute of Science and Technology is a graduate-level university located in Masdar City focused on renewable energy and sustainability.
- **Integrated transport system:** A driverless personal rapid transit system and extensive pedestrian pathways aim to minimize car use.

Pros:
- **Environmental sustainability:** High reliance on renewable energy sources and green building standards reduce carbon footprint.
- **Economic opportunities:** There are plenty of opportunities that attract businesses and researchers in the renewable energy and sustainability sectors.
- **High quality of life:** Focus on green spaces and pedestrian-friendly infrastructure enhances livability.

Cons:
- **High costs:** Significant initial investment in infrastructure and technology.
- **Scalability issues:** High-tech solutions may be difficult to implement on a larger scale or in less affluent regions.
- **Dependency on technology:** Overreliance on technology can lead to vulnerabilities if systems fail or are compromised.

Significance:

Masdar City is significant as a pioneering example of what a sustainable city can look like. It serves as a model for integrating renewable energy, green architecture, and innovative technology into urban planning.

Case Study: Songdo, South Korea

Major Developments:
- **Ubiquitous network:** High-speed data network with extensive use of IoT devices for real-time monitoring and management.
- **Smart grid technology:** Advanced energy management systems that optimize energy consumption.
- **Waste management:** Automated waste collection system that uses underground pipes to transport waste to processing facilities.
- **Green spaces:** Over 40% of the city's area is designated as green space.

Pros:
- **Efficiency:** Real-time data allows for efficient management of resources and services.
- **High livability:** Extensive green spaces and smart infrastructure improve quality of life.
- **Economic growth:** Attracts businesses and investors due to its advanced infrastructure and technology.

Cons:

- **Privacy concerns:** Extensive data collection raises concerns about privacy and data security.
- **High costs:** Implementing and maintaining advanced technologies can be expensive.
- **Technological dependence:** Heavy reliance on technology can be problematic if systems fail.

Significance:

Songdo is a benchmark for smart city development, showcasing how IoT and advanced technologies can be integrated into urban infrastructure to create more efficient and livable cities.

Case Study: Yachay: Ecuador's City of Knowledge

Major Developments:

- **Educational hub:** Home to Yachay Tech University, focusing on STEM education and research.
- **Innovation ecosystem:** Designed to attract researchers, tech companies, and start-ups.
- **Sustainability initiatives:** Emphasis on renewable energy, green spaces, and sustainable infrastructure.
- **Global collaboration:** Partnerships with international universities and research institutions.

Pros:

- **Knowledge economy:** Promotes economic growth through education and innovation.
- **Sustainability:** Focus on renewable energy and sustainable practices.
- **Global reach:** Attracts international talent and collaboration.

Cons:

- **Initial costs:** High initial investment in infrastructure and educational facilities.
- **Long-term viability:** Success depends on sustained investment and international collaboration.
- **Access:** May not be accessible to all due to its focus on high-tech industries.

Significance:
Yachay represents a forward-thinking approach to urban development, aiming to build a knowledge-based economy through education, research, and innovation.

Case Study: Hudson Yards: New York City's Smart Neighborhood, New York

Major Developments:
- **Microgrid:** An advanced energy system that ensures efficient energy use and resilience.
- **Smart waste management:** Uses pneumatic tubes to transport waste, reducing truck traffic and emissions.
- **High-speed data infrastructure:** Extensive fiber optic network for high-speed Internet access.
- **Public spaces:** Incorporates parks, plazas, and public art installations.

Pros:
- **Resilience:** Microgrid and advanced infrastructure enhance energy efficiency and reliability.
- **Livability:** Focus on public spaces and green areas improves quality of life.
- **Economic growth:** Attracts businesses and residents due to its advanced infrastructure and amenities.

Cons:
- **High costs:** Development and maintenance of high-tech infrastructure are expensive.
- **Gentrification:** Risk of increasing property values and displacing lower-income residents.
- **Technological dependence:** Reliance on advanced technology can be a vulnerability.

Significance:
Hudson Yards is a prime example of integrating smart city technologies into an urban environment, demonstrating how advanced infrastructure can enhance resilience, livability, and economic growth.

Case Study: Amaravati: India's Planned Smart City

Major Developments:
- **IoT and big data:** Extensive use of IoT devices and big data analytics to manage urban services.
- **Green building:** Focus on sustainable building practices and renewable energy.
- **Public transportation:** Integrated public transport system with smart traffic management.
- **Citizen services:** Digital platforms for citizen engagement and service delivery.

Pros:
- **Sustainability:** Emphasis on green building and renewable energy reduces environmental impact.
- **Efficiency:** Smart technologies improve the efficiency of urban services.
- **Inclusivity:** Digital platforms enhance citizen engagement and access to services.

Cons:
- **Implementation challenges:** Large-scale implementation of smart technologies can be complex.
- **Digital divide:** Risk of excluding those without access to technology.
- **Cost:** Significant investment required for development and maintenance.

Significance:
Amaravati represents an ambitious effort to create a modern, sustainable, and technologically advanced city in India, showcasing the potential for smart city developments in emerging economies.

Final Words

The rise of smart cities such as Masdar City, Songdo, Yachay, Hudson Yards, and Amaravati represents a significant shift in urban development. These projects illustrate how integrating advanced technologies with sustainable practices can create urban environments that are not only intelligent and efficient but also livable and resilient. As these cities continue to develop, they will serve as models for future urban planning, demonstrating how innovation and sustainability can transform the way we live, work, and interact in the twenty-first century.

Resources

For more information, check out the following resources.

Books

- *Smart Cities: Big Data, Civic Hackers, and the Quest for a New Utopia* by Anthony M. Townsend
- *The Smart Enough City: Putting Technology in Its Place to Reclaim Our Urban Future* by Ben Green
- *Cognitive Computing: Theory and Applications* by Vijay V. Raghavan and George Z. Voyiadjis
- *Data and Goliath: The Hidden Battles to Collect Your Data and Control Your World* by Bruce Schneier
- *Smart Cities For Dummies* (John Wiley & Sons, 2020) by Jonathan Reichental

Watch List

- *The Human Scale* (documentary)
- *Urbanized* (documentary)

Websites

- NEOM: www.neom.com
- Masdar City: www.masdarcity.ae
- Amravati: www.amravaticorporation.in
- Hudson Yards: www.hudsonyardsnewyork.com
- Yachay: http://www.yachay.gob.ec

Take the Future Readiness Score at www.iankhan.com/frs or scan the QR Code

12

A New Age for Agriculture

We need to start thinking about how we're going to feed the world in the next 20 to 30 years.

—Bill Gates[1]

AGRICULTURE IS THE world's oldest profession. Today the tide has shifted, thanks to industrialization, automation, and technology. Our production levels are record high, and yet there is a need for more efficiency as the Earth's population is set to hit nine billion people in the next decade of two. This chapter looks at modern agriculture, its needs, and the area where it is rapidly transforming.

The Rise of a New Dawn

Growing up, I spent summers on my grandparents' farm, where the rhythm of life was dictated by the seasons and the sun. Early mornings were filled with the hum of tractors and the smell of freshly turned earth. I watched as workers toiled tirelessly, planting seeds and nurturing crops with methods handed down through generations. That was a world of tradition, of respect for the land, and of a deep understanding of nature's cycles.

Yet, even then, I could see the challenges mounting. The unpredictable weather, the struggle to maintain soil fertility, and the ever-present threat of pests and diseases loomed large. My grandfather's dedication was unwavering, but it was clear that the old ways were straining under the weight of modern demands.

Today, as I revisit those memories, I see a world of agriculture on the brink of a remarkable transformation. The fields that once relied solely on the wisdom of generations are now being revolutionized by technology and innovation. From carbon capture techniques that turn farms into carbon sinks to sustainable practices that harmonize productivity with environmental stewardship, the future of farming looks radically different from my grandfather's era.

This chapter delves into these groundbreaking advancements reshaping agriculture. We explore how carbon capture technologies are turning farms into pivotal players in the fight against climate change. We examine the principles of sustainability, highlighting practices that align agricultural productivity with environmental health. The rise of robotic farming heralds a future where precision and efficiency reign supreme, addressing labor shortages and optimizing resource use. Meanwhile, AI's integration into farming and dairy operations promises a leap toward unprecedented productivity and animal welfare.

But these advancements are not without challenges. Economic barriers, technological hurdles, and the need for policy support present significant obstacles. Yet, the potential rewards—enhanced food security, reduced environmental impact, and improved livelihoods for farmers—make this journey imperative.

As we navigate this chapter, consider the broader implications of these innovations. How can these technologies be integrated into existing farming practices? What role do consumers, policymakers, and technology developers play in this transformation? Join us as we explore the future of agriculture, a future where technology and sustainability converge to create a resilient and equitable food system for all.

What Is Carbon Capture?

In the face of escalating climate change concerns, the agricultural sector stands at a pivotal juncture, embracing innovative practices to mitigate its environmental impact. Among these innovations, carbon capture technology has emerged as a significant disruptor, offering a path to transform agriculture into a vital part of the solution to climate change. This technology, which involves capturing carbon dioxide (CO_2) from the atmosphere and either storing it underground or utilizing it in various ways, is increasingly being integrated into agricultural practices, marking a paradigm shift in how the industry approaches sustainability and environmental stewardship.

Historically, agriculture has been both a boon and a bane for the environment. Early farming practices, dating back thousands of years, involved slash-and-burn techniques that released significant amounts of CO_2 into the atmosphere. With the Industrial Revolution, the advent of chemical fertilizers and large-scale monoculture farming further exacerbated greenhouse gas emissions. However, the twenty-first century brings a renewed focus on reversing these trends, with carbon capture technologies leading the charge.

Agriculture has traditionally been viewed as a major source of greenhouse gas emissions, contributing to climate change through activities such as deforestation, fertilizer use, and livestock farming. However, carbon capture technology presents an opportunity to reverse this narrative, enabling the sector to actively remove CO_2 from the atmosphere. Through practices such as enhanced soil carbon sequestration, bioenergy with carbon capture and storage (BECCS), and the use of carbon-capturing crops, agriculture can transition from being part of the problem to an integral part of the climate solution.

What Is Enhanced Soil Carbon Sequestration?

One of the most promising avenues for carbon capture in agriculture is enhanced soil carbon sequestration. This practice involves adopting farming techniques that increase the amount of carbon stored in the soil, such as cover cropping, reduced tillage, and the application of biochar. These methods not only capture CO_2 but also improve soil health, water retention, and crop yields, demonstrating how environmental and agricultural objectives can align.

For example, General Mills has committed to advancing regenerative agriculture on one million acres of farmland by 2030. Their initiatives include supporting farmers to implement cover cropping and no-till practices, which enhance soil carbon sequestration and boost biodiversity.

How Does Bioenergy with Carbon Capture and Storage (BECCS) Work?

BECCS represents another disruptive approach, combining bioenergy production with carbon capture technology. By growing biomass crops that absorb CO_2 as they grow, then capturing and storing the CO_2 released during biomass energy production, BECCS offers a way to produce renewable energy while achieving negative emissions. Although still in the early stages of deployment, BECCS holds considerable potential for reducing atmospheric CO_2 levels.

The Drax Group in the UK is pioneering BECCS technology. Their project aims to make the Drax Power Station carbon negative by 2030, capturing millions of tonnes of CO_2 annually.

What Are Carbon-Capturing Crops?

The development of carbon-capturing crops through genetic engineering and breeding programs is an emerging field that could further enhance agriculture's role in carbon capture. These crops are designed to have deeper root systems, enabling them to store more carbon in the soil, or to be more efficient at photosynthesis, converting more CO_2 into biomass. This innovation not only aids in carbon capture but also can lead to higher productivity and resilience to climate change.

For instance, researchers at the Salk Institute are developing crops such as corn and soybeans with enhanced root systems that sequester more carbon, potentially transforming vast agricultural landscapes into carbon sinks.

What Are the Challenges and Considerations?

Despite the potential of carbon capture in agriculture, there are significant challenges and considerations to address. The cost and technological barriers to implementing carbon capture and storage on a wide scale remain high, requiring substantial investment in research, development, and infrastructure. There are also concerns about the long-term viability and safety of underground CO_2 storage, as well as the land use implications of scaling up BECCS and carbon-capturing crops, which could compete with food production.

What Is the Role of Policy Support and Market Mechanisms?

For carbon capture in agriculture to reach its full potential, supportive policies and market mechanisms are essential. Incentives for farmers to adopt carbon capture practices, such as carbon credits or subsidies for sustainable farming techniques, can accelerate the adoption of these technologies. Furthermore, establishing robust carbon markets and pricing mechanisms can provide the financial motivation needed to invest in carbon capture and storage infrastructure.

California's cap-and-trade program includes agriculture as a sector eligible for carbon credits, incentivizing farmers to adopt carbon sequestration practices. This model provides a financial framework that could be replicated globally.

What Is the Future of Carbon Capture in Agriculture?

Looking to the future, carbon capture in agriculture could play a critical role in meeting global climate goals. As technology advances and costs decline, the integration of carbon capture practices in agriculture could become more widespread, transforming the sector into a net carbon sink. This shift not only contributes to climate change mitigation but also supports sustainable development, food security, and rural economies.

Future Insights

The modern-day disruption of carbon capture technology in agriculture offers a promising pathway toward sustainability and climate resilience. By turning agricultural practices into solutions for carbon removal, the sector can significantly contribute to the global effort to combat climate change. While challenges remain, the continued evolution and support of carbon capture innovations hold the potential to revolutionize agriculture and ensure a sustainable future for the planet.

What Is Sustainability?

The agricultural sector is currently experiencing a profound transformation, driven by the urgent need for sustainability in the face of climate change, resource depletion, and a growing global population. This shift toward sustainable practices represents a significant disruption in traditional farming methods, which have often prioritized short-term yield over long-term environmental health. Today, sustainability in agriculture is not just a buzzword but a necessary paradigm shift, aimed at producing food in ways that protect the environment, public health, and animal welfare, while also ensuring economic viability for farmers and communities.

Sustainability in agriculture encompasses a broad range of practices, technologies, and philosophies that seek to harmonize with the natural world.

This approach involves reducing the use of nonrenewable resources, minimizing environmental impacts, promoting biodiversity, and supporting the socioeconomic well-being of farmers and rural communities. From organic farming and agroecology to precision agriculture and regenerative practices, the move toward sustainability is reshaping the agricultural landscape.

How Do Organic Farming and Agroecology Contribute to Sustainability?

At the heart of the sustainability movement in agriculture are organic farming and agroecology. These practices eschew synthetic fertilizers and pesticides in favor of natural processes that enhance soil health, conserve water, and support biodiversity. By relying on crop rotation, composting, and biological pest control, organic farming and agroecology not only produce nutritious food but also build resilient ecosystems capable of withstanding environmental stresses.

In Denmark, over 11% of the farmland is managed organically, supported by strong government policies and consumer demand for organic products. This model shows how national commitment can drive widespread adoption of sustainable practices.

How Does Precision Agriculture Use Technology for Sustainability?

Another critical component of modern sustainable agriculture is precision agriculture, which employs advanced technologies such as GPS, drones, and IoT sensors to optimize farming practices. This data-driven approach allows farmers to monitor crop health, soil conditions, and weather patterns in real time, making informed decisions that maximize efficiency and reduce waste. Precision agriculture minimizes the overuse of water, fertilizers, and pesticides, leading to lower environmental impact and higher yields.

John Deere's precision agriculture technologies, such as their advanced tractors and autonomous drones, enable farmers to implement sustainable practices effectively. These innovations help reduce resource use and improve crop yields, demonstrating the potential of technology to enhance sustainability.

What Is Regenerative Agriculture?

Regenerative agriculture takes the concept of sustainability further, aiming not just to minimize harm but to actively improve environmental health.

This holistic approach focuses on restoring soil fertility, increasing biodiversity, and sequestering carbon. Practices such as cover cropping, no-till farming, and holistic grazing work to rebuild organic matter in the soil, capturing carbon from the atmosphere and reversing the effects of climate change.

Gabe Brown, a farmer from North Dakota, is a leading advocate of regenerative agriculture. His farm has seen increased soil health and productivity through the implementation of regenerative practices, serving as a model for others.

What Are the Challenges to Achieving Sustainability?

Despite its benefits, the transition to sustainable agriculture faces numerous challenges. Economic barriers, including the high initial costs of adopting sustainable practices and the lack of access to markets for sustainable products, hinder widespread adoption. Additionally, there is a need for more education and training for farmers to implement and maintain sustainable practices effectively. Policy support is also crucial, as current agricultural subsidies and regulations often favor conventional, industrial farming methods over sustainable ones.

How Do Consumers and Technology Play a Role in Sustainability?

Consumers play a pivotal role in driving the shift toward sustainable agriculture through their purchasing choices. Demand for organic, locally sourced, and sustainably produced food encourages farmers to adopt eco-friendly practices. Meanwhile, technological innovation continues to offer new tools and solutions for sustainable farming, from biopesticides and drought-resistant crops to blockchain for supply chain transparency.

In Japan, the trend toward local and organic food has spurred the growth of farmers' markets and direct-to-consumer sales, highlighting the power of consumer demand in promoting sustainability.

What Is the Future of Sustainable Agriculture?

Looking forward, sustainable agriculture stands as a beacon of hope for addressing some of the most pressing issues facing humanity and the planet. As awareness grows and technologies evolve, sustainable practices are set to become more accessible and effective, paving the way for a food system that nourishes both people and the Earth. The future of agriculture lies in embracing sustainability not as an optional approach but as an essential strategy for survival and prosperity.

Future Insights

In conclusion, the disruption brought about by the focus on sustainability in agriculture heralds a new era of farming that is in harmony with the environment. By adopting sustainable practices, the agricultural sector can ensure food security, protect biodiversity, and mitigate the impacts of climate change, creating a resilient and equitable food system for future generations. The journey toward sustainable agriculture is complex and challenging, but it is also filled with opportunities for innovation, collaboration, and transformation, making it one of the most critical endeavors of our time.

The Advent of Robotic Farming

In the realm of agriculture, a sector as ancient as civilization itself, the advent of robotic farming stands as a testament to the incredible strides humanity has made in technology and innovation. This modern disruption is reshaping the agricultural landscape, offering solutions to some of the industry's most persistent challenges, including labor shortages, the need for sustainable practices, and the demand for increased efficiency and productivity. Robotic farming, through the integration of machine learning, other forms of AI, and advanced robotics, is not merely an evolution in agricultural practices but a revolutionary shift toward precision agriculture.

At the core of robotic farming is the use of autonomous systems and machinery to perform various agricultural tasks traditionally done by humans or with human-operated equipment. From autonomous tractors and drones to robotic harvesters and weed control systems, these technologies are designed to optimize the farming process, reducing the reliance on manual labor and enhancing the precision of agricultural operations. This shift toward automation and data-driven agriculture marks a significant departure from conventional farming methods, promising to increase efficiency, reduce waste, and improve the overall sustainability of agricultural practices.

John Deere's autonomous tractors and the BoniRob weeding robot developed by Bosch are leading examples of how robotic systems are transforming farming. These technologies enable precise applications, such as targeted herbicide use and efficient harvesting, which minimize environmental impact and boost productivity.

One of the most profound impacts of robotic farming is its ability to transform traditional agricultural practices. Robots equipped with sensors and AI algorithms can monitor crop health, soil conditions, and environmental factors in real time, allowing for precise application of water, fertilizers, and pesticides. This targeted approach minimizes the overuse of inputs, reducing environmental impact and lowering costs. Furthermore, robotic systems can operate around the clock, unaffected by weather conditions or labor constraints, ensuring that farming operations can continue seamlessly, maximizing yield and productivity.

In California, the use of robotic harvesters in vineyards has revolutionized grape picking, ensuring that harvesting is done at the optimal time for quality and yield. This technology addresses labor shortages and enhances the efficiency of the harvest process.

How Will Robotic Farming Help?

Robotic farming presents a viable solution to the labor shortages that have plagued the agricultural sector for years. With an aging farmer population and a decline in agricultural labor, automation relieves the pressure on farms to find and retain manual labor. Moreover, the precision and efficiency of robotic systems align with the principles of sustainable agriculture, reducing the carbon footprint of farming operations, conserving water, and promoting soil health. By addressing these critical challenges, robotic farming not only ensures the continuity of agricultural production but also advances the industry toward a more sustainable and resilient future.

Despite its potential, the widespread adoption of robotic farming faces several challenges. The high initial cost of robotic systems and the technological infrastructure required to support them can be prohibitive for small and medium-sized farms. There is also a need for technical knowledge and skills to operate and maintain these advanced systems, necessitating significant training and education for farmers and agricultural workers. Furthermore, regulatory and safety concerns surrounding autonomous machinery in open environments must be addressed to ensure the safe integration of these technologies into the agricultural landscape.

What Is the Future of Robotic Farming?

Looking ahead, the future of robotic farming is bright, with continuous advancements in technology promising to further enhance the capabilities and accessibility of robotic systems. Innovations in machine learning, other forms of AI, and sensor technology are expected to improve the autonomy, efficiency, and decision-making abilities of agricultural robots, making them more adept at complex tasks and adaptable to a wider range of crops and environments. As the technology matures and costs decrease, robotic farming could become mainstream, transforming agriculture into a high-tech industry characterized by precision, efficiency, and sustainability.

Future Insights

In conclusion, robotic farming embodies the disruptive power of technology in agriculture, offering new pathways to address the industry's most pressing challenges. By enhancing productivity, addressing labor shortages, and promoting sustainable practices, robotic farming holds the promise of revolutionizing agriculture, ensuring its viability and resilience in the face of a changing world. As we embrace this robotic revolution, it is imperative to navigate the challenges of adoption and integration, ensuring that the benefits of robotic farming are realized across the agricultural sector, from small family farms to large agribusinesses. The journey toward fully automated farming is complex, but the potential rewards for humanity and the planet make it a venture worth pursuing.

Robotic Cow Milking: Is That a Thing?

Robotic cow milking systems represent a significant disruption in the dairy industry, transforming traditional dairy farming into a more efficient, sustainable, and animal-friendly operation. This innovative approach to milking cows harnesses advanced robotics and information technology, automating the milking process and offering profound benefits that extend beyond mere convenience. As the global demand for dairy continues to grow, robotic milking systems (RMS) are proving to be a pivotal factor in meeting this demand sustainably, marking a departure from conventional practices toward a future of precision dairy farming.

What Are the Benefits and Challenges?

One of the most notable benefits of robotic milking systems is their positive impact on animal welfare. Cows in RMS-enabled farms typically experience less stress, as they have the freedom to decide when to be milked, leading to a more natural and comfortable living environment. This autonomy often results in increased milk yield per cow, as the stress reduction and increased milking frequency naturally stimulate milk production. Furthermore, the data collected by RMS can be used to monitor the health and well-being of each cow, enabling early detection of potential health issues and contributing to better herd health management.

For example, the Lely Astronaut, a popular robotic milking system, has been shown to increase milk yield by up to 10% while significantly improving cow health and welfare. This system's ability to monitor each cow individually allows farmers to tailor care and feeding practices, ensuring optimal productivity and well-being.

Robotic milking systems also contribute to the sustainability of dairy farming. By optimizing the milking process and reducing the need for manual labor, RMS can lead to more efficient use of resources, including energy, water, and feed. The precise application of feed and management of manure, facilitated by the detailed data collected by RMS, can significantly reduce the environmental footprint of dairy farming. This technology-driven approach aligns with broader sustainability goals, including reducing greenhouse gas emissions and promoting responsible resource management.

Despite their advantages, the adoption of robotic cow milking systems is not without challenges. The high initial investment required for RMS installation and the ongoing maintenance costs can be significant barriers, particularly for small to medium-sized farms. Additionally, the successful integration of RMS into a dairy operation requires a certain level of technological proficiency and a willingness to adapt to new farm management practices. Concerns about data privacy and the security of the digital infrastructure supporting RMS are also noteworthy, necessitating robust cybersecurity measures to protect sensitive information.

The Evolution of Urban Agriculture

Urban agriculture involves growing food within city environments, utilizing spaces such as rooftops, vacant lots, and vertical farms. This practice not only increases local food production but also promotes sustainability and community engagement.

(continued)

(*continued*)

It is significant for the following reasons:

- **Food security:** Reduces dependency on long supply chains and ensures fresh produce availability.
- **Environmental benefits:** Lowers carbon footprint by reducing transportation needs and promotes green spaces in cities.
- **Economic opportunities:** Provides jobs and stimulates local economies through farmer's markets and urban farms.

These are some innovative examples:

- **Vertical farms:** Companies such as AeroFarms and Plenty use advanced hydroponic systems to grow crops in urban settings, maximizing space and efficiency.
- **Rooftop gardens:** Brooklyn Grange in New York City operates the world's largest rooftop soil farms, producing fresh vegetables for local communities.
- **Community gardens:** Initiatives such as Detroit's urban garden projects engage residents in growing their own food, fostering community spirit and self-sufficiency.

Future Insights

In conclusion, robotic cow milking systems represent a modern-day disruption in agriculture, offering a pathway to more efficient, sustainable, and animal-friendly dairy farming. By automating the milking process, RMS not only addresses labor challenges but also enhances milk production, improves animal welfare, and contributes to environmental sustainability. While challenges to adoption remain, the potential benefits of RMS make it a compelling choice for the future of dairy farming.

As the industry continues to evolve, embracing technological advancements such as robotic milking will be key to meeting the growing global demand for dairy in a responsible and sustainable manner.

AI in Farming and Dairy Is Here

The integration of AI into farming and dairy operations marks a significant disruption in the agricultural landscape, ushering in an era of precision agriculture and revolutionizing traditional practices. This technological advancement leverages machine learning algorithms and other forms of AI to analyze vast amounts of data, enabling farmers to make more informed decisions, optimize yields, improve animal health, and enhance overall farm efficiency. As the global population continues to grow, and environmental concerns become increasingly pressing, AI in farming and dairy presents a sustainable pathway to meet the world's food production needs.

How Is AI Optimizing Crop Production?

AI's application in crop production involves analyzing data from various sources, including satellite images, sensors, and drones, to monitor crop health, soil conditions, and environmental factors. By processing this data, AI can identify patterns and predict outcomes, such as the optimal time for planting, watering, and harvesting. This precision approach not only maximizes yield but also conserves resources by ensuring that water, fertilizers, and pesticides are applied only where and when needed, minimizing waste and environmental impact.

The use of AI-driven platforms such as Climate FieldView, developed by the Climate Corporation, provides farmers with insights on crop performance and field conditions, helping them make data-driven decisions that enhance productivity and sustainability.

How Is AI Enhancing Dairy Farm Operations?

In dairy farming, AI is transforming herd management by monitoring animal health and behavior through wearable devices and camera systems. AI algorithms can detect early signs of illness, track fertility cycles, and monitor feeding patterns, providing dairy farmers with actionable insights to improve milk production and animal welfare. Additionally, AI-driven robotic milking systems allow for more efficient milking processes, further enhancing productivity and enabling cows to be milked according to their natural cycles, thereby improving their well-being.

The introduction of wearable technology such as FitBark for cows, which tracks their activity and health metrics, is revolutionizing dairy herd management by providing real-time data to farmers.

How Is AI Used in Predictive Analytics for Pest and Disease Control?

AI's predictive analytics capability is a game changer for pest and disease control in agriculture. By analyzing historical data and current conditions, AI models can forecast the likelihood of pest invasions or disease outbreaks, allowing farmers to take preemptive action. This not only helps to protect crops but also reduces the reliance on chemical pesticides, contributing to more sustainable farming practices and protecting the ecosystem.

Companies such as Taranis are using AI to analyze high-resolution images from drones to detect early signs of pest infestation and disease in crops, enabling timely interventions that save crops and reduce pesticide use.

What Are AI-Driven Decision Support Systems?

Decision support systems powered by AI are providing farmers with insights and recommendations on every aspect of farm management, from crop selection and rotation to resource allocation and market analysis. These systems process complex data sets to offer tailored advice, helping farmers to navigate the uncertainties of weather, market prices, and changing environmental conditions. By enhancing decision-making, AI-driven systems are making farms more resilient and adaptable to change.

What Are the Challenges in Implementing AI in Agriculture?

Despite the potential benefits, the implementation of AI in farming and dairy faces several challenges. The high cost of technology and infrastructure can be prohibitive, especially for small-scale farmers. There is also a significant learning curve associated with adopting new technologies, requiring education and training. Additionally, concerns about data privacy and ownership persist, as the collection and analysis of farm data involve sensitive information.

What Is the Future of AI in Agriculture?

Looking ahead, the future of AI in agriculture is bright, with ongoing advancements in technology promising to further enhance its capabilities and accessibility. The development of more sophisticated AI models, coupled with the proliferation of IoT devices and improvements in data analytics, will continue to drive innovation in the field. As AI technology becomes more affordable and user-friendly, its adoption is expected to increase, making precision agriculture the norm rather than the exception.

Future Insights

In conclusion, AI's disruption in farming and dairy represents a pivotal shift toward more efficient, sustainable, and productive agricultural practices. By leveraging the power of AI, the agricultural sector can meet the growing demand for food in a way that conserves resources, protects the environment, and enhances the well-being of both animals and humans. Despite the challenges, the potential of AI to transform agriculture is immense, offering a path to a more sustainable and food-secure future. As the sector continues to evolve, embracing AI and other technological innovations will be crucial for its success in the twenty-first century and beyond.

Final Words

As we jump into the transformative power of technology in modern agriculture, it becomes clear that the future of farming is being reshaped in ways our ancestors could never have imagined. From the nostalgic memories of traditional farming practices to the revolutionary advancements in carbon capture, sustainability, robotic farming, and AI, we stand on the brink of a new agricultural dawn. This chapter has explored how these innovations are addressing the critical challenges of our time, such as climate change, resource depletion, and food security, while also enhancing productivity and sustainability.

In conclusion, the journey toward modernizing agriculture through technology is complex and challenging, but it is also filled with opportunities for innovation, collaboration, and transformation. By embracing these advancements, we can create a food system that not only meets the needs of a growing global population but also protects and enhances the environment. The future of agriculture lies in our ability to integrate technology and sustainability, ensuring a resilient and equitable food system for generations to come.

Resources

Books

- *The Omnivore's Dilemma* by Michael Pollan
- *Growing a Revolution* by David R. Montgomery
- *The One-Straw Revolution* by Masanobu Fukuoka

Watch List

- *The Biggest Little Farm* (film, 2018)
- *Sustainable* (film, 2016)
- *Inhabit: A Permaculture Perspective* (film, 2015)

Take the Future Readiness Score at www.iankhan.com/frs or scan the QR Code

PART

13

The Theory of Future Readiness

FUTURE READINESS IS the capability of an organization to not resist, withstand, or counter the effects of change in its operating environment, but to be able to flow with the change and adapt to it and serve a greater purpose.

This chapter provides an overview about the theory of future readiness and its evolution over the last 20 years. I will introduce you to various aspects of the theory and why we choose the measurements that make the Future Readiness Score worth exploring.

The Need to Measure Disruption to Be Part of It

In today's rapidly changing world, understanding and measuring disruption is crucial for businesses to remain relevant and competitive. Disruption is not just a buzzword; it's a fundamental shift that alters the way industries operate. To be part of this change, companies must develop robust metrics and frameworks to assess the impact and trajectory of disruptive forces. By quantifying these changes, businesses can identify opportunities, anticipate challenges, and develop strategies that align with the evolving landscape.

There are countless examples of businesses and organizations operating to their finest. In this book I have covered numerous examples of such organizations. Here are some more to consider.

Amazon and Retail Disruption   Amazon, under the leadership of Jeff Bezos, revolutionized the retail industry by integrating technology and data analytics into every aspect of its operations. Amazon's use of metrics to track consumer behavior, inventory management, and supply chain efficiency allowed it to disrupt traditional retail giants such as Walmart. By measuring and analyzing key data points, Amazon was able to anticipate market trends and consumer needs, resulting in a significant competitive advantage. Today, Amazon's annual revenue exceeds $469.8 billion, demonstrating the power of leveraging disruption through data-driven strategies.

Tesla and Automotive Innovation   Elon Musk's Tesla has disrupted the automotive industry by focusing on electric vehicles (EVs) and sustainable energy solutions. Tesla's approach involves rigorous measurement and analysis of battery performance, energy consumption, and autonomous driving capabilities. This data-centric strategy has enabled Tesla to continuously innovate and improve its products. For instance, Tesla's Autopilot system uses real-time data from millions of miles driven to enhance its autonomous driving algorithms. As a result, Tesla has become the world's most valuable automaker, with a market capitalization of more than $600 billion as of August 2024.

Netflix and Media Transformation   Netflix, led by Reed Hastings, transformed the media industry by transitioning from a DVD rental service to a streaming giant. Netflix's ability to measure viewer preferences and viewing habits through sophisticated algorithms allowed it to personalize content recommendations and produce original shows that resonate with audiences. This data-driven approach led to significant subscriber growth, with Netflix reaching over 230 million global subscribers in 2023. By measuring disruption and adapting to changing consumer behaviors, Netflix has remained a dominant force in the entertainment industry.

The Case for Measuring Future Readiness

Stanford Professor and AI luminary Erik Brynjolfsson once said that the heart of science is measurement. Measurements are necessary to maintain proper growth. In fact, the management of measuring success and failure is a key component of being able to adapt to change.

Measuring disruption helps businesses anticipate market trends and stay ahead of competitors. For example, IBM's Watson AI uses predictive analytics to forecast industry trends and provide insights into future market conditions.

This allows IBM to develop innovative solutions and maintain its leadership in the technology sector.

By quantifying the impact of disruptive forces, companies can allocate resources more effectively. For instance, PwC's "Global Entertainment & Media Outlook"[1] report uses data analytics to project industry growth and identify areas of opportunity. Companies that utilize such insights can invest in high-growth segments and optimize their strategies for maximum impact.

Measuring future readiness enhances organizational resilience by identifying potential risks and vulnerabilities. Deloitte's "Global Risk Management Survey"[2] highlights how businesses can use risk assessment tools to prepare for disruptions. By understanding potential threats, companies can develop contingency plans and mitigate the impact of unforeseen events.

Quantifying disruption fosters a culture of innovation by encouraging continuous improvement. Google's Project Aristotle used data to understand what makes teams successful. The findings revealed that psychological safety, dependability, and structure were key drivers of team performance. By measuring these factors, Google was able to create an environment that nurtures innovation and collaboration.

Luckily, the idea of future readiness is extremely well supported by other research organizations. Here are some statistics that stand out.

- According to a McKinsey Global Institute report, businesses that leverage data and analytics to inform their strategies are 23 times more likely to acquire customers, six times more likely to retain customers, and 19 times more likely to be profitable.[3]
- A study by Gartner found that 56% of companies that invest in digital transformation initiatives report a significant increase in revenue.[4]
- The International Data Corporation (IDC) predicts that global spending on digital transformation technologies will reach $2.3 trillion by 2023, underscoring the growing importance of measuring and adapting to disruption.[5]

The Debate: The Need to Measure Future Readiness

Proponents of measuring future readiness argue that it is essential for survival in a rapidly evolving market. By tracking key performance indicators (KPIs) and using data analytics, businesses can gain actionable insights that drive strategic decision-making. This proactive approach allows companies to identify emerging trends, optimize operations, and maintain a competitive edge.

However, some skeptics argue that overreliance on metrics can stifle creativity and lead to analysis paralysis. They contend that not all aspects of disruption can be quantified and that intuition and experience also play a crucial role in navigating change. While metrics are important, they should be balanced with qualitative insights to provide a holistic view of the business landscape.

The need to measure disruption and future readiness is evident in the successes of industry leaders such as Amazon, Tesla, and Netflix. By developing robust metrics and frameworks, businesses can navigate the complexities of disruption, anticipate market trends, and foster a culture of innovation. While it is important to balance quantitative and qualitative insights, the benefits of measuring future readiness far outweigh the potential drawbacks. In a world where change is the only constant, being equipped with the right tools and knowledge is key to thriving in the face of disruption.

The Need for Leadership to Evolve as Disruptive Forces Shape Our World

As disruptive forces reshape our world, leadership must evolve to guide organizations through uncertainty. Traditional leadership models, rooted in stability and predictability, are no longer sufficient. Modern leaders must embrace agility, innovation, and a forward-thinking mindset. They need to foster a culture that encourages experimentation, learning from failures, and adapting to new realities. By doing so, they can navigate their organizations through the complexities of disruption and harness its potential for growth.

Evolving Leadership

As I looked deeper into use cases of companies becoming undisruptable and leaders focused on future readiness, some leaders and the organizations they led really stood out as amazing examples I could share. Here are a few.

Microsoft and Satya Nadella's Leadership   When Satya Nadella became CEO of Microsoft in 2014, he faced a company that was struggling to innovate and keep pace with industry changes. Nadella shifted Microsoft's focus toward cloud computing and AI, fostering a culture of collaboration and continuous learning. His leadership style emphasized empathy, growth mindset, and inclusivity. This transformation led to a resurgence in Microsoft's relevance and profitability, with the company's market capitalization surpassing $2 trillion by 2021. Nadella's ability to pivot and embrace new technologies exemplifies the need for evolved leadership in times of disruption.

Apple and Tim Cook's Strategic Vision   Tim Cook, who succeeded Steve Jobs as CEO of Apple, maintained the company's innovative edge by focusing on operational excellence and sustainable growth. Cook's leadership style, characterized by a strong emphasis on ethical business practices and social responsibility, helped Apple navigate complex global markets and maintain its position as a technology leader. Under his guidance, Apple has continued to launch groundbreaking products and services, contributing to its status as one of the most valuable companies globally, with a market capitalization exceeding $2.8 trillion in 2023.

SpaceX and Elon Musk's Bold Leadership   Elon Musk's leadership at SpaceX showcases the importance of visionary thinking and risk-taking in the face of disruption. Musk's ambitious goal to make space travel affordable and colonize Mars has driven SpaceX to achieve remarkable milestones, such as the first privately funded spacecraft to reach the International Space Station and the development of reusable rockets. His relentless pursuit of innovation and willingness to embrace failure as a learning opportunity have positioned SpaceX as a leader in the aerospace industry, with significant implications for the future of space exploration.

In a rapidly changing world, leaders must be agile and innovative to respond to new challenges and opportunities. A study by McKinsey found that organizations with agile leaders are 70% more likely to be in the top quartile of organizational health. Agile leaders prioritize flexibility, encourage cross-functional collaboration, and adapt quickly to changing market conditions. This approach enables businesses to stay ahead of the curve and capitalize on emerging trends.

Modern leaders need to create an environment where experimentation is encouraged, and failure is viewed as a stepping stone to success. Google's "20% time" policy, which allows employees to spend 20% of their time on projects that interest them, has led to the creation of successful products such as Gmail and Google Maps. This culture of innovation drives continuous improvement and keeps organizations at the forefront of their industries.

Forward-thinking leaders anticipate future trends and prepare their organizations to meet them. They invest in research and development, stay informed about technological advancements, and engage with thought leaders and innovators. Amazon's investment in machine learning and other forms of AI, for instance, has enabled it to enhance customer experiences and streamline operations. Jeff Bezos's long-term vision and willingness to invest in future technologies have been critical to Amazon's sustained growth and innovation.

Future Insights

A lot of data supported my theory and as a result helped in making the case for future readiness as a new path for leadership and profitability. Here are some statistics that I found favorable.

- According to a survey by Deloitte, 94% of executives believe that leadership development programs are critical to their business success.
- A *Harvard Business Review* study found that companies with high agility scores achieved 25% higher profit margins than their less agile counterparts.
- Research by Gallup shows that organizations with strong leadership are 50% more likely to outperform their peers in terms of revenue growth.

The Debate: The Need for Leadership Evolution

Proponents of evolved leadership argue that the rapidly changing business environment necessitates a new approach to leadership. Traditional models focused on stability and hierarchy are ill-suited for navigating disruption. Evolved leaders who embrace agility, innovation, and a forward-thinking mindset are better equipped to drive organizational success in the face of uncertainty.

However, some critics argue that too much emphasis on agility and experimentation can lead to a lack of focus and strategic direction. They contend that while innovation is important, it must be balanced with operational excellence and disciplined execution. Effective leaders should find a middle ground that leverages the strengths of traditional and modern leadership approaches.

The need for leadership to evolve in response to disruptive forces is evident in the successes of leaders such as Satya Nadella, Tim Cook, and Elon Musk. By embracing agility, fostering a culture of experimentation, and developing a forward-thinking mindset, modern leaders can guide their organizations through the complexities of disruption and harness its potential for growth. While it is important to balance innovation with operational excellence, the benefits of evolved leadership in navigating a rapidly changing world far outweigh the potential drawbacks. In an era of constant change, adaptive and visionary leadership is essential for sustaining success and driving future growth.

How to Become Undisruptable If You Don't Know What Is Being Disrupted and How

To become undisruptable, it is essential to have a deep understanding of what is being disrupted and how. This involves continuous learning, staying informed about industry trends, and engaging with thought leaders and innovators. Businesses should invest in research and development, collaborate with start-ups, and participate in industry forums. By doing so, they can gain insights into emerging technologies and market shifts, enabling them to adapt proactively rather than reactively.

Let us take a look into some use cases of this in action.

IBM and Continuous Learning   IBM's reinvention under the leadership of Ginni Rometty exemplifies the importance of continuous learning. Faced with declining revenue from traditional hardware and software sales, IBM shifted its focus toward cloud computing, AI, and blockchain. The company invested heavily in training its workforce on these new technologies, launching initiatives such as the IBM Skills Academy and partnering with universities to develop relevant curricula. By prioritizing learning and staying ahead of industry trends, IBM successfully transformed itself into a leader in AI and cloud services, achieving a market capitalization of over $120 billion.

Google and Industry Engagement   Google's approach to staying undisruptable involves active engagement with industry trends and thought leaders. Through initiatives such as Google Ventures, the company invests in innovative start-ups across various sectors, gaining early access to emerging technologies and market shifts. Google also hosts events such as Google I/O, where developers and industry experts gather to share insights and advancements. This proactive engagement allows Google to remain at the forefront of technological innovation and maintain its competitive edge in the rapidly evolving tech landscape.

General Electric and Innovation Hubs   General Electric (GE) faced significant challenges as traditional manufacturing industries experienced disruption. Under the leadership of Jeff Immelt, GE established innovation hubs known as GE Garages, which focus on additive manufacturing, robotics, and IoT. These hubs serve as collaboration spaces where GE partners with start-ups, researchers, and customers to develop and test new technologies. This investment in innovation and collaboration enabled GE to stay relevant and competitive, particularly in the industrial Internet space.

Understanding disruption requires a commitment to continuous learning and adaptation. Companies that prioritize employee development and stay informed about industry trends can better anticipate changes and adapt their strategies accordingly. For example, Amazon's commitment to continuous learning is evident in its Corporate Learning and Development program, which offers employees opportunities to upskill and reskill in response to evolving business needs.

Engaging with thought leaders and innovators provides businesses with valuable insights into emerging technologies and market trends. This engagement can take various forms, including attending industry conferences, participating in forums, and collaborating with academic institutions. For instance, Microsoft collaborates with leading universities and research institutions through its Microsoft Research division, gaining access to cutting-edge developments in AI, quantum computing, and more.

Investing in research and development (R&D) is crucial for staying ahead of disruption. Companies that allocate significant resources to R&D can drive innovation and develop new products and services that meet changing market demands. Apple's consistent investment in R&D has enabled it to launch groundbreaking products such as the iPhone, iPad, and Apple Watch, maintaining its position as a leader in consumer technology.

There is promising data available that helps strengthen the idea of research, development, and learning overall.

- According to PwC's Global Innovation 1000 study, the top 10 most innovative companies spend an average of 8.4% of their revenue on R&D, compared to the global average of 4.5%.
- A survey by Deloitte found that 94% of business leaders believe continuous learning is critical for their organization's success in the next five years.
- Research by McKinsey shows that companies that invest in innovation are 2.4 times more likely to experience revenue growth compared to those that don't.

The Debate: The Importance of Proactive Adaptation

Proponents of proactive adaptation argue that businesses must continuously evolve to remain undisruptable. This involves monitoring industry trends, investing in new technologies, and fostering a culture of innovation. By staying ahead of disruption, companies can seize new opportunities and mitigate risks, ensuring long-term success.

However, some critics argue that an excessive focus on adaptation can lead to strategic drift, where companies lose sight of their core competencies and market position. They contend that while staying informed about industry trends is important, businesses must balance this with a clear strategic vision and disciplined execution.

To become undisruptable, businesses must have a deep understanding of what is being disrupted and how. This requires continuous learning, engaging with thought leaders, investing in R&D, and staying informed about industry trends. Examples from IBM, Google, and GE highlight the importance of proactive adaptation and collaboration in navigating disruption. While it is important to balance adaptation with strategic focus, the benefits of staying ahead of disruption far outweigh the potential drawbacks. In a world where change is constant, being informed and adaptable is key to maintaining a competitive edge and achieving long-term success rather than uninformed and rigid.

The Basis for Our Future Readiness Research

For the past two decades, I have dedicated myself to exploring the dynamics of disruption and future readiness. Working with some of the world's top brands, I have witnessed firsthand the transformative power of innovation and strategic foresight. This journey has involved deep dives into various industries, understanding the unique challenges they face, and identifying the common threads that lead to success in a disruptive environment.

From Insight to Innovation

My journey involved the following:

Exploring Disruption Across Industries My journey began with a fascination for how industries transform and adapt to change. By engaging with sectors such as manufacturing, health care, retail, and technology, I gained a comprehensive understanding of the forces driving disruption. For instance, in health care, the adoption of AI for diagnostic purposes has significantly improved patient outcomes and operational efficiency. In retail, e-commerce giants such as Amazon have leveraged data analytics to revolutionize customer experience and supply chain management.

Collaborating with Top Brands Working with leading global brands such as Microsoft, Intel, and American Banker, I had the opportunity to witness the implementation of cutting-edge technologies and strategies. These collaborations allowed me to understand how organizations can harness the power of innovation to remain competitive. For example, Microsoft's shift to cloud computing under Satya Nadella's leadership exemplifies how strategic foresight and agility can drive business transformation and growth.

Developing the Future Readiness Score Recognizing the need for a structured approach to navigating disruption, I created the Future Readiness Score. This metric helps organizations assess their preparedness for future challenges and opportunities. The score evaluates factors such as technological adoption, leadership agility, and organizational resilience, providing a road map for businesses to enhance their future readiness. Companies that have adopted this framework report significant improvements in their ability to anticipate and respond to market shifts.

Thought Leadership and Advocacy As a futurist and technology expert, I have shared my insights through various platforms, including keynote speeches, documentaries, and publications. My work has been featured on CNN, BBC, *Bloomberg*, and *Fast Company*, where I discuss emerging technologies such as AI, blockchain, and the metaverse. By engaging with a global audience, I aim to raise awareness about the importance of future readiness and inspire organizations to embrace innovation.

Producing Documentaries and Writing Books To further explore and disseminate knowledge about disruptive technologies, I have produced several documentaries and authored multiple books. My documentaries, available on platforms such as Amazon Prime Video and Emirates Airlines, delve into topics such as blockchain, AI, and the future of work. My books, including *Metaverse For Dummies* and *The Quick Guide to Prompt Engineering*, provide readers with practical insights into navigating the digital landscape.

Key Insights from Two Decades of Exploration

These are my key insights from the past 20 years:

The Power of Strategic Foresight One of the most significant lessons from my journey is the importance of strategic foresight. Organizations that proactively identify and prepare for potential disruptions are better positioned to capitalize on new opportunities and mitigate risks. This involves continuously scanning the horizon for emerging trends, investing in R&D, and fostering a culture of innovation.

Embracing Agility and Resilience   In a rapidly changing world, agility and resilience are critical to success. Companies must be willing to pivot their strategies, experiment with new business models, and adapt to evolving market conditions. Leaders play a crucial role in driving this transformation by encouraging a mindset of continuous learning and flexibility.

The Role of Technology in Driving Change   Technological advancements are at the heart of most disruptive changes. Whether it's AI, blockchain, or IoT, these technologies have the potential to reshape industries and redefine competitive landscapes. Businesses must stay abreast of technological developments and integrate them into their operations to stay ahead of the curve.

Collaboration and Ecosystem Building   No organization can navigate disruption alone. Building partnerships with start-ups, research institutions, and industry peers is essential for fostering innovation and gaining diverse perspectives. Collaborative ecosystems enable the sharing of knowledge, resources, and best practices, enhancing the collective ability to thrive in a disruptive environment.

Measuring and Managing Future Readiness   The creation of the Future Readiness Score emphasized the importance of measuring and managing future readiness. By evaluating their current state and identifying areas for improvement, organizations can develop targeted strategies to enhance their resilience and adaptability. This systematic approach provides a clear framework for navigating the complexities of disruption.

Future Insights

Over the past 20 years, my quest to understand disruption and future readiness has been both challenging and rewarding. Through collaborations with top brands, thought leadership, and the development of innovative tools such as the Future Readiness Score, I have gained invaluable insights into what it takes to succeed in a disruptive world. As we move forward, the lessons learned from this journey will continue to guide organizations in their pursuit of innovation, resilience, and sustained growth. By embracing strategic foresight, agility, and technological integration, businesses can navigate the uncertainties of the future and emerge stronger and more competitive.

How the Need to Measure the Future Led to the Theory of Future Readiness

The realization that businesses need a systematic approach to navigating the future led to the development of the theory of future readiness. This theory provides a comprehensive framework for organizations to assess their preparedness for future challenges and opportunities. It emphasizes the importance of measuring key indicators of disruption and innovation, enabling businesses to develop actionable insights and strategies.

The Genesis of the Theory of Future Readiness

The concept of future readiness emerged from the observation that many organizations were caught off guard by rapid technological advancements and market shifts. Leaders recognized the necessity of a structured methodology to evaluate and enhance their ability to foresee and adapt to changes. This need became particularly evident during my collaborations with various industries, where I noticed a recurring pattern: those who proactively measured and managed their readiness for the future were more successful in navigating disruptions.

The downfall of Blockbuster and the rise of Netflix perfectly illustrate the importance of future readiness. Blockbuster failed to anticipate the shift toward digital streaming, while Netflix continuously adapted its business model in response to technological advancements and changing consumer preferences. Netflix's commitment to innovation and strategic foresight enabled it to disrupt the media industry and become a dominant player.

Developing the Theory of Future Readiness

The theory of future readiness was developed to address this gap. It is built on the premise that future-proofing an organization requires a holistic and systematic approach. This theory encompasses several key components:

Defining a Clear Vision Organizations must articulate a clear and compelling vision that aligns with future trends and addresses emerging market needs. This vision serves as a guiding star, helping businesses stay focused on long-term goals amid short-term disruptions.

Fostering a Culture of Innovation Encouraging experimentation and embracing failure as a learning opportunity are crucial for continuous improvement. Agile methodologies allow organizations to pivot quickly and respond effectively to new challenges.

Leveraging Advanced Technologies Integrating technologies such as AI, blockchain, and IoT into business operations can drive efficiency and open new avenues for growth. Data analytics plays a critical role in identifying trends and making informed decisions.

Developing Future-Ready Leaders Leadership development programs that emphasize adaptability, strategic thinking, and emotional intelligence are essential. Leaders must inspire and guide their teams through uncertainty and change.

Integrating Sustainable Practices Ensuring that business strategies are environmentally sustainable and ethically sound is increasingly important. This approach not only addresses regulatory requirements but also aligns with consumer values.

Why Measurements Are Necessary

The cornerstone of the theory of future readiness is the measurement of key indicators. By quantifying various aspects of readiness, organizations can gain a clear understanding of their strengths and areas for improvement. The Future Readiness Score was created to provide a scientific basis for this assessment.

Key indicators include the following:

Technological Adoption Evaluating the extent to which an organization has integrated advanced technologies into its operations.

Market Responsiveness Assessing the ability to anticipate and respond to market changes and consumer behavior.

Innovation Capacity Measuring the frequency and impact of new ideas, products, or services introduced.

Leadership Agility Gauging the flexibility and adaptability of leadership in decision-making and strategic direction.

Sustainability Metrics Tracking environmental impact, resource efficiency, and ethical practices.

GE exemplifies how measuring future readiness can drive transformation. Faced with declining performance, GE adopted the Industrial Internet of Things (IIoT) and predictive analytics to enhance operational efficiency. By systematically measuring and improving its readiness, GE managed to revitalize its industrial operations and regain competitiveness.

Benefits of the Theory of Future Readiness

The following are the benefits of the theory:

Proactive Adaptation Organizations that adopt the theory of future readiness can proactively adapt to changes, rather than reacting to them. This approach reduces the risk of being blindsided by disruptions and positions businesses to capitalize on emerging opportunities.

Informed Decision-Making By leveraging data and analytics, businesses can make informed decisions that are aligned with their strategic vision. This reduces uncertainty and enhances the accuracy of forecasting future trends.

Enhanced Resilience Measuring and managing future readiness enhances organizational resilience. Companies become better equipped to withstand shocks and stresses, whether they are technological, economic, or environmental.

Sustainable Growth The integration of sustainable practices ensures that growth is not only robust but also responsible. This aligns with global efforts to address climate change and promotes long-term viability.

What Is the Future Readiness Score™?

The Future Readiness Score is a scientifically developed metric designed to assess an organization's preparedness for future challenges and opportunities. This comprehensive tool evaluates key aspects of an organization's structure, strategy, and operations to determine how well it can adapt to and thrive in the face of disruption. By providing a clear and quantifiable measure of future readiness, the Future Readiness Score helps businesses identify strengths, pinpoint areas for improvement, and develop targeted strategies for sustainable growth and resilience.

The following are the benefits of the Future Readiness Score:

Strategic Insights The Future Readiness Score provides strategic insights that help organizations align their vision and operations with future market demands.

Improved Decision-Making By leveraging data-driven insights, businesses can make informed decisions that enhance their agility and innovation capabilities.

Enhanced Resilience The comprehensive assessment helps organizations build resilience by identifying and mitigating potential risks.

Competitive Advantage   Companies with a high Future Readiness Score are better positioned to seize new opportunities and maintain a competitive edge in their industry.

Sustainable Growth   Emphasizing sustainability and ethical practices ensures that growth is both robust and responsible, aligning with global efforts to address environmental challenges.

The theory of future readiness provides a structured approach for businesses to navigate disruption and thrive in a rapidly changing world. By focusing on vision, innovation, technology, leadership, and sustainability, organizations can build resilience and agility. This framework not only prepares businesses for future challenges but also positions them to seize new opportunities, ensuring long-term success and relevance in an ever-evolving landscape.

The development of the theory of future readiness was driven by the need for businesses to systematically navigate the future. By measuring key indicators of disruption and innovation, organizations can develop actionable insights and strategies that enhance their resilience and adaptability. The theory of future readiness provides a comprehensive framework that enables businesses to stay ahead of the curve, seize new opportunities, and achieve sustained success in a rapidly evolving landscape.

The Future Readiness Score is an essential tool for organizations seeking to thrive in an era of rapid change and disruption. By providing a comprehensive assessment of an organization's preparedness, it helps businesses develop targeted strategies for future success. The insights gained from the Future Readiness Score enable organizations to enhance their resilience, foster innovation, and achieve sustainable growth, ensuring they remain competitive and undisruptable in a constantly evolving landscape.

As a reader of this book, you are invited to take a complimentary Future Readiness Score assessment. Visit www.iankhan.com/frs, fill in the form, and get started!

As we continue to explore and refine this theory, it will serve as a vital tool for organizations striving to become undisruptable in an era of constant change. By embracing the principles of future readiness, businesses can transform uncertainty into a strategic advantage and drive meaningful growth in the face of disruption.

Final Words

In today's rapidly evolving business landscape, the concept of future readiness is not just a competitive advantage but a necessity. The theory of future readiness and the Future Readiness Score offer a comprehensive framework for organizations to measure and enhance their preparedness for future challenges and opportunities. By focusing on key pillars such as vision, innovation, technology, leadership, and sustainability, businesses can build resilience and agility, ensuring long-term success and relevance in an ever-changing world.

The journey to becoming undisruptable starts with understanding and measuring disruption. Examples from industry leaders such as Amazon, Tesla, and Netflix demonstrate the power of data-driven strategies and proactive adaptation. These organizations have successfully navigated disruption by leveraging robust metrics, fostering a culture of innovation, and continuously evolving their leadership approaches.

The development of the Future Readiness Score is a significant step forward in providing businesses with the tools they need to thrive in an era of constant change. By quantifying future readiness, organizations can gain actionable insights, make informed decisions, and foster continuous improvement. This metric not only highlights areas for growth but also helps companies mitigate risks and seize emerging opportunities.

As we continue to refine and apply the theory of future readiness, it will serve as a vital tool for organizations striving to navigate the complexities of disruption. By embracing the principles of future readiness, businesses can transform uncertainty into a strategic advantage, driving meaningful growth and ensuring they remain competitive and undisruptable in a constantly evolving landscape.

Resources

Check out these resources to learn more about disruption and jobs in the future.

Books

- *The Lean Startup* by Eric Ries
- *Metaverse For Dummies* by Ian Khan
- *The Quick Guide to Prompt Engineering* by Ian Khan

TED Talks

- "The Lean Startup" by Eric Ries
- "What Will Future Jobs Look Like?" by Andrew McAfee
- "The Jobs We'll Lose to Machines—And the Ones We Won't" by Anthony Goldbloom

Take the Future Readiness Score at www.iankhan.com/frs or scan the QR Code

14

The Critical Need to Measure Future Readiness

Unless we measure how disruptable we are, we will never be able to create anything that is undisruptable.

—Ian Khan

Introduction

Imagine standing in a vast cornfield, the sun setting behind the horizon, casting long shadows over the rows of crops. This scene, reminiscent of my summers on my family farm, is a testament to the timeless rhythms of nature. However, the agricultural landscape today is transforming in ways my grandparents could only dream of. Fields are now high-tech hubs of innovation, and the same need for transformation applies to businesses globally.

In today's rapidly evolving business landscape, the concept of future readiness has become paramount. Organizations must be prepared not only to face imminent disruptions but also to leverage emerging opportunities to stay ahead. But how can companies accurately assess their readiness for the future? This question has driven the development of a comprehensive and standardized metric: the Future Readiness Score (FRS).

Why is measuring future readiness essential? In the face of accelerating technological advancements, shifting market dynamics, and unpredictable disruptions, understanding and quantifying future readiness is crucial.

Businesses that lack this insight are often ill-prepared to navigate changes, leading to missed opportunities and heightened risks.

According to McKinsey, 85% of executives acknowledge the necessity of transformation, yet only 23% believe their companies excel at executing it.[1] This gap underscores the urgent need for a robust measurement system.

The Top 50 Metrics in Business

To track organizational progress, success, capacity, profitability, and growth, companies use a variety of metrics. Metrics are absolutely important to be able to measure and track, modify, and adapt to changing business circumstances. Think about it, without any metrics, it would be practically

1. Revenue growth rate
2. Net profit margin
3. Gross profit margin
4. Operating profit margin
5. Return on investment (ROI)
6. Earnings before interest, taxes, depreciation, and amortization (EBITDA)
7. Return on equity (ROE)
8. Return on assets (ROA)
9. Debt-to-equity Ratio
10. Current ratio
11. Operational efficiency
12. Cost per unit
13. Inventory turnover ratio
14. Days sales outstanding (DSO)
15. Days inventory outstanding (DIO)
16. Days payable outstanding (DPO)
17. Supply chain cycle time
18. Order fulfillment cycle time
19. Production downtime
20. First pass yield (FPY)
21. Customer satisfaction (CSAT)
22. Net Promoter Score (NPS)
23. Customer retention rate
24. Customer churn rate
25. Customer lifetime value (CLV)
26. Customer acquisition cost (CAC)
27. Customer effort score (CES)
28. Average order value (AOV)
29. Customer complaint resolution time
30. Customer engagement score
31. Employee engagement score
32. Employee turnover rate
33. Absenteeism rate
34. Employee productivity
35. Training and development participation
36. Time to hire
37. Employee Net Promoter Score (eNPS)
38. Internal promotion rate
39. Diversity and inclusion metrics
40. Employee satisfaction with benefits
41. Innovation rate
42. Research and development (R&D) expenditure
43. Time to market
44. Patents filed
45. Market share
46. Revenue from new products
47. Growth rate of new customer acquisition
48. Business development activities
49. Expansion into new markets
50. Brand equity

impossible to run any meaningful organization. As a summary of the incredible work that has been done over the past, here is a recollection of the top 50 most popular and successful metrics available in business today.

These metrics offer a comprehensive view of an organization's performance, health, and other critical aspects. A big challenge, however, is that a metric to measure future readiness does not exist, or has not existed, until the FRS and the unique way in which it measures future readiness.

The Journey Until Now

Reflecting on my career, I recall a pivotal moment that shaped my understanding of future readiness. As a consultant, I had the opportunity to study some of the world's top companies, from tech giants such as Google and Apple to industry leaders such as Amazon and Microsoft. I was fascinated by their innovation and resilience, but one question kept nagging me: How do they measure their preparedness for the future?

Despite being successful organizations, I was unable to find a single metric is being used as a standard to quantify future readiness. Each organization had its unique approach, often focusing heavily on one area, such as technology investments, while neglecting others. This realization highlighted the critical need for a comprehensive, standardized metric—one that could provide a holistic view of an organization's readiness for future challenges and opportunities.

Our understanding of future readiness is grounded in extensive research and case studies. Studies by McKinsey, Gartner, *Forbes*, and the *Wall Street Journal* have been instrumental in shaping our approach. For instance, McKinsey's study on transformation execution revealed that while many executives recognize the need for change, few excel at implementing it. Gartner's research highlighted the benefits of data-driven decision-making, showing that organizations leveraging data are 23% more likely to outperform their competitors. These insights underscore the importance of a comprehensive measurement system for future readiness. Over a period of two years, we studied over 250 different studies to be able to understand the connection between a specific business area and future readiness.

Areas of the Future Readiness Score

The FRS encompasses seven critical components, or pillars as we call them.

- **Pillar 1, engagement:** Measures how engaged and motivated employees are within the organization.
- **Pillar 2, learning:** Assesses the organization's commitment to continuous learning and development.

- **Pillar 3, people:** Focuses on the skills, diversity, and well-being of the workforce.
- **Pillar 4, culture:** Examines the organizational culture and its alignment with future goals.
- **Pillar 5, collaboration:** Looks at strategic partnerships and collaborations.
- **Pillar 6, innovation:** Consists of all technology investments and initiatives.
- **Pillar 7, execution:** Measures the effectiveness of strategy implementation and operational execution.

Methodology Framework and Overview

The FRS methodology involves a multistep process to ensure comprehensive and accurate measurement:

- **Data collection:** Gather data from various sources, including employee surveys, financial reports, customer feedback, and operational metrics.
- **Analysis:** Analyze the data to identify patterns, strengths, and areas for improvement.
- **Scoring:** Assign scores to each component based on the analysis, providing a clear picture of the organization's future readiness.
- **Benchmarking:** Compare the scores against industry standards and best practices to contextualize the results.
- **Reporting:** Present the findings in a detailed report, highlighting key insights and actionable recommendations.

The data used in the FRS spans five years, encompasses more than half a million data points, and covers 5000 companies. This extensive dataset ensures that the FRS is both comprehensive and reliable.

As a reader of this book, you are invited to take a complimentary Future Readiness Score assessment. Visit www.IanKhan.com/Undisrupted, fill in the form, and get started!

FRS: A Tool for Management Consensus

How can a single, comprehensive metric such as the FRS foster management consensus? The FRS serves as a common language for all stakeholders within an organization, bridging gaps between departments and aligning everyone toward shared objectives. By providing a holistic view of an organization's readiness, the FRS enables cohesive decision-making and strategic alignment.

Consider the impact of the Net Promoter Score (NPS), a single metric introduced by Fred Reichheld in 2003. NPS revolutionized how companies measure customer loyalty by asking a simple question: "On a scale of 0 to 10, how likely are you to recommend our company to a friend or colleague?" This straightforward approach provided a clear, quantifiable measure of customer satisfaction and loyalty. It quickly became a critical tool for management teams worldwide, helping to unify efforts across departments toward enhancing customer experience.

According to an article in the *Harvard Business Review* (HBR), companies that adopt NPS as a key metric see significant improvements in customer retention, employee satisfaction, and revenue growth.[2]

These are reasons why the FRS can achieve similar consensus:

- **Clear communication:** Like NPS, the FRS distills complex information into a simple, understandable score. This clarity helps all team members—from executives to frontline employees—understand where the organization stands in terms of future readiness.
- **Unified focus:** The FRS highlights key areas needing improvement, ensuring that all departments work toward common goals. This unified focus is crucial for cohesive strategy execution.
- **Data-driven decisions:** With the FRS providing a comprehensive view of readiness across multiple dimensions, management can make informed decisions based on data rather than intuition. This leads to more effective and strategic planning.

The Score's Year-on-Year Benefits

How does the FRS help companies year on year? By consistently measuring and tracking future readiness, organizations can identify trends, monitor progress, and make continuous improvements. The year-on-year benefits of using the FRS include the following.

Benchmarking and Trend Analysis

- Just as companies use year-on-year NPS scores to benchmark performance and identify trends in customer satisfaction, organizations can use the FRS to track their readiness over time. This helps in recognizing patterns and making proactive adjustments. *HBR's* research on NPS shows that companies monitoring their NPS year-on-year can identify shifts in customer sentiment and adapt strategies accordingly.

Continuous Improvement

- Regularly measuring the FRS encourages a culture of continuous improvement. By identifying areas of weakness and making targeted improvements, organizations can enhance their readiness incrementally.
- Toyota's kaizen approach, which focuses on continuous improvement, has been key to its long-term success. Applying a similar mindset to future readiness ensures that organizations stay ahead of emerging challenges.

Strategic Adjustments

- The FRS allows companies to make strategic adjustments based on real-time data. This agility is crucial in a fast-changing business environment where flexibility and responsiveness are key to success.
- Microsoft's Future Ready campaign uses continuous data collection and analysis to make strategic adjustments, ensuring sustained growth and innovation.

Employee and Stakeholder Engagement

- Using the FRS can enhance employee and stakeholder engagement by providing a clear understanding of the organization's direction and progress. Engaged employees are more likely to contribute to the company's success.
- Gallup's research on employee engagement shows that companies with high engagement scores are more productive and profitable. The FRS can similarly drive engagement by highlighting areas for improvement and celebrating successes.

The Strategic Importance of Measuring Future Readiness

Measuring future readiness as a score provides a clear, actionable framework for organizations to navigate the complexities of a rapidly changing business environment. By offering clarity, focus, and data-driven insights, the FRS helps management teams align their efforts and make informed strategic decisions. The year-on-year benefits of using the FRS include continuous improvement, strategic agility, enhanced engagement, and proactive risk management.

As Satya Nadella, CEO of Microsoft, succinctly puts it, "Data and AI are the key drivers of business transformation and growth in the digital era."[3] By leveraging the FRS, organizations can harness the power of data to ensure they are not just prepared for future challenges but are also positioned to seize emerging opportunities, making them truly undisruptable in the long term.

Businesses That Missed the Boat

The following are some case studies that highlight the critical importance of future readiness. Companies that fail to anticipate and adapt to changing market conditions, technological advancements, and consumer preferences are at significant risk of decline. By focusing on future readiness and leveraging comprehensive metrics such as the FRS, organizations can avoid these pitfalls and position themselves for long-term success.

Nokia: Missing Opportunities

Nokia was once the undisputed leader in mobile phones, commanding over 40% of the global market share in 2007. However, by 2013, its market share had plummeted to just 3%.

The following were the key reasons for failure:

- **Lack of software innovation:** While Nokia excelled in hardware, it lagged in software development, failing to compete with iOS and Android platforms.
- **Poor strategic decisions:** Nokia underestimated the importance of the smartphone revolution and clung to its outdated Symbian operating system.
- **Ineffective leadership:** Frequent leadership changes and lack of clear vision hindered Nokia's ability to adapt quickly.

The following were the impacts:

- **Market position:** Nokia lost its leadership position and had to sell its mobile division to Microsoft in 2013.
- **Financial losses:** Billions in lost revenue and significant layoffs.

Kodak: Failing to Embrace Digital

Kodak was a pioneer in photography, inventing the digital camera in 1975. Despite this innovation, Kodak filed for bankruptcy in 2012.

The following were the key reasons for failure:

- **Resistance to change:** Kodak feared that digital photography would cannibalize its film business, leading to a lack of investment in digital technologies.
- **Market misjudgment:** Misjudging the speed at which digital photography would replace film, Kodak missed out on capitalizing on its own invention.
- **Operational inertia:** Slow decision-making processes and internal resistance to change prevented Kodak from adapting quickly.

The following were the impacts:

- **Bankruptcy:** Kodak filed for bankruptcy in 2012 after years of declining sales.
- **Market exit:** The company exited the consumer camera market, a domain it once dominated.

Blockbuster: Ignoring Digital Disruption

Blockbuster was a giant in the video rental industry, with over 9000 stores worldwide at its peak in the early 2000s.

The following were the key reasons for failure:

- **Ignoring market trends:** Blockbuster ignored the shift toward digital streaming and online rentals, underestimating the threat posed by Netflix and other digital platforms.
- **Inflexible business model:** Sticking to its traditional rental model, Blockbuster failed to innovate or adapt to changing consumer preferences.
- **Missed opportunities:** Blockbuster had the opportunity to buy Netflix in 2000 for $50 million but declined, believing their model was superior.

The following were the impacts:

- **Store closures:** Blockbuster declared bankruptcy in 2010, leading to the closure of most of its stores.
- **Market exit:** The company eventually ceased operations, unable to compete with digital streaming services.

Final Words

Organizations must focus on future readiness at multiple levels. The more data available, the more insights you can use to make decisions. Future readiness relates to profitability, stability, and the future of an organization's success in many ways. With over 45 data points available to understand the seven key areas of future readiness the FRS can be a very useful tool for your organization's future. Today in America, 65.3% of businesses close their doors 10 years after opening.[4] This is a staggering fact and something that can be addressed to some extent by ensuring how undisruptable you are, how well you are positioned for the future.

Measuring future readiness should be made mandatory for organizations to thrive in an era of rapid technological advancements and unpredictable market shifts. The benefits of the FRS are manifold, including enhanced clarity, benchmarking capabilities, actionable insights, and continuous improvement. Regular tracking of the FRS helps organizations make strategic adjustments, engage employees and stakeholders, and mitigate risks. Historical case studies such as Nokia, Kodak, and Blockbuster illustrate the dire consequences of failing to anticipate and adapt to change.

As we navigate the complexities of the modern business environment, leveraging tools such as the FRS can ensure that organizations are not just surviving but thriving. Embracing a culture of innovation, data-driven decision-making, and continuous improvement will position companies to seize emerging opportunities and remain resilient against future disruptions.

Resources

Here are some good resources to learn more about the topics in this chapter.

Books and Articles

- *The Lean Startup* by Eric Ries
- *Exponential Organizations* by Salim Ismail
- *The Innovator's Dilemma* by Clayton M. Christensen
- YouTube: *The Future of Work: How Companies Can Adapt to the Changing Workplace* by McKinsey & Company
- *Harvard Business Review: The Explainer: Disruptive Innovation*

Watch List
- *The Age of AI* (BBC documentary)
- *Disruptor 50: Companies Changing the World* (CNBC)

Take the Future Readiness Score at www.iankhan.com/frs or scan the QR Code

15

FRS Pillar 1: Engagement

The most important thing in communication is hearing what is not said.

—Peter Drucker

THE FIRST PILLAR of the theory of future readiness is engagement. In the journey of creating the Future Readiness Score, we looked at more than 250 independent industry studies to identify what really matters for an organization's success. Engagement came out to be one of the top seven! This chapter will drill down into what engagement is and how you should go about creating a plan to have a better engaged business.

What Is Engagement?

Engagement, in the context of business, refers to the emotional and psychological commitment an individual or group has toward an organization. Engagement can be internal, involving employees and management, or external, involving customers, partners, and other stakeholders. High levels of engagement typically correlate with greater productivity, higher employee satisfaction, and improved business outcomes.

Internal engagement focuses on the organization's workforce, encompassing everything from employee satisfaction and morale to commitment and involvement in the company's mission and goals. Internal engagement is crucial as it directly affects productivity, innovation, and retention rates. Companies such as Google and Microsoft are renowned for their high levels of internal engagement, which have contributed significantly to their success. Google's innovative approach to employee engagement, which now has spread to many industries at large, includes initiatives such as flexible work arrangements, wellness programs, and continuous learning opportunities. These efforts have resulted in high employee satisfaction and retention rates, contributing to Google's reputation as one of the best places to work.

External engagement involves interactions with customers, partners, investors, and the community. This type of engagement is vital for building brand loyalty, enhancing customer satisfaction, and fostering strong partnerships. Starbucks exemplifies external engagement through its comprehensive customer loyalty programs and active social media presence. The company's mobile app and Starbucks Rewards program are designed to engage customers continuously, offering personalized experiences and rewards. This strategy has helped Starbucks build a loyal customer base and maintain strong brand recognition globally.

A lot of work on organizational engagement is available today. For example, William A. Kahn is widely recognized for his seminal research on engagement, particularly in the workplace. His 1990 study introduced the concept of "personal engagement," which describes the simultaneous employment and expression of one's preferred self in work tasks, promoting connections, presence, and active role performance.[1]

Recommending Authors

Other works on organizational development focusing on engagement include those by the following authors:

- **Kurt Lewin:** Often considered the founding father of organizational development, he introduced concepts such as action research and the change model (unfreeze, change, refreeze).
- **Richard Beckhard:** An influential figure who defined organizational development as an effort planned, organization-wide, and managed from the top to increase organization effectiveness.
- **Douglas McGregor:** Known for theory X and theory Y, which explore management styles and their impact on employee motivation.

How to Use Engagement Channels

Engagement channels are the media through which organizations communicate and interact with their internal and external audiences. Effective use of these channels is critical for fostering strong engagement.

Internal channels include platforms such as Slack, Microsoft Teams, and company intranets, which facilitate seamless communication and collaboration. Regular employee surveys and feedback systems, such as those used by Salesforce, help gauge employee sentiment and identify areas for improvement. Salesforce's approach to internal engagement includes town halls and all-hands meetings where employees can voice concerns and share ideas directly with senior management. This open communication culture ensures that everyone feels heard and valued.

External channels encompass social media, email marketing, customer service platforms, and public relations. Companies such as Amazon leverage social media and email marketing to keep customers informed and engaged. Amazon's customer service platforms, including its AI-driven chatbots and 24/7 support, ensure that customers receive timely assistance, enhancing overall satisfaction. Public relations efforts, such as community events and media engagements, help build a positive public image and foster trust with the broader community.

How Engagement Explains Profitability

High levels of engagement, both internal and external, are directly linked to profitability. Engaged employees are more productive, innovative, and loyal, reducing turnover costs and enhancing operational efficiency. Similarly, engaged customers are more likely to be repeat buyers and brand advocates, driving revenue growth.

Companies with high employee engagement scores are 21% more profitable, according to Gallup research.[2] This profitability stems from several factors: engaged employees are more likely to go the extra mile, leading to higher productivity; they are less likely to leave the organization, reducing turnover costs; and they often provide better customer service, enhancing customer satisfaction. Additionally, *Forbes* reports that firms with strong customer engagement see a 25% increase in customer retention rates.[3] Engaged customers are more likely to be loyal, make repeat purchases, and recommend the company to others, all of which drive revenue growth.

Creating a culture that values and promotes engagement requires intentional strategies and consistent effort. Companies such as Zappos have successfully built such a culture by prioritizing employee happiness and customer satisfaction. Zappos's approach includes empowering employees to make decisions that enhance the customer experience and investing in their professional development. This focus on engagement has translated into high customer satisfaction and loyalty, as well as a positive workplace environment.

Steps to Engage Stakeholders

Stakeholder engagement is necessary to create an undisruptable organization. The stronger your ties with them, the stronger your business. Let's start with the basics.

1. **Identify key stakeholders:** Understand who your stakeholders are and what their needs and expectations are.
2. **Develop an engagement plan:** Establish clear, consistent, and tailored communication strategies for different stakeholder groups.
3. **Foster two-way engagement:** Encourage feedback and active participation from stakeholders through surveys, forums, and interactive platforms.
4. **Monitor and adjust:** Regularly assess the effectiveness of engagement strategies and make necessary adjustments based on feedback and performance metrics.

Best Practices

In the previous step we looked at the essential basics of what an engagement plan must have. But how about setting the course and moving forward? We have seen too many organizations that fail to carry out a well-thought-out plan. Here are some essential steps for successful practices:

1. **Set clear objectives:** Define what successful engagement looks like and set measurable goals.
2. **Allocate resources:** Ensure that sufficient resources, including time and budget, are dedicated to engagement activities.
3. **Leverage technology:** Utilize modern tools and platforms to facilitate engagement and track progress.
4. **Train and empower employees:** Provide training to employees on effective engagement practices and empower them to take initiative.
5. **Evaluate and iterate:** Continuously evaluate engagement efforts and iterate based on what works and what does not.

Leveraging the Power of Channels

Engagement is vital for an organization's success, affecting productivity, employee satisfaction, customer loyalty, and overall business outcomes. To effectively engage with both internal and external stakeholders, organizations can utilize various channels.

Here's an in-depth look at these channels, their use, and how they contribute to engagement.

Start a Newsletter
- **What it is:** A regularly distributed publication, typically via email, containing news, updates, and relevant information about the organization.
- **How it engages:** Newsletters keep stakeholders informed about company developments, successes, and upcoming events. They help maintain regular communication and foster a sense of inclusion and belonging.
- **Recommendation:** Use newsletters to highlight achievements, share employee stories, announce upcoming events, and provide industry insights. Ensure the content is engaging, visually appealing, and relevant to the audience.
- **Insight:** According to HubSpot, companies that blog receive 97% more links to their website, and newsletters can drive significant traffic to these blogs, enhancing visibility and engagement.

Use Social Media Platforms
- **What it is:** Platforms such as Facebook, LinkedIn, Twitter, and Instagram, used for social interaction and content sharing.
- **How it engages:** Social media allows real-time interaction with a wide audience, fostering direct communication, feedback, and engagement. It helps in building a community around the brand.
- **Recommendation:** Regularly post updates, engage with followers, respond to comments and messages promptly, and use multimedia content (videos, images) to enhance engagement. Leverage social media analytics to understand what content resonates best with your audience.
- **Insight:** Sprout Social reports that 77% of consumers are more likely to buy from a brand they follow on social media.

Leverage TV & Broadcast

- **What it is:** Broadcast and cable television used for commercial advertising, company news segments, and industry-related programming.
- **How it engages:** TV reaches a broad audience and can effectively communicate the company's message through visual and auditory means. It is especially useful for brand awareness and reputation building.
- **Recommendation:** Create engaging commercials or sponsor industry-related programs to reach potential customers and partners. Use TV to share major company milestones and community involvement.
- **Insight:** Nielsen data shows that TV advertising generates $4.20 in sales for every $1 spent, highlighting its effectiveness in driving engagement and sales.

Create Branded Content

- **What it is:** Content produced by the company that provides value to the audience while subtly promoting the brand.
- **How it engages:** Branded content, such as blogs, videos, and podcasts, provides valuable information that resonates with the audience, fostering trust and brand loyalty.
- **Recommendation:** Focus on creating high-quality, informative, and entertaining content that aligns with the interests and needs of your audience. Avoid overtly promotional content; instead, aim to educate and inspire.
- **Insight:** According to the Content Marketing Institute, 70% of consumers feel closer to a brand as a result of branded content.

Get in Print Magazines and Newspapers

- **What it is:** Print or digital publications providing news and information on a wide range of topics.
- **How it engages:** Newspapers can be used for press releases, company announcements, and thought leadership articles, reaching a diverse audience.
- **Recommendation:** Regularly publish press releases and op-eds in relevant newspapers. Highlight company achievements, industry insights, and community involvement.
- **Insight:** The American Press Institute found that 69% of adults in the United States read newspapers, either in print or online, providing a significant audience for company news.

Write Editorials

- **What it is:** Opinion pieces written by company leaders or guest writers, offering insights and perspectives on industry trends and issues.
- **How it engages:** Editorials position the company as a thought leader, fostering trust and credibility within the industry.
- **Recommendation:** Encourage senior leaders to write editorial pieces for industry publications. Focus on current industry challenges and provide unique perspectives or solutions.
- **Insight:** According to the Edelman Trust Barometer, thought leadership content increases trust in a company by 34%.

Partner with Business Publications

- **What it is:** Industry-specific magazines, journals, and online platforms that provide news and insights relevant to business professionals.
- **How it engages:** Business publications are a credible source of information for industry professionals. Publishing in these outlets enhances the company's reputation and visibility among peers and potential clients.
- **Recommendation:** Contribute articles, case studies, and research findings to leading business publications. Highlight your company's expertise and innovations.
- **Insight:** The Content Marketing Institute reports that 92% of marketers believe business publications enhance their company's authority in the industry.

Internal Engagement Ideas

- Primarily, internal engagement refers to an organization's efforts to connect and engage with employees. Primarily targeted at building a highly cohesive team, internal engagement can take many shapes. Here are some ideas.

Provide Employee Volunteer Time

- **What it is:** Programs that encourage employees to volunteer for community service during work hours.
- **How it engages:** Volunteer programs enhance employee satisfaction and foster a sense of purpose and community involvement, enhancing employee morale and corporate image.
- **Recommendation:** Offer paid volunteer time off (VTO) and organize company-wide volunteer events. Highlight these efforts in internal

and external communications to showcase your company's commitment to social responsibility.

- **Insight:** According to UnitedHealth Group, 87% of employees who volunteered through their workplace reported an improved perception of their employer.[4]

Offer Employee Free Time

- **What it is:** Allocated time for employees to pursue personal interests or hobbies during work hours.
- **How it engages:** Allowing free time boosts creativity, reduces burnout, and improves overall job satisfaction.
- **Recommendation:** Implement flexible work hours and encourage employees to take breaks and pursue hobbies. Share success stories of how employees use their free time to enhance their skills or contribute to the community.
- **Insight:** A study by the *Journal of Occupational and Organizational Psychology* found that employees with flexible schedules are 10% more engaged and 20% more productive.

Permit Personal Project Time

- **What it is:** Dedicated time for employees to work on personal or side projects during work hours.
- **How it engages:** Personal project time fosters innovation, skill development, and employee engagement by allowing individuals to pursue their passions.
- **Recommendation:** Allocate a certain number of hours per week for employees to work on projects of their choice. Provide resources and support for these initiatives and celebrate their successes within the company.
- **Insight:** Google's 20% time policy, which allows employees to spend 20% of their time on personal projects, has led to the creation of major products such as Gmail and AdSense.[5]

Allow for Community Projects Time

- **What it is:** Time allocated for employees to participate in projects that benefit the local community.
- **How it engages:** Involvement in community projects enhances corporate social responsibility, boosts employee morale, and strengthens community relations.

- **Recommendation:** Partner with local organizations and create opportunities for employees to contribute to community projects. Publicize these efforts through internal and external channels.
- **Insight:** A study by Deloitte found that 70% of employees believe that volunteer opportunities boost morale more than company-sponsored happy hours.

Organize Town Hall Meetings
- **What it is:** Company-wide meetings where employees can interact directly with senior management, ask questions, and receive updates.
- **How it engages:** Town hall meetings foster transparency, build trust, and encourage open communication between employees and leadership.
- **Recommendation:** Hold regular town hall meetings and ensure they are interactive and inclusive. Use these meetings to address employee concerns, share company performance, and discuss future plans.
- **Insight:** According to Gallup, companies with open communication practices are 25% more likely to have a lower turnover rate.[6]

Hold Annual Meetings
- **What it is:** Yearly gatherings where stakeholders, including employees, investors, and partners, review the company's performance and strategic direction.
- **How it engages:** Annual meetings provide a comprehensive overview of the company's achievements, challenges, and future plans, fostering a sense of collective purpose and alignment.
- **Recommendation:** Use annual meetings to celebrate successes, address challenges, and outline strategic goals. Encourage feedback and participation from all stakeholders.
- **Insight:** The *Harvard Business Review* notes that companies conducting regular annual reviews are 30% more likely to meet their long-term goals.[7]

Get Everyone Together at Company Events
- **What it is:** Social and professional gatherings organized by the company, such as retreats, parties, and team-building activities.
- **How it engages:** Company events enhance team cohesion, improve employee morale, and create a positive work environment.

- **Recommendation:** Organize regular company events that cater to diverse interests and encourage participation. Use these events to strengthen interpersonal relationships and reinforce company values.
- **Insight:** A study by Eventbrite found that 84% of employees feel more engaged when their company organizes regular social events.[8]

Great Examples of Highly Engaged Organizations

The following are some examples of companies that focus on engagement as a core business value and do a great job at it.

Google: Internal Engagement

Google is a prime example of a company that excels in internal engagement. The company offers numerous programs to boost employee engagement, including flexible work arrangements, wellness programs, and continuous learning opportunities. Google's innovative approach includes initiatives such as the Googleplex, a state-of-the-art campus designed to foster creativity and collaboration.

The Googleplex, the corporate headquarters of Google located in Mountain View, California, is a prime example of innovative workplace design that integrates organizational culture with physical space. Designed by Clive Wilkinson Architects, the Googleplex reflects Google's values of flexibility, collaboration, and work-life balance.

The Googleplex features a variety of unique elements such as "Glass Tent" offices that provide light and views while ensuring privacy and rapid construction, which was crucial during Google's rapid expansion. The campus also includes yurts made of recycled denim for meetings, emphasizing sustainability and adaptability. The layout encourages informal interactions through strategically placed social nodes, such as tech stops similar to Apple's Genius Bars, and communal areas such as kitchens and lounges adjacent to workspaces.

Google's organizational culture is built on principles of innovation, creativity, and transparency. The campus includes numerous amenities to support employee well-being and productivity, such as organic gardens, multiple cafés, gyms, and recreation areas. This environment fosters a sense of community and belonging, crucial for maintaining high levels of employee engagement and satisfaction.

Overall, the Googleplex exemplifies how physical space can support and enhance a company's culture and operational efficiency, making it a landmark in corporate campus design.

Starbucks: External Engagement

Starbucks exemplifies external engagement through its comprehensive customer loyalty programs and active social media presence. The Starbucks Rewards program, integrated with its mobile app, offers personalized experiences and rewards to customers. Additionally, Starbucks engages with its customers through social media platforms, addressing concerns and sharing updates. This strategy has helped Starbucks build a loyal customer base and maintain strong brand recognition globally.

Starbucks exemplifies external engagement through its comprehensive customer loyalty programs and active social media presence. The Starbucks Rewards program, integrated with its mobile app, offers personalized experiences and rewards to customers. This program allows customers to earn stars for every purchase, which can be redeemed for free drinks and food items, providing a highly personalized and engaging customer experience. Additionally, the app features mobile ordering and payment options, enhancing convenience and encouraging repeat business.

Starbucks also leverages social media platforms to engage with its customers effectively. By addressing customer concerns, sharing updates, and promoting new products, Starbucks maintains an active and responsive online presence. This engagement strategy helps build a loyal customer base and enhances brand recognition globally. Starbucks's social media activities include interactive posts, customer feedback responses, and visually appealing content that aligns with their brand values and marketing campaigns.

These strategies have contributed to Starbucks's strong brand loyalty and recognition, making it one of the most successful companies in the global coffee industry.

Salesforce: Balanced Engagement

Salesforce effectively balances internal and external engagement, contributing to its strong market position and loyal customer and employee base.

Internal Engagement   Internally, Salesforce fosters an open communication culture with regular town halls and all-hands meetings. These events encourage transparency and allow employees to stay informed about company updates, ask questions, and share their feedback directly with leadership. Additionally, Salesforce emphasizes employee well-being and professional development through various programs and initiatives. The company's commitment to equality and inclusion is evident through its diverse workplace policies and support for various employee resource groups.

External Engagement Externally, Salesforce engages with customers through its community platform, Salesforce Trailblazer Community. This platform enables users to connect, share experiences, and provide feedback, creating a vibrant and supportive user community. The Trailblazer Community also offers access to a wealth of resources, including forums, events, and training materials, helping customers maximize their use of Salesforce products. Furthermore, Salesforce actively engages with customers on social media and through its comprehensive content marketing strategy, which includes blogs, webinars, and case studies.

Impact This dual approach to engagement has strengthened Salesforce's market position by fostering a loyal customer and employee base. Internally, the open communication culture and focus on employee development have created a motivated and dedicated workforce. Externally, the active engagement with customers through the Trailblazer Community and other channels has built a robust and supportive customer network, enhancing customer satisfaction and retention.

Steps Toward Higher Engagement

By prioritizing engagement and implementing effective strategies, organizations can build stronger relationships with their stakeholders, drive business success, and ensure they are future-ready.

These are some next steps:

1. **Assess current engagement levels:** Use surveys and feedback tools to evaluate current engagement levels within your organization.
2. **Develop an engagement strategy:** Create a comprehensive engagement strategy that addresses both internal and external stakeholders.
3. **Implement and monitor:** Roll out the engagement initiatives and continuously monitor their effectiveness.
4. **Refine and improve:** Based on feedback and performance data, refine and improve engagement practices to ensure ongoing success.

Final Words

These are the key takeaways from this chapter: Engagement is a critical component of future readiness and business success. Both internal and external engagement are necessary for holistic organizational growth. Effective engagement strategies drive profitability, customer loyalty, and employee satisfaction. Consistent evaluation and adjustment of engagement strategies are crucial for sustained success. The Future Readiness Score assesses engagement as a core pillar.

Resources

Books

- *Drive* by Daniel H. Pink
- *The Employee Experience Advantage* by Jacob Morgan
- *First, Break All the Rules* by Marcus Buckingham and Curt Coffman
- *Influence* by Robert B. Cialdini

Take the Future Readiness Score at www.iankhan.com/frs or scan the QR Code

16

FRS Pillar 2: Learning

The capacity to learn is a gift; the ability to learn is a skill; the willingness to learn is a choice.

—*Brian Herbert*

IN THIS CHAPTER, we look at a fundamental pillar of future readiness: *learning*. Today there are more ways to learn than ever have been. In fact, we are overlearning, and the question is more about what we are learning. Take a dive!

What Is Learning?

Learning in the context of business refers to the continuous process of acquiring knowledge, skills, and competencies that are essential for an organization's growth and adaptability. It encompasses both formal education and informal knowledge sharing within the organization. For both organization as well as individuals, learning is a critical pillar of the Future Readiness Score (FRS) because it equips employees and leaders with the tools they need to innovate, adapt to changes, and drive the company forward.

The following are all the reasons why learning is essential for future readiness.

Learning Fosters Innovation and Adaptability   Learning fosters innovation by encouraging employees to think creatively and explore new ideas. It also enhances adaptability, enabling the organization to respond effectively to market changes and technological advancements. Companies that prioritize learning are better positioned to innovate and stay ahead of the competition.

In fact, according to a study by Deloitte, companies that cultivate a strong learning culture are 92% more likely to innovate.

Learning Enhances Employee Engagement and Retention A commitment to learning demonstrates that the organization values its employees' growth, leading to higher engagement and retention rates. Employees who have access to learning opportunities feel more valued and are more likely to remain loyal to the company.

In fact, LinkedIn's Workplace Learning Report found that 94% of employees would stay at a company longer if it invested in their career development.

Learning Improves Performance and Productivity Continuous learning helps employees improve their performance by acquiring new skills and knowledge relevant to their roles. This leads to increased productivity and efficiency, contributing to the overall success of the organization.

In fact, the American Society for Training and Development (ASTD) reports that companies with comprehensive training programs have 218% higher income per employee than those without formalized training.

Learning Builds a Competitive Advantage In a rapidly changing business environment, a skilled and knowledgeable workforce is a significant competitive advantage. Organizations that invest in learning are better equipped to handle disruptions and seize new opportunities.

In fact, a study by the *Harvard Business Review* found that companies with strong learning cultures are 52% more productive and 17% more profitable than their peers.

Types of Learning

The following are all different types of learning.

Formal Learning

Formal learning involves structured programs and courses designed to impart specific skills and knowledge. This type of learning is typically delivered through educational institutions or professional training organizations.

These are examples of this type of learning:

- **Workshops and seminars:** Short-term training sessions focused on specific skills or knowledge areas.
- **Degree programs:** Long-term educational programs leading to academic degrees.
- **Certification courses:** Programs that provide industry-recognized credentials.

Informal Learning

Informal learning occurs outside a structured curriculum and involves self-directed learning, peer collaboration, and experiential learning.

These are examples of this type of learning:

- **On-the-job training:** Learning by performing tasks and gaining hands-on experience.
- **Mentorship programs:** Guidance and knowledge sharing between experienced employees and newcomers.
- **Peer collaboration:** Learning through discussions and collaboration with colleagues.

E-learning

E-learning utilizes digital platforms and tools to deliver educational content and training programs. It offers flexibility and accessibility, allowing employees to learn at their own pace.

These are examples of this type of learning:

- **Online courses:** Web-based courses covering various topics.
- **Webinars:** Live or recorded online sessions on specific subjects.
- **Learning management systems (LMS):** Platforms that manage, deliver, and track e-learning activities.

Experiential Learning

Experiential learning involves learning through direct experience and reflection. This hands-on approach helps individuals apply theoretical knowledge to real-world situations.

These are examples of this type of learning:

- **Simulations:** Virtual or physical simulations that mimic real-life scenarios.
- **Role-playing:** Acting out situations to practice and develop skills.
- **Project-based learning:** Completing projects that require problem-solving and critical thinking.

How Learning Is Measured in the Future Readiness Score

The FRS includes learning as one of its eight core pillars. This comprehensive metric evaluates the effectiveness of an organization's learning initiatives through various dimensions:

Internal Learning

- **Training programs:** The availability and quality of training programs designed to enhance employees' skills and knowledge.
- **Professional development:** Opportunities for career advancement and continuous learning.
- **Knowledge sharing:** Mechanisms in place for knowledge sharing and collaboration among employees.

External Learning

- **Industry best practices:** Adoption of industry best practices and standards.
- **Benchmarking:** Regular benchmarking against competitors and industry leaders.
- **Customer feedback:** Utilizing customer feedback to drive improvements and innovation.

Case Studies: Learning in Action

Let us take a deeper look into some examples of organizations that have really mastered the learning pillar of future readiness.

Microsoft: A Culture of Continuous Learning

Microsoft exemplifies a strong learning culture with its commitment to continuous improvement and skill development. The company's growth mindset philosophy encourages employees to embrace challenges, learn from failures, and continuously seek personal and professional development. Microsoft provides a variety of learning resources, including online courses, mentorship programs, and collaborative projects. This commitment to learning has been instrumental in Microsoft's transformation under CEO Satya Nadella, contributing to its resurgence as a leading tech giant.

AT&T: Skill Transformation Through Learning

AT&T faced a significant challenge with the rapid evolution of technology and the need for new skills. In response, the company launched a comprehensive re-skilling initiative, investing $1 billion in employee education and training programs. AT&T partnered with leading educational institutions to offer courses in areas such as data science, cybersecurity, and software development. This initiative not only prepared employees for future roles but also positioned AT&T as a forward-thinking and adaptable organization.

AT&T reported that 140 000 employees had enrolled in its re-skilling programs, resulting in a more agile and future-ready workforce.

Top Learning Providers

To implement an effective learning strategy, partnering with top learning providers can be crucial. Here are some renowned learning providers:

- **LinkedIn Learning:** Offers a vast library of courses covering various professional skills.
- **Coursera:** Provides courses from top universities and companies, allowing employees to earn recognized certifications.
- **Udemy:** Features a wide range of courses on numerous topics, including business, technology, and personal development.
- **Skillsoft:** Specializes in corporate learning solutions, offering customized training programs.
- **edX:** Partners with leading institutions to offer high-quality courses and programs.
- **Khan Academy:** Offers free, high-quality education on a wide range of subjects.
- **Pluralsight:** Focuses on technology skills development with expert-led courses.

Successful Practices for Organizational Learning

Establishing a learning culture for your business is not just about providing your employees with educational material and expecting magic. Here are some essential areas to consider and work on as you look at becoming a learning organization.

- **Leadership commitment:** Ensure that leadership is committed to fostering a learning culture and sets an example by participating in learning activities.
- **Employee involvement:** Involve employees in the development of learning programs and encourage their input to ensure relevance and engagement.

- **Diverse learning opportunities:** Offer a variety of learning opportunities, including formal training, informal learning, and experiential learning.
- **Regular feedback:** Collect and act on feedback from employees regarding the effectiveness of learning programs.
- **Recognition and rewards:** Recognize and reward employees who actively participate in and benefit from learning initiatives.

Steps for Enabling Learning in Your Organization

Creating an effective learning environment within your organization is crucial for fostering innovation, improving performance, and ensuring future readiness. This basic plan outlines the steps necessary to enable a culture of continuous learning, leveraging various types of learning and top learning providers.

Step 1: Assess Learning Needs

Objective: Identify the skills and knowledge gaps within your organization.

Actions:
- **Conduct surveys and assessments:** Use surveys, interviews, and skills assessments to understand the current capabilities of your employees and identify areas for improvement.
- **Analyze business goals:** Align the learning needs with the strategic goals of the organization to ensure that learning initiatives support overall business objectives.
- **Benchmark against industry standards:** Compare your organization's skills and capabilities with industry standards to identify gaps and opportunities for improvement.

Step 2: Develop a Comprehensive Learning Strategy

Objective: Create a strategic plan that outlines the learning initiatives needed to address identified gaps and support business goals.

Actions:
- **Define learning objectives:** Clearly articulate the learning objectives that align with the organization's strategic goals.

- **Select learning methods:** Choose a mix of formal, informal, e-learning, and experiential learning methods that best suit the needs of your employees.
- **Create a learning road map:** Develop a road map that outlines the timeline, resources, and key milestones for implementing learning initiatives.

Step 3: Invest in Learning Resources

Objective: Allocate the necessary resources to support learning initiatives.

Actions:
- **Budget allocation:** Secure funding for learning programs, tools, and resources.
- **Partner with learning providers:** Collaborate with top learning providers such as LinkedIn Learning, Coursera, Udemy, Skillsoft, edX, Khan Academy, and Pluralsight to offer high-quality training programs.
- **Leverage technology:** Implement learning management systems (LMS) and e-learning platforms to facilitate and track learning activities.

Step 4: Encourage Knowledge Sharing

Objective: Foster a culture of knowledge sharing and collaboration among employees.

Actions:
- **Establish mentorship programs:** Pair experienced employees with less experienced ones to facilitate knowledge transfer and professional development.
- **Promote peer collaboration:** Create opportunities for employees to collaborate on projects, share insights, and learn from each other.
- **Use internal communication platforms:** Utilize tools such as Slack, Microsoft Teams, and intranets to facilitate communication and knowledge sharing.

Step 5: Implement Learning Programs

Objective: Roll out the learning initiatives and ensure their effective implementation.

Actions:

- **Launch training programs:** Begin with priority training programs that address the most critical skills and knowledge gaps.
- **Offer flexible learning options:** Provide employees with access to a variety of learning options, including online courses, workshops, seminars, and on-the-job training.
- **Monitor participation and progress:** Track employee participation and progress using LMS and other tracking tools.

Step 6: Measure and Improve

Objective: Regularly evaluate the effectiveness of learning initiatives and make necessary adjustments.

Actions:

- **Collect feedback:** Use surveys and feedback tools to gather input from employees about their learning experiences.
- **Analyze learning outcomes:** Assess the impact of learning programs on employee performance, productivity, and business outcomes.
- **Adjust and enhance programs:** Based on feedback and analysis, refine and improve learning programs to ensure they meet the evolving needs of the organization and its employees.

Final Words

The following are the key takeaways from this chapter:

- Learning is a critical component of future readiness and business success.
- Continuous learning fosters innovation, adaptability, and a competitive advantage.
- Investing in employee development enhances engagement, retention, and performance.
- Regular evaluation and improvement of learning initiatives are essential for sustained success.

Resources

I highly recommend picking one or more books from the following list to advance your knowledge about how our mind works, how we learn, and how learning can benefit your organization.

Books

- *Mindset: The New Psychology of Success* by Carol S. Dweck
- *The Power of Habit: Why We Do What We Do in Life and Business* by Charles Duhigg
- *Deep Work: Rules for Focused Success in a Distracted World* by Cal Newport

Take the Future Readiness Score at www.iankhan.com/frs or scan the QR Code

17

FRS Pillar 3: People

Take care of your employees, and they'll take care of your business. It's as simple as that.

—*Richard Branson*

The Importance of People for Business

In the realm of business, the importance of people cannot be overstated. Employees are the lifeblood of any organization, driving innovation, productivity, and growth. The Future Readiness Score (FRS) recognizes the critical role that people play in ensuring an organization's success and resilience. This chapter explores the various aspects of managing and nurturing people, highlighting why they are indispensable to future readiness.

Driving Innovation and Growth

People are the primary drivers of innovation and growth within an organization. Their creativity, skills, and dedication fuel the development of new products, services, and solutions that keep the company competitive. By investing in people, organizations can harness their potential to drive significant advancements and achieve sustained growth.

According to a report by McKinsey, companies that invest in their employees' skills and development are 1.5 times more likely to be innovative leaders in their industry.

Enhancing Productivity and Efficiency

Engaged and motivated employees are more productive and efficient. When employees feel valued and supported, they are more likely to go above and beyond in their roles, contributing to higher levels of organizational performance.

Gallup research indicates that organizations with high employee engagement levels experience 21% higher productivity.

Creating a Positive Work Environment

A positive work environment is essential for employee well-being and performance. This includes providing a safe, inclusive, and supportive workplace where employees feel respected and valued. Organizations that prioritize a positive work culture are more likely to attract and retain top talent.

For example, Google is known for its exceptional work environment, offering various perks and creating a culture of innovation and collaboration. This approach has helped Google consistently rank as one of the best places to work.

Recognizing and Rewarding Contributions

Recognition and rewards are powerful motivators. Acknowledging employees' hard work and achievements fosters a culture of appreciation and motivates them to continue performing at their best.

For example, Salesforce has a robust recognition program that celebrates employees' contributions, including awards, shout-outs, and performance bonuses. This practice has significantly contributed to Salesforce's high employee satisfaction and retention rates.

Examples of CEOs Motivating from the Top Down

Every CEO has a different style of leadership, and once in a while a leader has such a profound impact on their business that they become legends. Take a look at exemplary leadership as shown by the following individuals.

- **CEO eating lunch with employees:** Doug Conant, former CEO of Campbell Soup Company, made a point of regularly eating lunch in the company's cafeteria and sitting with different employees. This practice helped him build a strong rapport with the workforce, fostering a sense of inclusiveness and trust.

As a result, under Conant's leadership, employee engagement scores increased significantly, and Campbell Soup Company's market value increased by over 30%.

- **CEO flying economy:** Tony Hsieh, the late CEO of Zappos, was known for flying economy class despite his wealth. His actions demonstrated humility and a commitment to frugality, reinforcing the company's culture of equality and cost consciousness.[1]

As a result, Zappos's customer satisfaction and employee engagement rates were among the highest in the retail industry, contributing to its strong performance and reputation.

Supporting Work-Life Balance Work-life balance is crucial for maintaining employee health and productivity. Organizations that support flexible work arrangements and provide resources for managing work-life balance are more likely to have a happy and productive workforce.

In fact, the American Psychological Association found that employees with higher work-life balance report 20% higher job satisfaction and 25% lower stress levels.[2]

Providing Health and Wellness Programs Investing in health and wellness programs demonstrates that the organization cares about its employees' overall well-being. These programs can include physical health initiatives, mental health support, and access to wellness resources.

For example, Johnson & Johnson offers comprehensive health and wellness programs, including fitness facilities, mental health support, and wellness challenges.[3] These initiatives have led to a healthier, more engaged workforce.

Professional Development Opportunities Providing opportunities for professional development is essential for employee growth and retention. This includes offering training programs, mentorship, and career advancement opportunities.

For example, IBM's commitment to employee growth is evident in its extensive training programs and career development resources. IBM's Think Academy provides continuous learning opportunities, helping employees stay ahead in their fields.

Encouraging Continuous Learning   A culture of continuous learning ensures that employees remain adaptable and equipped with the latest skills and knowledge. Encouraging employees to pursue further education and certifications benefits both the individual and the organization.

Supporting data: LinkedIn's Workplace Learning Report found that 68% of employees prefer to learn at work, emphasizing the importance of providing learning opportunities within the organization.

Embracing Diversity and Inclusion   Diversity and inclusion are critical for fostering innovation and ensuring a dynamic and resilient workforce. Organizations that embrace diversity in all its forms are better positioned to understand and meet the needs of a diverse customer base.

In fact, a Boston Consulting Group study found that companies with more diverse management teams have 19% higher revenue due to innovation.

Adapting to Remote and Hybrid Work Models[4]   The future of work is increasingly leaning toward remote and hybrid work models. Organizations that adapt to these changes and provide the necessary tools and support for remote work can enhance productivity and employee satisfaction.

For example, Microsoft's adoption of flexible work arrangements has allowed employees to work remotely while maintaining high levels of productivity and collaboration. This flexibility has been instrumental in Microsoft's continued success during the COVID-19 pandemic.

Investing in employees is a crucial strategy for ensuring future readiness and fostering a competitive advantage. Here are some financial insights on how much companies typically invest in their employees annually:

Training and Development

- **US average:** According to the Association for Talent Development (ATD), US companies spend an average of $1299 per employee annually on training and development.
- **Large organizations:** Larger organizations (10 000+ employees) tend to spend more, averaging around $1800 per employee per year on training and development initiatives.

Health and Wellness Programs

- **Average spending:** A study by the International Foundation of Employee Benefit Plans found that US employers spend an average of $742 per employee per year on health and wellness programs.

- **Comprehensive programs:** Companies with comprehensive wellness programs, including mental health support and fitness facilities, can spend upward of $1200 per employee annually.

Employee Benefits and Perks
- **General benefits:** According to the Bureau of Labor Statistics (BLS), benefits account for approximately 32% of total compensation costs for employers in the United States, translating to around $11 000 to $15 000 per employee per year, depending on the industry and organization size.
- **Additional perks:** Companies known for exceptional employee perks, such as Google and Facebook, invest significantly more. For example, Google's wide range of employee benefits and perks are estimated to add up to several thousand dollars per employee annually.

Professional Development and Education
- **Tuition reimbursement:** Many companies offer tuition reimbursement programs, with average spending ranging from $4000 to $5250 per employee per year. This amount can vary based on the company's policies and the level of education pursued by the employees.
- **Leadership development programs:** Investments in leadership development programs can range from $500 to $5000 per participant annually, depending on the program's depth and duration.

Employee Recognition Programs
- **Recognition and rewards:** Organizations typically spend around 1%–2% of their payroll on employee recognition and reward programs. For a company with a payroll of $50 million, this translates to $500 000–$1 million annually on recognition initiatives.

Case Studies: People-Centric Organizations

Here are some examples of people-centric organizations:

Google: Valuing Employee Well-Being Google's commitment to employee well-being is reflected in its numerous perks and benefits, such as free meals, on-site health care, and wellness programs. Google's inclusive and innovative culture has made it one of the most desirable places to work globally.

Salesforce: Recognizing and Rewarding Employees Salesforce's robust recognition programs and emphasis on employee growth have contributed to its reputation as a great place to work. The company's culture of appreciation and support fosters high levels of engagement and loyalty among employees.

Johnson & Johnson: Prioritizing Health and Wellness   Johnson & Johnson's comprehensive health and wellness programs demonstrate its commitment to employee well-being. These initiatives have resulted in a healthier, more engaged workforce, contributing to the company's long-term success.

Here are some ways you can enhance people management in your organization:

- **Assess employee needs:** Conduct surveys and focus groups to understand the needs and expectations of your employees.
- **Develop a people-centric strategy:** Create a strategy that prioritizes employee well-being, development, and recognition.
- **Implement health and wellness programs:** Offer comprehensive health and wellness programs to support your employees' physical and mental health.
- **Provide professional development opportunities:** Invest in training programs, mentorship, and career advancement resources.
- **Foster a positive work environment:** Create a culture of respect, inclusion, and support to ensure a positive work environment.
- **Leverage technology for remote work:** Provide the necessary tools and support for remote and hybrid work models.

Final Words

People are the cornerstone of future readiness and business success. Investing in employees' well-being, growth, and recognition enhances productivity, innovation, and retention. A positive, inclusive, and supportive work environment is crucial for attracting and retaining top talent. Adapting to the future of work, including remote and hybrid models, is essential for maintaining a competitive edge.

The next steps to achieve this include conducting an employee needs assessment to understand the current needs and expectations of your employees. Developing a people-centric strategy that prioritizes employee well-being, development, and recognition is key. Implementing health and wellness programs to support your employees' physical and mental health will further enhance their performance and satisfaction. Providing professional development opportunities through training programs, mentorship, and career advancement resources is essential for continuous growth.

Creating a culture of respect, inclusion, and support will foster a positive work environment. Recognizing and rewarding employees' contributions through recognition programs will celebrate their achievements and boost morale. Leveraging technology for remote work by providing the necessary tools and support for remote and hybrid work models ensures flexibility and efficiency. Supporting continuous learning by encouraging employees to engage in professional development and offering access to courses, workshops, and educational resources is vital for ongoing improvement. Partnering with top learning providers to offer high-quality training programs can significantly enhance these efforts.

By prioritizing people and implementing effective strategies, organizations can build a strong, engaged, and resilient workforce, driving business success and ensuring future readiness.

Resources

Here are some resources to learn more about pillar 3.

Books

- *Drive: The Surprising Truth About What Motivates Us* by Daniel H. Pink
- *First, Break All the Rules: What the World's Greatest Managers Do Differently* by Marcus Buckingham and Curt Coffman
- *The Culture Code: The Secrets of Highly Successful Groups* by Daniel Coyle

TED Talks

- "How Great Leaders Inspire Action" by Simon Sinek
- "The Power of Vulnerability" by Brené Brown

Netflix Documentaries

- *Inside Bill's Brain: Decoding Bill Gates*
- *The Playbook*

Take the Future Readiness Score at www.iankhan.com/frs or scan the QR Code

18

FRS Pillar 4: Culture

Culture eats strategy for breakfast.

—*Peter Drucker*

ANOTHER PILLAR OF future readiness, culture is sometimes not the core priority of leaders. It does, however, play a key part in ensuring that the organization is positioned for success and future readiness. This chapter explores organizational culture and its further development.

Why Is Culture a Key to Future Readiness?

Company culture is often described as the personality of an organization. It encompasses the values, beliefs, and behaviors that shape how employees interact, make decisions, and work toward common goals. A strong, positive culture is crucial for fostering engagement, innovation, and resilience, making it a key parameter for organizational success and a vital component of the Future Readiness Score (FRS).

Company culture is the invisible glue that binds an organization together, guiding its internal and external actions. It manifests in everyday behaviors, decision-making processes, and the overall work environment. When employees share a common set of values and goals, they are more likely to work cohesively toward achieving organizational objectives.

Culture is a significant driver of employee engagement and productivity. When employees feel valued and aligned with the organization's mission,

207

they are more likely to be engaged and committed to their work. This engagement leads to higher productivity, better problem-solving, and greater innovation. For instance, Google's innovative and inclusive culture encourages creativity and collaboration, leading to high employee satisfaction and productivity. Such a culture not only retains talent but also attracts top professionals who want to work in an environment that values and nurtures their contributions.

Innovation thrives in a culture that promotes openness, risk-taking, and continuous learning. Organizations such as 3M have successfully cultivated such environments. 3M's "15% rule" allows employees to spend a portion of their time on projects of their own choosing. This policy has led to the development of numerous successful products, including the Post-it note. Companies that foster a culture of innovation are often at the forefront of their industries, continuously adapting to changes and leading market trends.

A positive company culture also translates to exceptional customer service. Employees who are satisfied and motivated are more likely to deliver superior customer experiences. Zappos, known for its customer-centric culture, has built a reputation for exceptional service. This dedication to customer satisfaction has resulted in strong customer loyalty and positive word-of-mouth marketing, driving the company's success.

The Power of Company Culture

Why is company culture important?

- **Engagement:** A strong culture fosters employee engagement and commitment. Gallup research shows that highly engaged teams see a 41% reduction in absenteeism and a 17% increase in productivity.
- **Innovation:** Cultures that encourage risk-taking and continuous learning drive innovation. McKinsey found that organizations with a strong culture of innovation are three times more likely to be top financial performers.
- **Customer satisfaction:** Positive internal culture often translates to superior customer service. *Harvard Business Review* notes that companies with a strong customer-focused culture see 20% higher customer satisfaction rates.

Netflix's Culture of Freedom and Responsibility

Netflix's culture of freedom and responsibility is another example of how a strong cultural foundation can lead to success. By empowering employees to make decisions and encouraging them to take ownership of their work, Netflix has created an environment where innovation thrives. This culture has enabled Netflix to disrupt the entertainment industry and achieve global success. The "Netflix Culture Deck," which outlines these principles, has been viewed more than 20 million times and has influenced the HR practices of numerous companies worldwide.

What Is the Netflix Culture Deck?

Netflix's approach to corporate culture, encapsulated in its famous "Netflix Culture Deck," is a testament to the power of fostering a workplace environment that prioritizes freedom and responsibility. This culture has not only enabled Netflix to thrive but has also set a benchmark for other companies aiming to innovate and disrupt their industries.

The 124-slide presentation outlines the core principles and values that guide Netflix's approach to management and operations. Key elements include:

- **Freedom and responsibility:** Employees are given significant autonomy to make decisions and are expected to act in the company's best interests.
- **Context, not control:** Leaders set clear context for decisions and strategies, rather than micromanaging.
- **Highly aligned, loosely coupled:** Teams are aligned on strategic goals but have the freedom to work independently.

To better understand the impact of the Netflix strategy, here are some of the areas in business where Netflix's approach has made big gains:

- **Employee autonomy and innovation:** Netflix's strategy of giving employees freedom has led to groundbreaking innovations. For instance, the introduction of the streaming service in 2007, which revolutionized the entertainment industry, was largely driven by employee insights and initiative. In a study by Reed Hastings and Erin Meyer, they found that Netflix's approach significantly enhances creativity and efficiency, as employees are empowered to explore new ideas without bureaucratic constraints.

- **Decision-making and accountability:** The culture of responsibility at Netflix ensures that employees are accountable for their actions. This has fostered a high-performing environment where employees are motivated to make decisions that drive success. According to a 2019 report by McKinsey, companies that empower their employees to make decisions quickly and independently are 1.5 times more likely to experience rapid revenue growth.
- **Global success and market leadership:** Netflix's subscriber base grew from 23 million in 2011 to over 230 million in 2023, a growth trajectory attributed to its innovative culture. This global success underscores the effectiveness of their unique cultural approach. By encouraging risk-taking and learning from failures, Netflix has maintained a competitive edge in the rapidly evolving media landscape.

Learning from the Netflix Strategy

To emulate Netflix's culture of freedom and responsibility, consider the following tips:

- **Empower employees:** Give your team the autonomy to make decisions and trust them to act in the company's best interests.
- **Set clear context:** Focus on providing strategic context rather than controlling every aspect of execution.
- **Promote accountability:** Foster a culture where employees are accountable for their outcomes and learn from their failures.
- **Encourage innovation:** Create an environment where employees feel safe to experiment and innovate without fear of failure.
- **Focus on talent density:** Strive to build a high-performing team by retaining only the best talent.

By adopting these principles and fostering a culture that values freedom and responsibility, companies can create an environment where innovation thrives, and success is a natural outcome. As Netflix's journey shows, the key to disruption and global success lies in empowering employees to be their best selves.

> Did you know that Reed Hastings, Netflix's cofounder, has often shared that the culture deck was created to articulate the kind of company they wanted to build. In his book, *No Rules Rules*, Hastings explains how eliminating formal policies on expenses, travel, and vacations has led to greater responsibility among employees.

Patagonia's Mission-Driven Culture

Patagonia exemplifies how a mission-driven culture can attract both loyal customers and passionate employees. Patagonia's commitment to environmental and social responsibility is not just a marketing strategy but a core aspect of its culture. This alignment between mission and culture has helped Patagonia grow and maintain a competitive edge in the outdoor apparel market. With annual revenues exceeding $1 billion, Patagonia's transparent and mission-driven approach has consistently fostered growth and customer loyalty.

> Patagonia is a prime example of how a mission-driven culture can attract loyal customers and passionate employees. Its commitment to environmental and social responsibility goes beyond marketing, becoming a core aspect of its identity. This alignment between mission and culture has enabled Patagonia to grow and maintain a competitive edge in the outdoor apparel market.

What Defines Patagonia's Mission-Driven Culture?

Patagonia's mission statement, "We're in business to save our home planet," encapsulates its dedication to environmental stewardship and ethical practices. This mission drives all aspects of the company's operations, from product design to employee engagement.

Key elements of Patagonia's culture include:

- **Environmental activism:** Actively engaging in environmental campaigns and initiatives.
- **Sustainable practices:** Emphasizing eco-friendly materials and processes.
- **Transparency:** Maintaining open communication about its practices and impact.
- **Community engagement:** Supporting grassroots environmental organizations and encouraging employee activism.

> Patagonia employees are deeply engaged in the company's mission. For example, employees are given up to two months paid leave to work for environmental causes, which has led to significant contributions to various environmental projects worldwide.

Here is how the Patagonia strategy has shaped their business in key areas of impact.

- **Environmental commitment and product innovation:** Patagonia's commitment to sustainability is evident in its product innovation. The company uses recycled materials in 69% of its products and aims to be carbon neutral by 2025. This focus not only reduces environmental impact but also appeals to eco-conscious consumers. According to a 2020 Nielsen report, 73% of global consumers say they would definitely or probably change their consumption habits to reduce their environmental impact.
- **Employee engagement and retention:** Patagonia fosters a work environment that aligns with its mission, leading to high employee engagement and retention. The company offers extensive benefits, such as on-site childcare and paid internships with environmental organizations, which reinforce its commitment to work-life balance and environmental activism. A 2018 study by Deloitte found that mission-driven companies have 30% higher levels of innovation and 40% higher levels of retention.
- **Customer loyalty and brand advocacy:** Patagonia's transparency and ethical practices resonate strongly with customers. The company's "Worn Wear" program encourages customers to buy used products and repair rather than replace them, fostering loyalty and reducing environmental impact. This approach has earned Patagonia a Net Promoter Score (NPS) of 83, far exceeding the average for the retail industry, which hovers around 30.

> Patagonia's founder, Yvon Chouinard, has always championed the idea that businesses should prioritize the planet over profits. His book *Let My People Go Surfing* details how Patagonia integrates its mission into every aspect of the business.

Learning from Patagonia's Strategy

To emulate Patagonia's mission-driven culture, consider the following tips:

- **Define and communicate your mission:** Clearly articulate a mission that resonates with both your employees and customers.

- **Embed sustainability:** Integrate sustainable practices into your operations, from sourcing materials to product design.
- **Engage employees:** Offer programs and benefits that align with your mission and support your employees' passions and values.
- **Be transparent:** Maintain open communication about your practices, successes, and challenges.
- **Support community initiatives:** Encourage and facilitate employee involvement in community and environmental initiatives.

By adopting a mission-driven approach similar to Patagonia's, companies can create a culture that not only attracts and retains top talent but also builds a loyal customer base committed to shared values. As Patagonia's journey demonstrates, aligning business practices with a higher purpose can lead to sustained growth and a significant positive impact on the world.

Starting, Fostering, and Following Through

Creating a strong company culture starts with clear values and a shared vision. Leadership plays a critical role in embodying and promoting these values. When leaders consistently demonstrate the organization's values through their actions, they set a powerful example for employees to follow. Moreover, regular communication about the company's mission, vision, and values helps reinforce the cultural framework.

Fostering an inclusive and supportive work environment is also essential. Employees should feel safe to express their ideas, take risks, and learn from failures. Providing opportunities for professional development and continuous learning not only enhances individual capabilities but also strengthens the organization's overall competence.

Recognition and rewards are powerful tools for reinforcing desired behaviors and fostering a positive culture. Acknowledging employees' contributions and celebrating successes, both big and small, can significantly boost morale and motivation. Organizations should also provide platforms for employees to give feedback and share their experiences. This two-way communication helps build trust and ensures that the culture evolves in line with employees' needs and expectations.

Pixar's Culture of Openness

At Pixar, the "brain trust" meetings are a cornerstone of its collaborative culture. These meetings bring together diverse teams to provide candid feedback on projects, fostering a culture of openness and continuous improvement. This collaborative approach has been key to Pixar's success in creating some of the most beloved animated films.

> Pixar's culture of collaboration, epitomized by its "brain trust" meetings, has been a cornerstone of its remarkable success in the animation industry. These meetings foster a culture of openness and continuous improvement, enabling Pixar to produce some of the most beloved animated films.

The development of *Inside Out* is a prime example of Pixar's collaborative culture. Director Pete Docter credits the brain trust meetings for helping to refine the complex narrative, resulting in a film that grossed more than $857 million worldwide and won the Academy Award for Best Animated Feature.

What Are Pixar's "Brain Trust" Meetings?

The "brain trust" is a unique meeting format where directors, writers, and key creative staff come together to provide candid feedback on ongoing projects. These meetings are characterized by:

- **Honest feedback:** Participants are encouraged to provide blunt, constructive criticism.
- **Diverse perspectives:** Bringing together a variety of voices to enhance creativity and problem-solving.
- **Egalitarian environment:** No hierarchy in these meetings, ensuring all ideas are valued.

So how did the Pixar strategy enhance their business and which areas of business gained the most? Here is an overview:

- **Impact on film quality:** Pixar's approach to feedback and collaboration has directly improved the quality of its films. For instance, during the production of *Toy Story*, the brain trust meetings were crucial in refining the story and characters, leading to a groundbreaking success that grossed over $373 million worldwide. This iterative process has been integral to the success of films such as *Finding Nemo*, *The Incredibles*, and *Inside Out*, all of which have received critical acclaim and box office success.

- **Employee engagement and innovation:** The collaborative culture at Pixar fosters high levels of employee engagement and innovation. Employees feel their contributions are valued, leading to higher job satisfaction and creativity. A Gallup study highlights that companies with highly engaged employees outperform their peers by 147% in earnings per share, underscoring the financial benefits of such a culture.
- **Continuous improvement and adaptability:** The brain trust meetings exemplify Pixar's commitment to continuous improvement. For example, during the making of *Ratatouille*, extensive feedback sessions led to significant changes in the storyline and character development, which ultimately contributed to the film's success. This willingness to adapt and improve has kept Pixar at the forefront of the animation industry.

> Ed Catmull, cofounder of Pixar, has often emphasized the importance of a supportive yet candid environment for creativity. In his book *Creativity, Inc.*, he details how the brain trust meetings are designed to strip away fear and encourage open dialogue.

Learning from Pixar's Approach

To emulate Pixar's collaborative culture, consider the following tips:

- **Establish open feedback channels:** Create regular forums where employees can provide and receive candid feedback.
- **Hire diverse teams:** Encourage collaboration across different departments to bring diverse perspectives to projects.
- **Foster a safe environment:** Ensure that all team members feel safe to share their ideas and criticisms without fear of retribution.
- **Use an iterative process:** Implement an iterative process for project development, allowing for continuous refinement and improvement.
- **Provide leadership support:** Ensure that leadership actively supports and participates in these collaborative efforts.

Final Words

Investing in a strong company culture is not just beneficial but essential for achieving long-term success and future readiness. By fostering a positive, inclusive, and innovative culture, organizations can enhance engagement, drive innovation, and ensure sustained growth.

By adopting these principles, companies can cultivate a collaborative culture that not only enhances creativity and innovation but also drives sustained success. Pixar's journey highlights how fostering an environment of openness and continuous improvement can lead to extraordinary achievements in any industry.

Company culture is a critical pillar of the FRS and a fundamental driver of organizational success. By fostering a positive, inclusive, and innovative culture, organizations can enhance employee engagement, drive innovation, and deliver exceptional customer experiences. The success stories of companies such as Google, 3M, Zappos, Netflix, Patagonia, and Microsoft illustrate the transformative power of a strong company culture.

As businesses navigate the complexities of the modern world, investing in and nurturing their culture will be essential for achieving long-term success and future readiness.

Resources

Check out the following books and TED Talks to learn more about the topics covered in this chapter.

Books

- *Drive: The Surprising Truth About What Motivates Us* by Daniel H. Pink
- *Leaders Eat Last: Why Some Teams Pull Together and Others Don't* by Simon Sinek
- *The Culture Code: The Secrets of Highly Successful Groups* by Daniel Coyle

TED Talks

- "The Power of Vulnerability" by Brené Brown
- "How Great Leaders Inspire Action" by Simon Sinek

Take the Future Readiness Score at www.iankhan.com/frs or scan the QR Code

19

FRS Pillar 5: Collaboration

If you want to go fast, go alone. If you want to go far, go together.
—African Proverb

A CORE PILLAR of the future readiness operating system, collaboration works wonders when done right. This chapter covers types of collaboration, how to activate collaboration, and how to use it as a superpower.

What Is Collaboration?

In today's interconnected world, collaboration and partnerships are crucial for achieving success. Whether it's internal collaboration within an organization or external partnerships with other companies, suppliers, or customers, working together can drive innovation, efficiency, and growth. This chapter explores the various dimensions of collaboration, highlighting its importance and providing use cases that demonstrate how collaborative efforts can lead to remarkable achievements.

- **Innovation:** Collaborative efforts lead to diverse perspectives and ideas, fostering innovation. According to a study by McKinsey, organizations that promote collaborative working are five times more likely to be high-performing.

- **Efficiency:** Collaboration streamlines processes and reduces redundancy, improving overall efficiency. *Forbes* reports that companies implementing effective collaboration tools see a 30% increase in productivity.
- **Growth:** External partnerships provide access to new markets and resources, driving mutual growth. Deloitte found that companies leveraging external collaborations are twice as likely to achieve their innovation goals.

Internal Collaboration

Internal collaboration involves working together within an organization across different departments, teams, and roles. It fosters a culture of open communication, shared goals, and mutual support, leading to improved problem-solving and innovation.

According to a joint study by The Institute for Corporate Governance and Babson College, organizations that promote collaborative working are five times more likely to be high performing.[1]

For example, at Pixar, collaboration between different departments (animation, storytelling, and technology) has been key to creating successful films. Regular "brain trust" meetings encourage open feedback and collective problem-solving, ensuring high-quality outcomes.

External Collaboration

External collaboration involves partnerships with other organizations, suppliers, customers, or even competitors. These partnerships can provide access to new markets, technologies, and resources, driving mutual growth and success.

Research by Deloitte shows that companies leveraging external collaborations are twice as likely to achieve their innovation goals.[2]

For example, the collaboration between Starbucks and PepsiCo to create the bottled Frappuccino demonstrates how external partnerships can open new market opportunities. By combining Starbucks' coffee expertise with PepsiCo's distribution capabilities, the product became a significant success.[3]

How Can You Collaborate Effectively?

Collaboration can help you find a way to success through various means. You could collaborate internally within the organization, externally, or in a cross-functional manner. There are many ways to look at joint outcomes and succeeding together. While I do not want to hold you from thinking big and wide, here are some areas of collaboration worth looking at and asking yourself whether these have been fully activated.

How Can You Collaborate with Competitors?

While it may seem counterintuitive, collaborating with competitors can lead to significant benefits. This approach, known as *coopetition*, allows companies to pool resources, share risks, and drive industry-wide innovation.

For example, the partnership between Apple and Samsung in the semiconductor space is a notable example of competitive collaboration. Despite being fierce competitors in the smartphone market, Apple relies on Samsung's advanced chip manufacturing capabilities for its devices. This collaboration allows both companies to leverage their strengths and drive technological advancements.[4]

In fact, a study by *Harvard Business Review* found that companies engaged in coopetition experienced higher innovation rates and market growth compared to those that solely competed.[5]

How Can You Collaborate with Suppliers?

Building strong relationships with suppliers can enhance supply chain efficiency, reduce costs, and ensure quality. Collaborative efforts with suppliers can lead to innovations in product development and manufacturing processes.

Use case: Toyota's close collaboration with its suppliers through the Toyota Production System (TPS) has been a key factor in its manufacturing efficiency and quality control. By sharing best practices and jointly developing improvements, Toyota and its suppliers achieve mutual benefits.

Research by the *Supply Chain Management Review* indicates that companies with strong supplier collaboration see a 20% reduction in procurement costs and a 15% improvement in quality.[6]

How Can You Collaborate with Customers?

Engaging customers in the innovation process can lead to products and services that better meet their needs and expectations. Customer collaboration involves seeking feedback, co-creating solutions, and building long-term relationships.

For example, LEGO's collaboration with its customer community through the LEGO Ideas platform allows fans to submit and vote on new product ideas.

Successful ideas are turned into official LEGO sets, leading to higher customer satisfaction and increased sales.

A 2022 report by PwC found that companies that actively involve customers in their innovation processes are 60% more likely to report revenue growth.[7]

Foresight

Creating a culture that values and promotes collaboration is essential. This involves encouraging open communication, fostering trust, and providing tools and platforms that facilitate collaborative efforts.

For example, Microsoft's use of collaboration tools such as Teams has significantly improved internal communication and project management. By integrating these tools, Microsoft has enhanced productivity and fostered a more connected workforce.

According to *Forbes*, companies that implement effective collaboration tools and strategies see a 30% increase in productivity.[8]

Technology plays a crucial role in enabling collaboration. From cloud-based platforms to project management software, the right technology can streamline communication, document sharing, and project tracking.

For example, Slack's collaboration platform has transformed how teams communicate and collaborate on projects. Its integration with various tools and applications has made it a preferred choice for organizations looking to enhance their collaborative efforts.

Gartner reports that 80% of companies using collaboration tools have seen improvements in team performance.[9]

Interesting Case Studies

A lot has been covered in this chapter and yet there is more data to share. Here are some other industry use cases that shed a light on collaboration and its impact on business, when done right.

Google and NASA: What Can We Learn from Their Partnership?[10]   Google partnered with NASA to launch the Quantum Artificial Intelligence Lab. This collaboration aims to advance machine learning and other forms of artificial intelligence using quantum computing. By pooling their expertise and resources, Google and NASA are pushing the boundaries of technology and innovation.

This collaboration has already led to significant advancements in quantum computing, with potential applications in various industries.

Ford and Lyft: How Does Their Partnership Shape the Future of Transportation?[11] Ford and Lyft have collaborated to develop autonomous vehicles for ride-sharing services. This partnership combines Ford's expertise in vehicle manufacturing with Lyft's ride-sharing platform, aiming to create a sustainable and efficient transportation solution.

According to Deloitte, partnerships like these are essential for developing the infrastructure and technology needed for autonomous vehicles.

Ready to Change How Your Business Collaborates?

With all the use cases shared, it can be daunting to take the first step. Well, here is a simple approach to consider. Think of it as simple plan that you can modify, change, and adapt based on your organization's specific needs.

1. **Assess collaboration needs:** Understand the current state of collaboration within your organization and identify areas for improvement.
2. **Develop a collaboration strategy:** Create a comprehensive strategy that promotes both internal and external collaboration.
3. **Implement collaboration tools:** Invest in technology that facilitates communication and project management.
4. **Foster a collaborative culture:** Encourage open communication, trust, and mutual respect among employees.
5. **Engage in competitive collaboration:** Look for opportunities to collaborate with competitors for mutual benefit.
6. **Strengthen supplier relationships:** Build strong, collaborative relationships with suppliers to enhance supply chain efficiency.
7. **Involve customers in innovation:** Engage customers in the innovation process to create products and services that meet their needs.

Final Words

In today's interconnected world, collaboration and partnerships are indispensable for achieving success. Within organizations, internal collaboration fuels innovation and enhances problem-solving capabilities, fostering a dynamic environment where creative solutions can thrive. Externally, collaboration opens doors to new markets, advanced technologies, and additional resources, thereby broadening the scope and potential impact of the organization's efforts.

Furthermore, competitive collaboration, where companies work together despite being rivals, can stimulate industry-wide innovation and growth, setting new benchmarks for progress. Building strong relationships with suppliers and customers is also vital, as these connections can significantly boost efficiency and drive further innovation. Through these collaborative efforts, organizations can harness the collective expertise and strengths of various stakeholders, paving the way for sustainable success and advancement.

Resources

Check out the following resources.

Books

- *Collaborative Intelligence: Thinking with People Who Think Differently* by Dawna Markova and Angie McArthur
- *The Five Dysfunctions of a Team: A Leadership Fable* by Patrick Lencioni
- *Team of Teams: New Rules of Engagement for a Complex World* by General Stanley McChrystal

Watch List

- "How Too Many Rules at Work Keep You from Getting Things Done," TED Talk by Yves Morieux
- "How Diversity Makes Teams More Innovative," TED Talk by Rocío Lorenzo
- *Your Brain: Who's in Control?* Full documentary, NOVA | PBS

Take the Future Readiness Score at www.iankhan.com/frs or scan the QR Code

20

FRS Pillar 6: Innovation

Everything begins with an idea.

—*Earl Nightingale*

How Are Future Readiness and Innovation Linked?

Future readiness is the capability of individuals, organizations, and societies to anticipate, adapt, and thrive in a rapidly evolving landscape. As technology accelerates change across industries, future readiness demands a proactive approach to innovation, ensuring resilience and competitiveness in an unpredictable world. Embracing the unknown and preparing for it involves more than just reacting to changes; it requires anticipating future trends and building capabilities to harness them.

Innovation serves as the engine propelling future readiness. It's the process of translating new ideas into tangible outcomes, whether products, services, or processes that enhance value. By embedding innovation into their core strategies, organizations can navigate uncertainties with agility, leveraging cutting-edge technologies to redefine their operations and markets.

As Alan Kay aptly said, "The best way to predict the future is to create it."[1] Innovation empowers organizations to be creators of their destiny rather than passive participants.

Among the seven pillars of future readiness—innovation, agility, resilience, digital literacy, strategic foresight, leadership, and sustainability—innovation stands out as the catalyst that drives progress in all other areas.

- **Agility:** Innovation enhances agility by fostering a culture that welcomes change and encourages experimentation. This allows organizations to pivot quickly in response to market shifts.
- **Resilience:** Innovative solutions build resilience by creating adaptive systems that can withstand and recover from disruptions.
- **Digital literacy:** Staying at the forefront of technological advancements through innovation ensures a workforce proficient in the latest tools and techniques.
- **Strategic foresight:** Innovation involves anticipating future trends and proactively developing solutions, aligning closely with strategic foresight.
- **Leadership:** Visionary leaders who prioritize innovation inspire their teams to think creatively and embrace new challenges.
- **Sustainability:** Sustainable innovation drives the development of eco-friendly products and processes, contributing to long-term environmental and social goals.

Examples of Innovative Companies

According to the US Bureau of Labor Statistics, 18% of small business don't last to the end of their first year. In a report in *USA Today*, stats indicate that there are hundreds and millions of micro, small, medium, and large businesses across the world. On a different spectrum, there are over 1453 unicorns across the world. These are businesses generating $1 billion or more per year. What determines the success of a business, and what can business leaders rely on when making bets on their expertise? Here are some businesses that have pioneered directions and succeeded. These are some of my favorite undisrupted leaders within their segment.

Tesla: Transforming the Automotive Industry Through Innovation

Tesla's innovation lies in its commitment to sustainability and cutting-edge technology. By focusing on electric vehicles (EVs), Tesla has transformed the automotive industry, setting new standards for performance, efficiency, and sustainability.

Electric Powertrains: Leading the Charge Tesla's electric powertrains are at the heart of its innovation. These powertrains are more efficient and environmentally friendly than traditional internal combustion engines, offering numerous benefits:

- **Efficiency:** Tesla's electric motors convert more energy from the battery to the wheels compared to internal combustion engines, resulting in higher efficiency.
- **Environmental impact:** Electric powertrains produce zero tailpipe emissions, significantly reducing the environmental impact of driving.
- **Performance:** Tesla's powertrains deliver instant torque, providing superior acceleration and driving experience.

The success of the Tesla Roadster, Model S, and Model 3 highlights how electric powertrains can outperform traditional engines in both performance and sustainability.

Autopilot and Full Self-Driving (FSD): The Future of Autonomous Driving Tesla's Autopilot system uses advanced artificial intelligence (AI) to enable autonomous driving. Constantly improving through over-the-air updates, Autopilot and FSD represent the future of driving:

- **Advanced AI:** Tesla's neural network processes vast amounts of data from the vehicle's sensors to navigate roads and traffic autonomously.
- **Safety:** Autopilot's features, such as adaptive cruise control and lane-keeping assist, enhance safety by reducing human error.
- **Convenience:** Features such as Navigate on Autopilot and Smart Summon make driving more convenient and less stressful.

Tesla's continuous updates ensure that vehicles improve over time, reflecting the company's commitment to innovation and customer satisfaction.

Gigafactories: Revolutionizing Manufacturing Tesla's Gigafactories are designed to mass-produce batteries and EVs, significantly reducing production costs and scaling up the adoption of electric vehicles:

- **Economies of scale:** Gigafactories enable Tesla to produce batteries and EVs at a larger scale, driving down costs.

- **Innovation in production:** Advanced manufacturing techniques, such as the use of automation and innovative battery production methods, enhance efficiency.
- **Sustainability:** Gigafactories are powered by renewable energy sources, aligning with Tesla's mission to accelerate the world's transition to sustainable energy.

The Gigafactories in Nevada, Shanghai, and Berlin are key to Tesla's strategy of global expansion and dominance in the EV market.

SpaceX: Pioneering Space Exploration

SpaceX, founded by Elon Musk, aims to make space travel more affordable and accessible. Its innovations include reusable rockets, fully reusable spacecraft, and a satellite Internet constellation, showcasing its ability to revolutionize space missions and beyond.

Reusable Rockets: The Falcon 9   One of SpaceX's most revolutionary innovations is the Falcon 9 rocket, designed for reusability. Traditional rockets are expendable, meaning each mission requires a brand-new rocket, contributing to astronomical costs. SpaceX envisioned a different approach: reusable rockets that could return to Earth, be refurbished, and launched again.

- **Challenges and failures:** The path to achieving reusability was fraught with challenges. Early attempts to land the Falcon 9's first stage were met with spectacular failures. Rockets exploded on impact, missed their targets, or toppled over upon landing. These failures, though costly and demoralizing, provided invaluable data and learning opportunities.
- **Breakthroughs and successes:** After numerous trials and errors, SpaceX successfully landed a Falcon 9 booster in December 2015. This historic achievement marked the first time an orbital-class rocket returned to Earth intact. Since then, SpaceX has refined its techniques, achieving over 50 successful landings and reusing boosters multiple times, significantly reducing the cost of space missions.

Starship: The Future of Interplanetary Travel   SpaceX's Starship project aims to build a fully reusable spacecraft capable of carrying humans to Mars and beyond. Starship represents a quantum leap in space travel technology, combining cutting-edge materials, advanced propulsion systems, and innovative design.

■ **Challenges and failures:** The development of Starship has encountered several setbacks. Early prototypes, such as the Starhopper and Starship Mk1, faced explosive failures during testing. These incidents highlighted the complexities of developing a spacecraft capable of withstanding the rigors of interplanetary travel.

■ **Breakthroughs and successes:** Despite these setbacks, SpaceX continued to iterate rapidly. The successful high-altitude flight and landing of Starship SN15 in May 2021 demonstrated significant progress. Each test flight, whether a success or failure, brought SpaceX closer to its goal of making life multiplanetary.

Starlink: Global Broadband Coverage Beyond traditional space missions, SpaceX has ventured into satellite Internet with its Starlink project. Starlink aims to provide global broadband coverage through a constellation of low Earth orbit (LEO) satellites.

■ **Challenges and failures:** Deploying thousands of satellites and ensuring reliable connectivity presented numerous technical challenges. Early launches faced issues with satellite collisions, signal interference, and regulatory hurdles.

■ **Breakthroughs and successes:** SpaceX overcame these challenges through relentless innovation and iteration. As of 2023, Starlink provides Internet services to over a million users worldwide, including remote and underserved areas. The project showcases SpaceX's ability to diversify its technological capabilities and address global connectivity issues.

Resiliency in SpaceX's Journey SpaceX's trajectory is a testament to the importance of resilience in innovation. The company's ability to learn from failures and persist in the face of adversity has been crucial to its success.

■ **Cultural resilience:** SpaceX fosters a culture that embraces failure as a stepping stone to success. Each failure is analyzed in detail, and lessons learned are quickly applied to future iterations. This iterative approach ensures continuous improvement and innovation.

■ **Leadership:** Elon Musk's visionary leadership has been pivotal. His willingness to take risks and his unwavering belief in SpaceX's mission have inspired the team to push through challenges. Despite what some of us may think about his uncanny marketing and attention-seeking techniques, Elon has been deemed as one of the most remarkable minds of the modern times.

- **Team resilience:** SpaceX's engineers and scientists work in a high-pressure environment where rapid prototyping and testing are the norms. Their resilience and dedication have been instrumental in overcoming technical and logistical hurdles.

SpaceX's story is a powerful example of how innovation, coupled with resilience and a relentless drive to succeed, can lead to groundbreaking achievements and the transformation of industries.

Early Adopter Companies: Pioneers of Innovation

What unites these early adopter companies is their ability to see beyond the present, recognizing and embracing emerging trends before they became mainstream. Their willingness to take risks and invest in new technologies has not only transformed their respective industries but also set new standards for innovation and customer experience.

- Netflix embraced streaming technology when it was still a nascent field, foreseeing the shift toward on-demand content consumption.
- Uber leveraged the rise of smartphones and GPS technology to revolutionize urban transportation and spark the gig economy.
- Airbnb tapped into the sharing economy trend, transforming the hospitality industry by offering unique and personalized travel experiences.
- Slack identified the need for better workplace communication tools, creating a platform that enhanced collaboration and productivity.

These companies demonstrated resilience in the face of challenges, continually iterating on their ideas and adapting to market demands. Their stories highlight the importance of being early adopters, not just in recognizing new opportunities but in shaping the future through bold, innovative actions. I'll go into more detail in the following sections.

Netflix: Revolutionizing Content Consumption

Netflix began its journey in 1997 as a DVD rental-by-mail service, disrupting traditional video rental stores. However, it wasn't until 2007 that Netflix made a bold pivot to streaming video, a move that would revolutionize the entertainment industry. As one of the first companies to embrace streaming technology, Netflix set a new standard for content consumption.

The decision to transition from physical DVDs to digital streaming was both visionary and risky. In the early 2000s, broadband Internet was not yet ubiquitous, and the technology to stream high-quality video was in its nascent stages. Despite these challenges, Netflix invested heavily in streaming technology, recognizing the potential for on-demand viewing.

By 2010, Netflix had solidified its position as a streaming giant, offering a vast library of movies and TV shows accessible from virtually any device with an Internet connection. This move not only disrupted the video rental industry but also challenged traditional cable and satellite TV providers. Netflix's early adoption of streaming technology positioned it as a leader in the digital entertainment revolution, influencing how people consume media globally.

Uber: Redefining Urban Transportation

Uber's launch in 2010 marked a seismic shift in urban transportation. Leveraging smartphone technology and GPS, Uber introduced a convenient and efficient way to book rides, disrupting the traditional taxi industry. Uber's innovation lay in its app, which allowed users to request a ride, track their driver's arrival in real time, and pay seamlessly through the app.

At a time when smartphones were becoming increasingly ubiquitous, Uber recognized the potential to streamline transportation using this technology. The company's early adoption of GPS and mobile app technology enabled it to offer a superior user experience compared to traditional taxi services.

Uber's impact extended beyond urban transportation. By providing flexible work opportunities, Uber sparked the gig economy, allowing individuals to work as drivers on their own schedules. This model of employment has since influenced various other sectors, contributing to the rise of on-demand services.

Airbnb: Transforming the Hospitality Industry

Airbnb's inception in 2008 introduced a new way for people to find and book accommodations. By capitalizing on the sharing economy trend, Airbnb provided a platform for homeowners to offer their properties as short-term rentals. This innovative approach transformed the hospitality industry, offering travelers more diverse and personalized lodging options.

Airbnb's founders saw an opportunity in the underutilized living spaces and the increasing popularity of peer-to-peer services. The company's early adoption of online platforms to connect hosts and guests facilitated its rapid growth. By 2011, Airbnb had listings in cities around the world, challenging traditional hotels and motels.

Airbnb's model not only offered cost-effective and unique accommodation options but also fostered a sense of community and cultural exchange. This innovation in hospitality redefined how people experience travel, making it more immersive and personalized.

Slack: Revolutionizing Workplace Collaboration

Slack, launched in 2013, transformed workplace communication with its innovative messaging platform. Recognizing the limitations of email and traditional communication tools, Slack integrated real-time messaging, file sharing, and third-party app integrations into a single platform, enhancing productivity and collaboration.

At a time when remote work and digital collaboration were becoming increasingly important, Slack's early adoption of real-time communication technology filled a crucial gap in the market. The platform's user-friendly interface and ability to integrate with other business tools made it an indispensable part of modern work environments.

Slack's impact was profound, changing how teams communicate and collaborate. By enabling more efficient information sharing and reducing email overload, Slack improved workplace productivity and fostered a more dynamic work culture. Its success has inspired numerous other companies to develop similar tools, cementing its place as a pioneer in digital workplace innovation.

Case Study: Moderna's COVID-19 Vaccine

In late 2019, as news of a novel coronavirus began to spread from Wuhan, China, the world braced for an unprecedented health crisis. By early 2020, COVID-19 had reached pandemic status, causing widespread illness, death, and economic upheaval. In this dire context, Moderna, a relatively young biotechnology company, emerged as a beacon of hope, leveraging its innovative mRNA technology to develop a vaccine at an unprecedented speed.

The Early Days: Laying the Foundation

Moderna's journey began years before the pandemic, rooted in its commitment to pioneering mRNA technology. Unlike traditional vaccines, which often use inactivated viruses or viral proteins to elicit an immune response, mRNA vaccines use genetic instructions to produce a protein that triggers immunity. This approach promised several advantages: faster development times, scalable production, and the ability to rapidly adapt to emerging pathogens.

Founded in 2010, Moderna had spent a decade refining its mRNA platform, overcoming numerous scientific and technical challenges. By 2019, the company had developed a robust pipeline of mRNA-based therapies and vaccines, but it was still largely untested in large-scale clinical applications. This foundational work proved invaluable when the COVID-19 crisis struck.

The Pandemic Strikes: Swift Action and Innovation

As COVID-19 began to spread globally, the urgency to develop a vaccine became paramount. In January 2020, Chinese scientists published the genetic sequence of SARS-CoV-2, the virus causing COVID-19. Within days, Moderna scientists designed an mRNA sequence encoding the virus's spike protein, the key target for neutralizing antibodies.

This rapid response was made possible by Moderna's innovative platform, which allowed for the quick synthesis and testing of mRNA constructs. By February 24, 2020, Moderna had shipped the first batch of its vaccine candidate, mRNA-1273, to the National Institutes of Health (NIH) for a Phase 1 clinical trial—a mere 42 days after the virus's genetic sequence was published.

Agile Processes: Adapting and Scaling

Moderna's ability to adapt and scale its production processes was another critical factor in its success. Traditional vaccine development is a lengthy process, often taking years. However, Moderna's mRNA technology, combined with its agile manufacturing processes, significantly shortened this timeline.

The company rapidly scaled up production capabilities, leveraging its state-of-the-art manufacturing facilities. This agility was crucial in meeting the massive demand for the vaccine once it proved effective in clinical trials. Moderna's mRNA platform enabled not only swift initial production but also the flexibility to quickly ramp up output as needed.

Collaborative Efforts: A Unified Front

Moderna's success was not achieved in isolation. Collaborative efforts with government bodies, academic institutions, and other organizations played a pivotal role. The US government's Operation Warp Speed provided significant funding and support, facilitating rapid development and distribution.

Partnerships with institutions such as the NIH ensured rigorous clinical testing, while collaborations with contract manufacturers expanded production capacity. This unified effort underscored the importance of public-private partnerships in addressing global health crises. Moderna's transparent communication and cooperation with regulatory agencies, such as the Food and Drug Administration (FDA), further expedited the vaccine's approval process.

Overcoming Challenges: Resilience and Determination

The path to success was not without obstacles. Moderna faced immense pressure to deliver a safe and effective vaccine amid a global pandemic. The accelerated timeline raised concerns about safety and efficacy, necessitating rigorous clinical trials and thorough regulatory scrutiny.

Moderna's team worked tirelessly, often around the clock, to ensure the vaccine met the highest standards. The company's culture of resilience and determination, fostered over years of innovation and challenge, was crucial in overcoming these hurdles. Each setback was met with a resolve to find solutions, driven by the urgent need to address the pandemic.

Achieving Success: A Historic Milestone

In December 2020, Moderna's mRNA-1273 vaccine received Emergency Use Authorization (EUA) from the FDA. Clinical trials had demonstrated the vaccine's efficacy at approximately 94%, a remarkable achievement given the speed of development. The rollout of the vaccine marked a historic milestone in the fight against COVID-19.

Moderna's success story is a powerful testament to how innovation can serve as an accelerant in addressing global challenges. The company's ability to leverage advanced technology, adapt and scale rapidly, and collaborate effectively transformed a potential catastrophe into an opportunity for progress. Moderna's mRNA vaccine not only provided a critical tool in combating the pandemic but also showcased the potential of mRNA technology for future medical breakthroughs.

Lessons Learned and the Path Forward

Moderna's journey with the COVID-19 vaccine offers valuable lessons for future preparedness:

- **Investment in innovation:** Decades of investment in mRNA technology laid the groundwork for a rapid response.

- **Agile manufacturing:** The ability to quickly scale production is crucial in a global health crisis.
- **Collaboration:** Public-private partnerships and global cooperation are essential in overcoming large-scale challenges.
- **Resilience:** A culture that embraces challenges and persists through setbacks is vital for success.

Looking forward, Moderna continues to explore the potential of mRNA technology in treating other diseases, such as cancer and rare genetic disorders. The success of mRNA-1273 has opened new avenues for medical innovation, promising a future where rapid and flexible responses to health challenges become the norm.

Moderna's story is not just one of scientific triumph but also of human resilience, collaboration, and the relentless pursuit of progress. It exemplifies how, with the right combination of innovation and determination, we can rise to meet even the most daunting challenges.

Embracing AI and Emerging Technologies: The Path to Innovation

In today's fast-paced digital world, the adoption of AI and other emerging technologies is crucial for organizations aspiring to be innovators. These technologies offer transformative potential, enabling businesses to enhance efficiency, create new products and services, and gain a competitive edge. Companies that successfully integrate AI and emerging technologies into their operations can anticipate trends, make data-driven decisions, and deliver unprecedented value to their customers.

Artificial intelligence stands at the forefront of technological innovation. AI encompasses a range of capabilities, from machine learning and natural language processing to robotics and computer vision. These technologies can process vast amounts of data, identify patterns, and make predictions, allowing businesses to operate more intelligently and efficiently.

Key Benefits of AI Adoption

- **Enhanced decision-making:** AI-driven analytics provide insights that help organizations make informed, strategic decisions. Predictive models can forecast market trends, customer behavior, and operational efficiencies.

- **Automation and efficiency:** AI automates repetitive and mundane tasks, freeing up human resources to focus on more strategic and creative activities. This leads to increased productivity and cost savings.
- **Personalization:** AI enables highly personalized customer experiences by analyzing individual preferences and behaviors. This personalization enhances customer satisfaction and loyalty.
- **Innovation in products and services:** AI can drive the development of new products and services that were previously unimaginable. From autonomous vehicles to intelligent virtual assistants, AI is the engine behind many groundbreaking innovations.

Case Study: OpenAI as an Innovator Company

OpenAI, founded in 2015, has become a beacon of innovation in the field of artificial intelligence. The organization's mission is to ensure that artificial general intelligence (AGI) benefits all of humanity. OpenAI's journey exemplifies how embracing emerging technologies can lead to transformative innovations.

Advanced Research and Breakthroughs   OpenAI is renowned for its cutting-edge research and development in AI. The organization has made significant strides in creating sophisticated AI models, including:

- **GPT (Generative Pre-trained Transformer) Series:** OpenAI's GPT models, particularly GPT-3 and the more recent GPT-4, have revolutionized natural language processing. These models can generate human-like text, understand context, and perform complex language tasks, from translation to content creation. GPT-3, with its 175 billion parameters, set a new benchmark in the AI community for its ability to generate coherent and contextually relevant text across diverse topics.
- **DALL-E and CLIP:** These models showcase AI's creative potential. DALL-E generates images from textual descriptions, pushing the boundaries of generative art. CLIP understands images and their associated text, enabling better interpretation and manipulation of visual content.
- **Robotics and reinforcement learning:** OpenAI has also made significant contributions to robotics, using reinforcement learning to train robots to perform tasks with high precision. Their research in this area paves the way for advancements in autonomous systems and robotics applications across various industries.

Collaboration and Open Source OpenAI's commitment to collaboration and open-source principles has amplified its impact. By sharing research findings, code, and best practices, OpenAI fosters a global community of researchers and developers who contribute to and benefit from its innovations.

- **OpenAI Gym:** An open-source tool kit for developing and comparing reinforcement learning algorithms. It provides a diverse range of environments for testing and training AI models.
- **OpenAI Codex:** This model powers GitHub Copilot, an AI pair programmer that assists developers by suggesting code snippets and automating routine coding tasks. Codex exemplifies how AI can augment human capabilities, making software development more efficient.

Ethical AI and Responsible Innovation OpenAI emphasizes the ethical implications of AI and strives to develop technologies that are safe and beneficial. The organization's principles include prioritizing long-term safety, ensuring broad distribution of benefits, and promoting transparency and accountability.

- **AI safety research:** OpenAI invests in research to address potential risks associated with AGI, such as ensuring robustness, preventing misuse, and aligning AI systems with human values.
- **Public engagement and policy:** OpenAI actively engages with policymakers, academics, and the public to foster understanding and dialogue about AI's societal impacts. By contributing to policy discussions, OpenAI aims to shape the responsible development and deployment of AI technologies.

Adopting Emerging Technologies: Strategies for Success Organizations looking to become innovators by adopting AI and emerging technologies can learn from OpenAI's approach. Here are key strategies to consider:

- **Invest in research and development:** Dedicate resources to exploring new technologies and developing expertise in AI. Continuous R&D ensures that your organization stays at the cutting edge of innovation.
- **Foster a culture of innovation:** Encourage experimentation and risk-taking within your organization. Create an environment where employees feel empowered to explore new ideas and technologies.

- **Collaborate and share knowledge:** Build partnerships with academic institutions, industry peers, and technology providers. Sharing knowledge and collaborating on research can accelerate innovation and lead to breakthroughs.
- **Focus on ethical AI:** Consider the ethical implications of AI and other emerging technologies. Implement guidelines and frameworks to ensure responsible development and deployment.
- **Leverage open source:** Utilize and contribute to open-source projects. Open-source tools and frameworks can accelerate development and foster a community of innovation.
- **Prioritize user experience:** Design technologies that enhance user experience. AI should be intuitive and accessible, providing tangible benefits to users.

Future Insights

The adoption of AI and emerging technologies is not just a pathway to innovation; it is a necessity for organizations aiming to thrive in the digital age. By leveraging these technologies, companies can enhance their capabilities, create new value, and drive transformative change. OpenAI's journey exemplifies the profound impact that embracing AI can have, setting a benchmark for other organizations to follow. As technology continues to evolve, the potential for innovation is boundless, and those who embrace it will lead the way into the future.

Final Words

Innovation is the cornerstone of future readiness, enabling individuals, organizations, and societies to anticipate, adapt, and thrive amid rapid technological advancements. It transforms ideas into powerful outcomes, enhancing value through new products, services, and processes. This proactive approach to innovation ensures resilience and competitiveness in an unpredictable world.

The seven pillars of future readiness are all driven by innovation. By fostering a culture that welcomes change and encourages experimentation, organizations can pivot quickly, build adaptive systems, stay ahead in technological advancements, and inspire creative leadership. Sustainable innovation also contributes to long-term environmental and social goals.

Case studies of innovative companies such as Tesla and SpaceX highlight how commitment to cutting-edge technology and resilience leads to groundbreaking achievements. Tesla revolutionized the automotive industry with its electric vehicles and autonomous driving technology, while SpaceX redefined space exploration with reusable rockets and ambitious interplanetary travel plans.

In conclusion, embracing innovation is essential for navigating uncertainties and shaping a successful future. Organizations that integrate innovation into their core strategies will lead the way, turning ideas into powerful realities and securing their place in an ever-evolving landscape.

Resources

Books

- *The Innovator's Dilemma* by Clayton Christensen
- *Zero to One* by Peter Thiel
- *Bold* by Peter H. Diamandis and Steven Kotler

Take the Future Readiness Score at www.iankhan.com/frs or scan the QR Code

21

FRS Pillar 7: Execution

Vision without execution is merely a dream. Execution transforms dreams into reality and is the bridge between aspirations and accomplishments.

—*Anonymous*

Why Is Execution a Key Pillar of Future Readiness?

Execution is the ability to effectively and efficiently turn strategies and plans into actions that achieve desired outcomes. It is the bridge between ideas and results, transforming innovative concepts and strategic goals into tangible success. For any organization aiming to be future-ready, execution is fundamental for several reasons:

- **Bringing vision to reality:** Without execution, even the most visionary strategies remain abstract. Execution translates plans into operational activities, ensuring that the vision is realized in practical terms.
- **Competitive advantage:** Organizations that excel in execution can outperform their competitors by rapidly adapting to changes, delivering products and services with consistency and quality, and responding swiftly to market demands.
- **Sustainable growth:** Effective execution ensures that resources are utilized optimally, risks are managed, and performance is continuously improved, leading to sustainable growth and long-term success.

- **Accountability and alignment:** Execution fosters a culture of accountability and alignment within an organization. Clear execution plans ensure that all team members understand their roles and responsibilities, working toward common goals.
- **Customer satisfaction:** Consistent and reliable execution enhances customer satisfaction by meeting or exceeding expectations, building trust, and fostering loyalty.

Examples of Flawless Execution

Planning without execution is wasted effort. Today we have the luxury of accessing information at our fingertips. Countless books, case studies, and examples of leadership and organizations executing their strategy are available. Here we look at some of the most profound and classic examples of exemplary execution of strategy. Well, these are some of my favorites, to say the least.

Apple: Launch of the iPhone

When Apple introduced the iPhone in 2007, it was not just a new product; it was a game changer in the tech industry. The flawless execution of the iPhone launch involved meticulous planning, innovative marketing, and seamless coordination across various departments.

Apple focused on a user-centric design, integrating cutting-edge technology with an intuitive user interface. The company also created a robust ecosystem of applications and services that complemented the iPhone.

The successful execution of the iPhone launch established Apple as a leader in the smartphone market, driving massive revenue growth and transforming the way people interact with technology.

Amazon: Launch of the Prime Membership Program

Amazon's Prime membership program, launched in 2005, is a quintessential example of strategic execution that revolutionized e-commerce and redefined customer expectations. The program initially promised unlimited two-day shipping for an annual fee, a proposition that set new standards for convenience and customer satisfaction.

The inception of Amazon Prime stemmed from a deep understanding of consumer pain points and market opportunities. Jeff Bezos, Amazon's CEO, envisioned a service that would enhance customer loyalty by addressing one of the biggest barriers to online shopping: shipping costs and delays. By offering a subscription model that guaranteed fast and free shipping, Amazon aimed to encourage repeat purchases and build a loyal customer base.

Key Strategies Behind Prime's Success The success of Amazon Prime can be attributed to several strategic initiatives and flawless execution:

Investment in Logistics and Fulfillment

- **Advanced logistics network:** Amazon invested heavily in building an advanced logistics network capable of supporting the Prime program. This included the development of numerous fulfillment centers strategically located near key markets to reduce shipping times.
- **Technology integration:** Amazon leveraged cutting-edge technology to optimize its supply chain operations. This included sophisticated algorithms for inventory management, predictive analytics to forecast demand, and automation to enhance efficiency in fulfillment centers.

Expanding Prime Benefits

- **Streaming services:** In 2011, Amazon expanded Prime to include access to Prime Video, offering a wide array of movies and TV shows. This move added immense value to the membership, attracting a broader audience.
- **Exclusive deals and early access:** Prime members were given access to exclusive deals and early access to select sales events, further enhancing the program's appeal.
- **Additional services:** Over the years, Amazon continued to add new benefits such as Prime Music, Prime Reading, and free Twitch subscriptions, making Prime a comprehensive membership offering that catered to various customer needs.

Customer-Centric Approach

- **Ease of use:** Amazon ensured that the Prime membership was easy to understand and use. The seamless integration of Prime benefits across the Amazon platform made it simple for customers to take advantage of the program.
- **Continuous improvement:** Amazon constantly sought customer feedback to refine and enhance Prime. This iterative approach ensured that the program evolved to meet changing customer preferences and needs.

Impact of Flawless Execution   The strategic execution of Amazon Prime had a profound impact on the company's growth and market dominance:

Boosted Customer Loyalty
- **Increased retention:** Prime members exhibited higher retention rates compared to non-members. The array of benefits and the value proposition of the membership created a strong incentive for customers to renew their subscriptions annually.
- **Higher spending:** Prime members also spent significantly more than non-members. The convenience of fast shipping and access to exclusive deals encouraged more frequent purchases, driving up average order values.

Market Penetration and Competitive Advantage
- **Global reach:** By 2021, Amazon Prime had over 200 million subscribers globally. The program's expansion into international markets further solidified Amazon's presence and competitiveness worldwide.
- **Competitive edge:** The success of Prime forced competitors to innovate and improve their own offerings. However, Amazon's early and sustained investment in logistics and customer experience gave it a significant head start, maintaining its edge in the market.

Revenue Growth
- **Subscription revenue:** The recurring revenue from Prime subscriptions became a substantial and predictable revenue stream for Amazon.
- **Ecosystem synergy:** The integration of various services under the Prime umbrella created a synergistic effect, driving usage across Amazon's ecosystem. For instance, Prime Video and Prime Music not only added value but also kept customers engaged with Amazon's platform, indirectly boosting e-commerce sales.

Detailed Execution Elements   Let us examine the key elements of execution in Amazons strategy.

Scalability and Flexibility
- Amazon designed Prime to be scalable, allowing it to grow and adapt to new markets and customer segments. The company's logistics infrastructure was built to handle increased demand, ensuring that the promise of two-day shipping could be maintained even as the customer base expanded.

- Flexibility in adding new benefits and services kept Prime relevant and valuable, demonstrating Amazon's ability to pivot and enhance its offerings in response to market trends and consumer preferences.

Data-Driven Decisions

- Amazon's execution of Prime was heavily data-driven. The company utilized vast amounts of customer data to personalize the shopping experience, optimize inventory management, and predict demand patterns. This ensured that the right products were available at the right time, reducing stockouts and enhancing customer satisfaction.

Marketing and Customer Education

- Effective marketing strategies played a crucial role in the adoption of Prime. Amazon used targeted campaigns to highlight the benefits of Prime, leveraging customer testimonials and promotional offers to attract new members.
- Amazon also invested in educating customers about the value of Prime, using detailed descriptions, videos, and FAQs to ensure potential subscribers fully understood the benefits they would receive.

Conclusion: Mastering Execution for Unmatched Success   Amazon Prime's journey from a bold concept to a cornerstone of e-commerce success exemplifies the power of strategic execution. By investing in logistics, continuously expanding benefits, and maintaining a relentless focus on customer satisfaction, Amazon not only revolutionized the retail industry but also set a benchmark for execution excellence.

For organizations looking to emulate Amazon's success, the key takeaway is clear: Flawless execution requires a blend of strategic vision, investment in infrastructure, adaptability, and a customer-centric approach. By mastering these elements, companies can transform innovative ideas into enduring success, securing their place as leaders in their respective industries.

Tesla: Model 3 Production

Tesla's execution of the Model 3 production is a testament to overcoming challenges and achieving success. Initially faced with production bottlenecks and quality issues, Tesla revamped its manufacturing processes to meet high demand.

Tesla implemented advanced automation in its gigafactories, streamlined its supply chain, and focused on continuous improvement. CEO Elon Musk's hands-on leadership and problem-solving approach played a crucial role.

The successful ramp-up of Model 3 production positioned Tesla as a major player in the automotive industry, driving significant growth in sales and market capitalization.

Microsoft Azure

Microsoft's execution of its Azure cloud services platform is a stellar example of how effective execution can drive business growth and innovation. Launched in 2010, Azure quickly rose to prominence in the competitive cloud services market, standing alongside giants such as Amazon Web Services (AWS) and Google Cloud. The platform's success can be attributed to Microsoft's strategic initiatives and flawless execution.

The inception of Azure came as Microsoft recognized the growing importance of cloud computing. With the rise of data-driven business models and the increasing need for scalable IT infrastructure, cloud services were becoming essential. Microsoft aimed to leverage its extensive enterprise relationships and technological expertise to create a robust cloud platform that could meet diverse business needs.

Key Strategies Behind Azure's Success   The success of Microsoft Azure can be attributed to several strategic initiatives and meticulous execution:

Leveraging Enterprise Relationships

- **Established trust:** Microsoft had long-standing relationships with enterprise customers, built on decades of providing reliable software solutions such as Windows, Office, and SQL Server. This trust was pivotal in encouraging businesses to adopt Azure.
- **Integrated solutions:** By integrating Azure with existing Microsoft products, such as Office 365 and Dynamics 365, Microsoft created a seamless experience for enterprise users, enhancing productivity and efficiency.

Investment in Data Center Infrastructure

- **Global network:** Microsoft invested heavily in building a global network of data centers, ensuring that Azure could provide reliable and low-latency services to customers around the world. This extensive infrastructure enabled Azure to offer high availability and resilience.

- **Cutting-edge technology:** The data centers were equipped with state-of-the-art hardware and advanced technologies, allowing Azure to deliver scalable and efficient cloud services. Microsoft's focus on innovation in data center design and operations played a critical role in Azure's performance.

Expanding Service Offerings

- **Broad spectrum of services:** Microsoft continuously expanded Azure's service offerings, covering infrastructure as a service (IaaS), platform as a service (PaaS), and software as a service (SaaS). This comprehensive suite of services catered to various business needs, from computing and storage to machine learning and other forms of AI.
- **Industry-specific solutions:** Azure developed specialized solutions for different industries, such as health care, finance, and retail. These tailored services addressed specific regulatory and operational requirements, making Azure more attractive to enterprise customers.

Prioritizing Security and Compliance

- **Robust security measures:** Security has always been a top priority for Microsoft. Azure implemented robust security measures, including encryption, identity and access management, and threat detection, to protect customer data and applications.
- **Compliance certifications:** Microsoft ensured that Azure met various industry-specific and global compliance standards, such as GDPR, HIPAA, and ISO 27001. This focus on compliance helped build trust with enterprise customers, particularly those in highly regulated industries.

Impact of Flawless Execution The strategic execution of Microsoft Azure had a profound impact on the company's growth and market leadership:

Market Penetration and Competitive Positioning

- **Rapid growth:** Azure experienced rapid growth, quickly becoming a leading player in the cloud computing market. Its comprehensive service offerings and extensive data center network positioned it as a formidable competitor to AWS and Google Cloud.
- **Competitive edge:** Azure's integration with Microsoft's enterprise software ecosystem gave it a unique competitive edge, making it the preferred choice for many businesses looking for a cohesive and efficient cloud solution.

Revenue Growth

- **Significant contribution:** Azure became a major revenue driver for Microsoft, contributing significantly to the company's overall growth. The recurring revenue from cloud services provided a stable and predictable income stream.
- **Diversification:** Azure's success helped Microsoft diversify its revenue sources, reducing its reliance on traditional software licensing and paving the way for a more balanced and resilient business model.

Innovation and Industry Leadership

- **Driving innovation:** Azure's extensive capabilities and continuous expansion fueled innovation within Microsoft and among its customers. Businesses could leverage Azure's advanced technologies to develop innovative solutions and improve operational efficiency.
- **Thought leadership:** Microsoft emerged as a thought leader in cloud computing, influencing industry standards and best practices. Azure's success showcased Microsoft's ability to adapt to new technological trends and lead in the digital transformation era.

Detailed Execution Elements   Let us take a peek into what Microsoft did that made them succeed.

Scalability and Flexibility

- Microsoft designed Azure to be highly scalable, capable of handling the demands of small start-ups to large enterprises. The platform's flexibility allowed it to adapt to the specific needs of various industries and use cases, from simple web hosting to complex AI workloads.

Data-Driven Insights and Decision-Making

- Azure's development and expansion were heavily data-driven. Microsoft utilized customer feedback, market analysis, and usage patterns to continuously refine and enhance Azure's services. This data-driven approach ensured that Azure remained relevant and competitive in a rapidly evolving market.

Customer Education and Support and Strong Partner Ecosystem

- **Customer education:** Microsoft invested in educating its customers about the benefits and capabilities of Azure. Through webinars, documentation, training programs, and a robust support network, Microsoft ensured that customers could effectively leverage Azure's features to achieve their business goals.

- **Partner ecosystem:** Microsoft built a strong partner ecosystem, collaborating with independent software vendors (ISVs), system integrators (SIs), and managed service providers (MSPs) to deliver comprehensive solutions and support to Azure customers.

Results   Microsoft Azure's journey from its launch to becoming a leading cloud services platform is a testament to the power of strategic execution. By leveraging its enterprise relationships, investing in data center infrastructure, expanding service offerings, and prioritizing security and compliance, Microsoft not only achieved massive success but also set new standards for the cloud computing industry.

Organizations looking to emulate Microsoft's success should focus on developing clear strategies, investing in critical infrastructure, continuously expanding and improving their offerings, and prioritizing customer trust through robust security and compliance measures. By mastering these elements of execution, businesses can drive innovation, achieve sustained growth, and secure their position as leaders in their respective markets.

Nike's Digital Transformation

Nike's digital transformation strategy is a prime example of how effective execution can enhance customer engagement and operational efficiency. By integrating digital technologies into its business model, Nike has significantly strengthened its direct-to-consumer (DTC) channels, ensuring a seamless and personalized shopping experience for its customers. This transformation has not only improved Nike's operational capabilities but also reinforced its position as a leading global brand.

In response to the evolving retail landscape and the increasing importance of online shopping, Nike embarked on a comprehensive digital transformation journey. Recognizing the potential of digital technologies to enhance customer experiences and streamline operations, Nike aimed to create a cohesive and integrated digital ecosystem. The objective was to bridge the gap between physical and digital channels, offering customers a unified and engaging brand experience.

Key Strategies Behind Nike's Success   Nike's digital transformation was driven by several strategic initiatives and meticulous execution:

Investment in E-Commerce Platforms

- **User-friendly website and mobile apps:** Nike invested heavily in developing a robust e-commerce platform and intuitive mobile applications. The website and apps were designed to offer a seamless and personalized shopping experience, with features such as product recommendations, virtual try-ons, and easy navigation.
- **Enhanced user experience:** By focusing on user experience (UX) design, Nike ensured that its digital platforms were visually appealing, easy to use, and highly functional. The aim was to replicate the in-store experience online, making it convenient for customers to browse and purchase products.

Digital Marketing and Customer Engagement

- **Data-driven marketing:** Nike leveraged data analytics to understand customer preferences and behavior. This allowed the company to create targeted marketing campaigns that resonated with different customer segments. Personalized emails, social media ads, and digital content were used to engage customers and drive traffic to Nike's online platforms.
- **Community building:** Nike utilized digital channels to build a sense of community among its customers. Through initiatives such as the Nike Run Club app and Nike Training Club app, the company provided value-added services that encouraged customer engagement and loyalty.

Supply Chain and Inventory Management Enhancements

- **Integrated supply chain:** Nike enhanced its supply chain management by integrating advanced technologies such as RFID (radio-frequency identification) and AI-powered analytics. This integration improved inventory visibility and accuracy, enabling Nike to manage stock levels efficiently and reduce lead times.
- **Omni-channel fulfillment:** By adopting an omni-channel fulfillment strategy, Nike allowed customers to purchase products online and pick them up in-store, or have them delivered from the nearest retail location. This flexibility enhanced customer convenience and satisfaction.

Direct-to-Consumer (DTC) Focus and Membership Programs

- **DTC strategy:** Nike's digital transformation placed a strong emphasis on strengthening its DTC channels. By reducing reliance on third-party retailers and focusing on selling directly to customers, Nike gained better control over the customer experience and increased profit margins.

- **Membership programs:** Nike introduced membership programs such as NikePlus, offering exclusive benefits, early access to products, and personalized experiences. These programs helped foster customer loyalty and drive repeat purchases.

Impact of Flawless Execution The strategic execution of Nike's digital transformation had a profound impact on the company's growth and market leadership:

Increased Online Sales and Global Reach
- **Surge in e-commerce revenue:** Nike's investment in digital platforms paid off with a significant increase in online sales. The company reported substantial growth in e-commerce revenue, particularly during the COVID-19 pandemic when physical stores faced closures and restrictions.
- **Global reach:** The digital transformation enabled Nike to reach customers globally, expanding its market presence and attracting new customer segments. The ability to shop online from anywhere in the world broadened Nike's customer base.

Improved Customer Experience
- **Personalized shopping:** The use of data analytics and AI allowed Nike to offer personalized shopping experiences. Customers received product recommendations tailored to their preferences, enhancing satisfaction and engagement.
- **Seamless integration:** The seamless integration of physical and digital channels ensured a consistent and cohesive brand experience. Customers could easily transition between online and offline shopping, enjoying the same level of service and convenience.

Stronger Brand Presence
- **Digital content and community:** Nike's focus on digital content and community building strengthened its brand presence in the digital space. The company's apps, social media channels, and online communities fostered a sense of belonging and loyalty among customers.

- **Innovation leadership:** Nike's successful digital transformation positioned it as a leader in retail innovation. The company's ability to adapt to changing market dynamics and leverage digital technologies set a benchmark for other brands.

Detailed Execution Elements   Let us take a peek into Nike's key execution elements.

Scalability and Adaptability

- Nike designed its digital platforms to be scalable, capable of handling increased traffic and expanding features as needed. This scalability ensured that the platforms could grow with the business and adapt to changing customer needs.
- The company's agile approach to digital transformation allowed it to quickly implement new technologies and adapt to market trends, ensuring continuous improvement and innovation.

Customer-Centric Approach

- Nike's execution strategy was deeply customer-centric. By focusing on delivering value and enhancing the customer experience, Nike ensured that its digital transformation resonated with consumers and met their evolving expectations.
- Feedback mechanisms and customer insights were integral to Nike's strategy, enabling the company to refine its digital offerings and stay ahead of competitors.

Partnerships and Ecosystem Development

- Nike collaborated with technology partners and digital agencies to develop and implement its digital strategies. These partnerships brought in specialized expertise and innovative solutions, accelerating Nike's digital transformation.
- The development of a digital ecosystem, including apps, social media channels, and online communities, created multiple touchpoints for customer engagement and interaction.

Results   Nike's digital transformation journey from traditional retail to a digitally integrated powerhouse is a testament to the power of strategic execution. By investing in e-commerce platforms, enhancing supply chain management, and focusing on customer engagement, Nike not only increased online sales but also improved customer experiences and strengthened its brand presence in the digital space.

Organizations looking to emulate Nike's success should focus on developing clear digital strategies, investing in critical digital infrastructure, continuously expanding and improving their digital offerings, and prioritizing customer engagement. By mastering these elements of execution, businesses can drive digital innovation, achieve sustained growth, and secure their position as leaders in the digital era.

Procter & Gamble's Supply Chain Optimization

Procter & Gamble (P&G), a global leader in consumer goods, recognized the critical importance of an efficient supply chain in maintaining its competitive edge and meeting consumer demands. By implementing a comprehensive supply chain optimization strategy, P&G significantly enhanced its operational efficiency and reduced costs. This strategic execution leveraged data analytics and automation to streamline operations, ultimately transforming P&G's supply chain into a model of efficiency and effectiveness.

P&G's decision to optimize its supply chain stemmed from the need to manage an increasingly complex global network of suppliers, manufacturing facilities, and distribution centers. The company aimed to enhance efficiency, reduce operational costs, and ensure consistent product availability to meet the demands of its vast consumer base. The goal was to create a more responsive and agile supply chain capable of adapting to market changes and customer needs.

Key Strategies behind P&G's Success   The success of P&G's supply chain optimization can be attributed to several strategic initiatives and meticulous execution:

Leveraging Advanced Analytics
- **Demand forecasting:** P&G utilized advanced analytics to forecast demand accurately. By analyzing historical sales data, market trends, and consumer behavior, the company could predict future demand with greater precision. This enabled P&G to plan production schedules and inventory levels more effectively, reducing stockouts and excess inventory.

- **Inventory optimization:** The company implemented sophisticated inventory optimization algorithms to maintain optimal stock levels across its supply chain. This approach ensured that the right products were available at the right locations, minimizing holding costs and improving product availability.

Investing in Automation Technologies

- **Automated production systems:** P&G invested in state-of-the-art automation technologies to enhance production efficiency. Automated systems streamlined manufacturing processes, reduced human error, and increased throughput. This investment in automation allowed P&G to scale production rapidly and meet varying demand levels.
- **Smart warehousing and logistics:** P&G incorporated automation into its warehousing and logistics operations. Automated guided vehicles (AGVs), robotic picking systems, and smart shelving systems improved the efficiency of warehousing operations. Advanced logistics management systems optimized routing and delivery schedules, ensuring timely and cost-effective distribution of products.

Data-Driven Decision-Making

- **Real-time monitoring:** P&G implemented real-time monitoring and analytics across its supply chain. Sensors, IoT devices, and advanced analytics platforms provided real-time visibility into inventory levels, production status, and logistics operations. This enabled P&G to make informed decisions quickly and address issues proactively.
- **Predictive maintenance:** By leveraging data analytics, P&G implemented predictive maintenance programs for its manufacturing equipment. Predictive algorithms analyzed machine performance data to predict potential failures and schedule maintenance activities before breakdowns occurred, minimizing downtime and maintaining production efficiency.

Impact of Flawless Execution   The strategic execution of P&G's supply chain optimization had a profound impact on the company's operational performance and market competitiveness:

Significant Cost Savings

- **Operational efficiency:** The implementation of automation technologies and advanced analytics led to significant improvements in operational efficiency. P&G reduced labor costs, minimized waste, and optimized resource utilization, resulting in substantial cost savings.

- **Inventory management:** By optimizing inventory levels and reducing excess stock, P&G minimized holding costs and improved cash flow. Efficient inventory management also reduced the risk of obsolescence and write-offs.

Improved Product Availability
- **Enhanced responsiveness:** The optimized supply chain allowed P&G to respond quickly to changes in demand. Accurate demand forecasting and inventory optimization ensured that products were available when and where needed, reducing stockouts and enhancing customer satisfaction.
- **Consistent quality:** Automation in production processes ensured consistent product quality. By minimizing human error and variability, P&G maintained high standards of quality across its product lines.

Increased Customer Satisfaction
- **Timely deliveries:** Efficient logistics operations and smart warehousing systems ensured timely deliveries to customers. P&G's ability to fulfill orders promptly and accurately improved customer trust and loyalty.
- **Product availability:** Consistent product availability across retail channels enhanced the shopping experience for consumers. P&G's commitment to meeting customer expectations reinforced its reputation as a reliable and customer-centric brand.

Detailed Execution Elements   Let us look at P&G's strategic execution elements that stand apart.

Scalability and Flexibility
- P&G designed its supply chain optimization initiatives to be scalable and adaptable. The company's investment in flexible automation systems and advanced analytics allowed it to scale operations as needed and adapt to market changes seamlessly.
- The ability to adjust production schedules and logistics plans quickly ensured that P&G could meet fluctuating demand and maintain service levels across different markets.

Collaboration and Integration
- P&G fostered close collaboration with its suppliers and logistics partners. Integrated supply chain management systems facilitated seamless communication and coordination, enhancing overall efficiency.

- The company's collaborative approach extended to internal teams as well. Cross-functional collaboration between manufacturing, logistics, and sales teams ensured that supply chain strategies were aligned with business objectives.

Continuous Improvement   With a focus on ensuring they do not fall behind, continuous improvement helped P&G become a clear market leader. Two things that stood out for me are:

- P&G's supply chain optimization was not a one-time initiative but an ongoing process. The company continuously monitored performance metrics, gathered feedback, and identified areas for improvement.
- By fostering a culture of continuous improvement, P&G ensured that its supply chain remained competitive and capable of meeting evolving market demands.

Results   Procter & Gamble's supply chain optimization journey from traditional operations to a highly efficient and automated system exemplifies the power of strategic execution. By leveraging advanced analytics, investing in automation technologies, and fostering a data-driven decision-making culture, P&G not only achieved significant cost savings but also improved product availability and customer satisfaction.

Organizations looking to emulate P&G's success should focus on developing clear supply chain strategies, investing in critical technologies, continuously expanding and improving their supply chain operations, and prioritizing collaboration and continuous improvement. By mastering these elements of execution, businesses can drive operational efficiency, achieve sustained growth, and secure their position as leaders in their respective industries.

Final Thoughts

Execution is a fundamental pillar of future readiness, enabling organizations to turn strategies into reality and achieve sustained success. By learning from the examples of industry leaders such as Apple, Amazon, Tesla, Microsoft, Nike, and P&G, organizations can develop robust execution strategies that drive innovation, efficiency, and growth.

To master execution, organizations should focus on clear vision and objectives, detailed planning, effective communication, resource allocation, performance monitoring, leadership and accountability, and continuous improvement. By embracing these principles, organizations can ensure they are well equipped to navigate the challenges of the future and seize opportunities for success.

The Top 50 Use Cases for Flawless Execution

Research these use cases to understand the role of execution in business.

1. Apple iPhone launch
2. Amazon Prime membership
3. Tesla Model 3 production
4. Microsoft Azure cloud services
5. Nike digital transformation
6. Procter & Gamble supply chain optimization
7. Netflix transition to streaming
8. Uber ride-sharing platform
9. Airbnb accommodation platform
10. Google search engine
11. SpaceX Falcon 9 reusability
12. Samsung Galaxy smartphone line
13. Toyota lean manufacturing (TPS, or Toyota Production System)
14. Intel microprocessor development
15. Starbucks global expansion
16. McDonald's franchise model
17. IBM Watson AI
18. Disney Plus streaming service
19. Salesforce CRM platform
20. Facebook ad platform
21. Alibaba singles' day sales
22. Zara fast fashion supply chain
23. Spotify music streaming
24. Zoom video conferencing
25. FedEx overnight delivery
26. General Electric six sigma implementation
27. Apple App Store
28. Southwest Airlines low-cost model

(continued)

(*continued*)

29. PayPal digital payments
30. LinkedIn professional networking
31. Adobe Creative Cloud
32. Siemens Industry 4.0 Solutions
33. Uber Eats food delivery
34. Slack workplace collaboration
35. Stripe online payments
36. Walmart supply chain management
37. Dell direct sales model
38. BMW electric vehicles (i Series)
39. Boeing 787 Dreamliner
40. Dropbox cloud storage
41. H&M fast fashion
42. Nestlé Nespresso
43. Unilever sustainable living plan
44. PepsiCo product diversification
45. JPMorgan Chase digital banking
46. Intel Inside branding campaign
47. Hyundai Genesis launch
48. Ford F-Series trucks
49. Mastercard contactless payments
50. Nike Air Jordan brand

These examples span various industries and highlight the importance of strategic execution in achieving success and maintaining a competitive edge.

Next Steps

Where do we go from here? Here is a skeleton of a plan to get started with making execution a top priority and to succeed.

Conduct a Strategic Review

- Assess your current execution processes and identify areas for improvement.
- Set clear, measurable goals and objectives aligned with your strategic vision.

Develop Comprehensive Execution Plans
- Create detailed plans that outline the steps, timelines, resources, and responsibilities required to achieve your objectives.
- Ensure flexibility in your plans to adapt to changing circumstances.

Implement Performance Monitoring Systems
- Establish robust performance tracking systems to monitor progress and identify bottlenecks.
- Use data-driven insights to make informed decisions and adjustments.

Foster a Culture of Accountability
- Encourage a culture where individuals take responsibility for their roles and deliverables.
- Implement regular review sessions and feedback mechanisms to maintain alignment and accountability.

Invest in Leadership Development
- Provide training and development programs for leaders to enhance their execution skills.
- Foster leadership qualities that inspire and motivate teams to achieve their best.

Leverage Technology and Tools
- Invest in project management and collaboration tools to streamline execution processes.
- Utilize data analytics and automation to enhance efficiency and decision-making.

Encourage Continuous Improvement
- Promote a culture of continuous improvement where feedback is valued and processes are regularly optimized.
- Encourage innovation and experimentation to find better ways of executing tasks.

Final Words

Execution is crucial for turning visions into reality, ensuring competitive advantage, and achieving sustainable growth. Effective execution involves translating plans into actionable steps, optimizing resources, and fostering accountability. By excelling in execution, organizations such as Apple,

Amazon, Tesla, and Microsoft have transformed their industries, demonstrating the importance of meticulous planning, strategic investments, and continuous improvement. Emphasizing execution ensures that innovative ideas lead to tangible success and long-term resilience.

To execute like there is no tomorrow, seek perfection in every task. However, remember that even the greatest plans can fail, and the most precisely executed strategies can go awry if not continuously monitored. Measure everything and chase the biggest goals relentlessly. As the final step of the future readiness framework, the execution pillar should not be viewed as the concluding phase but as a practice that must be consistently integrated throughout every phase of future readiness. This approach ensures sustained momentum, adaptability, and success in a rapidly changing business environment.

Resources

Books

- *Execution: The Discipline of Getting Things Done* by Larry Bossidy and Ram Charan
- *The Four Disciplines of Execution: Achieving Your Wildly Important Goals* by Chris McChesney, Sean Covey, and Jim Huling
- *Measure What Matters: How Google, Bono, and the Gates Foundation Rock the World with OKRs* by John Doerr
- *Good Strategy Bad Strategy: The Difference and Why It Matters* by Richard Rumelt

Take the Future Readiness Score at www.iankhan.com/frs or scan the QR Code

22

Future Readiness Metrics

If you cannot measure it, you cannot improve it.

—*Lord Kelvin*

IN THIS CHAPTER I have compiled some of the popular future readiness assessments and models currently available. While there may be other models being used and a combination of foresight tools together with future proofing methods being utilized, the following are what is currently available in the mainstream.

Future Readiness Score by Ian Khan

This book introduced you to the Future Readiness Score (FRS). Our methodology stems from a comprehensive framework designed to evaluate an organization's preparedness for future disruptions. The score incorporates multiple dimensions, such as technological adoption, innovation capacity, leadership vision, and organizational agility.

Visit the website at www.iankhan.com/frs.

Also make sure you take the FRS to know what your current state of future readiness is.

Future Readiness Indicator by International Institute for Management Development (IMD)

The IMD Future Readiness Indicator assesses companies on their preparedness to thrive in a rapidly changing business environment. It focuses on technology firms and uses a structured approach to rank their future readiness.

Visit the website at https://www.imd.org/future-readiness-indicator/home.

Future Readiness Index by Dubai Future Foundation

The Dubai Future Foundation's Future Readiness Index evaluates the readiness of governments and cities to embrace future opportunities and challenges. It aims to identify best practices and promote a forward-thinking mindset.

Visit the website at https://u.ae/en/about-the-uae/uae-in-the-future/dubai-future-readiness-index.

BCG's Future Preparedness Assessment

Created by Boston Consulting Group, this assessment measures how prepared companies are for future disruptions.

WEF Global Competitiveness Index

Developed by the World Economic Forum, this index measures the competitiveness of countries, which includes their readiness for future economic challenges.

KPMG Change Readiness Index

This index assesses how well countries and organizations can manage change, including technological advancements and economic shifts.

MIT Technology Review's Digital Evolution Index

Measures how countries are evolving digitally and their readiness for future digital opportunities.

Accenture's Future Systems Readiness Index

Evaluates organizations' systems and their readiness to leverage future technologies for business transformation.

Take the Future Readiness Score at www.iankhan.com/frs or scan the QR Code

23

Undisrupted Business Leader Profiles

THERE ARE COUNTLESS change makers who have disrupted the norm to shift our thinking, change how things are done, and to ultimately build a better world. This chapter is a collection of some of my favorite disruptors who created or continue to create shifts that we all should recognize. Their stories are nothing less than inspirational, powerful, and something to learn from about being undisrupted. This list is not a comprehensive listing of everyone who has been a disruptor or become the undisrupted but a curated selection of business achievers purely selected on the basis of how they have transformed the status quo.

Elon Musk

Elon Musk, born on June 28, 1971, in Pretoria, South Africa, stands as one of the quintessential disruptors of the twenty-first century. His story is not merely one of success but of reshaping entire industries and pushing humanity's limits. Musk's journey from a visionary entrepreneur to a global disruptor underscores his relentless pursuit of innovation, unwavering commitment to sustainability, and profound impact on the future of technology, transportation, and space exploration.

Musk's trajectory as a disruptor began in the digital payments arena with the creation of X.com in 1999, which later became PayPal. This venture revolutionized online commerce by providing a secure, user-friendly platform for digital transactions. PayPal's success, culminating in its acquisition by eBay for $1.5 billion in 2002, underscored Musk's ability to identify and exploit gaps in existing markets.

However, Musk's ambitions extended far beyond the digital landscape. He envisioned a future where humanity could combat climate change through sustainable energy and become a multi-planetary species. This vision laid the foundation for his ventures in electric vehicles (EVs), solar energy, and space exploration, through which he has profoundly disrupted traditional industries.

What Makes Musk a Disruptor?

Tesla, Inc.   Founded in 2003, Tesla has revolutionized the automotive industry by proving that EVs can be desirable, high-performing, and mainstream. Models such as the Roadster, Model S, and Model 3 have set new standards for electric mobility, accelerating the global transition away from fossil fuels.

SpaceX   Established in 2002, SpaceX's mission is to reduce space transportation costs and enable Mars colonization. Its achievements, including the first privately funded spacecraft to reach orbit and the International Space Station (ISS), reusable rockets, and the Starlink satellite constellation, have redefined space exploration and commercialization.

SolarCity and Tesla Energy   Musk's foray into renewable energy through SolarCity (now part of Tesla Energy) has disrupted the energy sector by mainstreaming solar power for residential and commercial use. Tesla's Solar Roof and Powerwall further integrate renewable energy generation and storage, underscoring Musk's vision for a sustainable energy ecosystem.

The Boring Company   Launched in 2016, The Boring Company seeks to alleviate urban traffic congestion through an innovative network of underground transportation tunnels. This venture challenges conventional urban transit solutions, offering a novel approach to city planning and mobility.

Neuralink   Founded in 2016, Neuralink aims to merge the human brain with artificial intelligence (AI) to enhance human cognition. Though still in its early stages, Neuralink represents Musk's belief in the potential of technology to augment human capabilities and address neurological conditions.

Jeff Bezos

Jeff Bezos, the founder of Amazon.com, Inc., stands as a quintessential example of a modern disruptor whose vision and innovative ventures have profoundly reshaped retail, technology, and even space exploration. Born on January 12, 1964, in Albuquerque, New Mexico, Bezos exhibited an early passion for technology and a keen interest in how things work, setting the stage for his future as a groundbreaking entrepreneur.

Bezos's journey into the realm of disruption began after his graduation from Princeton University with degrees in electrical engineering and computer science. His early career in finance and technology did not fully satisfy his entrepreneurial spirit, leading him to identify an untapped opportunity in the burgeoning World Wide Web. In 1994, he founded Amazon.com with the vision of creating the most customer-centric company in the world, initially focusing on books due to their wide selection and growing demand.

Key Achievements

- Amazon.com: Initially an online bookstore, Amazon quickly expanded to become the "everything store," offering an unprecedented variety of products. Its user-friendly platform, customer reviews, and innovative features such as 1-Click shopping revolutionized the e-commerce space, setting new standards for online retail.
- Amazon Prime: Launched in 2005, Amazon Prime redefined customer expectations for online shopping with its fast, free shipping. Prime evolved into a comprehensive subscription service offering streaming video, music, and more, further cementing Amazon's role in the lives of consumers.
- Amazon Web Services (AWS): Introduced in 2006, AWS became a cornerstone of the cloud computing revolution, providing businesses of all sizes with scalable, reliable, and cost-effective computing resources. AWS's impact extends beyond Amazon, powering start-ups to large enterprises, fundamentally changing the IT landscape.
- Kindle: The release of the Amazon Kindle in 2007 disrupted the publishing industry by popularizing e-books. The Kindle offered readers instant access to a vast library of content, transforming how people read and interact with books.
- Amazon Echo and Alexa: Launched in 2014, Amazon Echo and its voice-controlled intelligent personal assistant, Alexa, pioneered the market for smart speakers and home automation products, reshaping consumer technology interaction.

The Undisrupted Mindset

As Bezos stepped down as Amazon's CEO in 2021 to focus on Blue Origin and other ventures, his legacy continues to influence the company and the broader business and technological landscapes. His commitment to tackling climate change through the Bezos Earth Fund and exploring sustainable space colonization offers a glimpse into the future directions of his disruptive endeavors.

In conclusion, Jeff Bezos's profile as a disruptor is characterized by his ability to foresee and capitalize on emerging trends, creating solutions that address latent customer needs and drive technological innovation. His contributions to e-commerce, cloud computing, digital media, and space exploration have left an indelible mark on the world, reshaping industries and consumer behavior. As Bezos continues to explore new frontiers, his impact on the world and its future remains a testament to the power of visionary leadership and disruptive innovation.

Steve Jobs

Steve Jobs, cofounder of Apple Inc., is emblematic of what it means to be a disruptor. His legacy is not merely a collection of innovative products but a testament to how visionary leadership can redefine entire industries. He was born on February 24, 1955, in San Francisco, California. His journey from an adopted child interested in electronics to one of the most revered disruptors in technology demonstrates his unparalleled capacity to envision and actualize a future that others couldn't see.

Becoming a Disruptor

Jobs's disruptive path began with his early interest in electronics, fostered in a garage in Los Altos, California, where he and Steve Wozniak founded Apple Computer in 1976. Their first product, the Apple I, was a leap toward personal computing, but it was the introduction of the Apple II that truly revolutionized the industry, making personal computing accessible to the masses.

Key Achievements

- Macintosh: Launched in 1984, the Macintosh was the first commercially successful personal computer to feature a graphical user interface (GUI) and a mouse. This innovation made computing more intuitive and accessible, setting a new standard for user interaction.

- iPod: Introduced in 2001, the iPod transformed the music industry by offering an unprecedented way to store and listen to music. Its integration with iTunes, a platform for digital music distribution, disrupted traditional music sales, paving the way for digital content consumption.
- iPhone: The iPhone, unveiled in 2007, redefined the smartphone, combining a phone, an iPod, and an Internet communicator into one device. Its user-friendly design, multi-touch interface, and ecosystem of apps catalyzed the mobile revolution, changing how people communicate, work, and entertain themselves.
- iPad: Launched in 2010, the iPad created a new category between laptops and smartphones. Its portability, combined with a large touch screen, made it an ideal device for consuming and creating content, influencing various sectors from education to entertainment.
- Apple Stores: Jobs's vision extended to retail, where he reimagined the experience of buying technology. Apple Stores, with their minimalist design and focus on customer service, became temples of technology, enhancing brand loyalty and setting a benchmark for retailing.

Reed Hastings

Reed Hastings, cofounder and CEO of Netflix, is a paragon of disruption in the digital era. His journey from an entrepreneur with a vision to upend the traditional video rental business to leading a company that has redefined global entertainment is a testament to the transformative power of innovation and strategic foresight. He was born in 1960 in Boston, Massachusetts, and his path to becoming a disruptor was fueled by an early interest in technology and an entrepreneurial spirit honed through experiences that ranged from selling vacuum cleaners door-to-door to launching his first software company.

The Genesis of Disruption

Hastings's disruption of the entertainment industry began with a late fee on a rented movie, which sparked the idea for Netflix in 1997. Initially a DVD rental service that utilized the Internet for ordering and mail for delivery, Netflix introduced a novel subscription model with no late fees, challenging the established brick-and-mortar rental businesses. This customer-centric approach, focusing on convenience and value, laid the groundwork for what was to become a global entertainment phenomenon.

Key Achievements

- **Netflix's subscription model:** Revolutionizing the video rental industry, Netflix's subscription model allowed unlimited rentals for a flat monthly fee, eliminating the hassle of late fees and due dates. This innovation not only attracted millions of subscribers but also signaled the decline of traditional rental stores.
- **Streaming video on demand (SVOD):** In 2007, Netflix introduced streaming, allowing subscribers to watch movies and TV shows instantly on their computers. This pivot from DVD rentals to streaming content was a bold move that anticipated the shift toward digital consumption of entertainment, setting the stage for Netflix to become a leader in the streaming revolution.
- **Original content production:** With the launch of its first original series, *House of Cards*, in 2013, Netflix ventured into content production, transforming from a content distributor to a global entertainment powerhouse. This shift not only diversified Netflix's content offerings but also disrupted traditional TV production and distribution models, encouraging binge-watching and giving rise to a new era of television.
- **Global expansion:** Under Hastings's leadership, Netflix expanded its service worldwide, reaching over 190 countries by 2016. This global reach has allowed Netflix to cater to diverse audiences, creating and distributing content that transcends geographical and cultural boundaries, and solidifying its position as a global entertainment leader.

Sara Blakely

Sara Blakely, the founder of Spanx, Inc., epitomizes the essence of modern disruption through sheer determination, innovative thinking, and a keen understanding of consumer needs. She was born on February 27, 1971, in Clearwater, Florida. Blakely's journey from selling fax machines door-to-door to becoming the youngest self-made female billionaire showcases her disruptive influence in the fashion and business worlds.

From Idea to Disruption

Blakely's path to becoming a disruptor began with a simple yet profound need for comfortable, flattering undergarments that remained invisible under clothing. Frustrated by the lack of viable options, she invested her life savings of $5000 to develop a prototype that would later revolutionize women's shapewear. This was the inception of Spanx, a brand that would transform the lingerie industry with its innovative designs and inclusive approach to women's bodies.

Key Achievements

- **Spanx shapewear:** Blakely's first and most influential creation, the original footless pantyhose, solved a common problem for women, offering a smooth silhouette without the discomfort of traditional shapewear. Its success laid the foundation for Spanx, a brand that would extend to a wide range of products, including leggings, bras, and maternity wear, each designed with the aim of making women feel confident and comfortable.
- **Inclusive sizing and marketing:** Spanx distinguished itself by offering an inclusive range of sizes and utilizing real women in its marketing campaigns long before body positivity became a mainstream movement. This approach not only disrupted traditional beauty standards but also fostered a loyal customer base that felt seen and understood by the brand.
- **Direct-to-consumer model:** Blakely's decision to sell Spanx directly to consumers via online platforms and infomercials, bypassing the traditional retail model, was revolutionary at the time. This direct-to-consumer approach allowed for greater control over the brand's message, a deeper connection with customers, and the agility to respond quickly to market trends.

Mark Zuckerberg

Mark Zuckerberg, the cofounder and CEO of Facebook, Inc. (now Meta Platforms, Inc.), is a seminal figure in the digital age, embodying the quintessence of disruption. He was born on May 14, 1984, in White Plains, New York. Zuckerberg's journey from a Harvard dorm room to leading one of the most influential tech companies globally underscores his profound impact on how people connect, communicate, and perceive the digital world.

Pathway to Disruption

Zuckerberg's disruptive journey commenced at Harvard University in 2004 when he launched The Facebook, originally designed as a college networking site. This initiative, rooted in the simple idea of connecting people through an online platform, quickly transcended its initial scope, expanding beyond academic confines to become Facebook, a global social networking behemoth.

Key Achievements

- **Facebook:** Zuckerberg's flagship creation, Facebook, fundamentally altered human interaction, enabling billions worldwide to share their lives, ideas, and emotions online. It democratized information sharing and created a new paradigm for personal and professional networking.
- **News Feed:** Introduced in 2006, the News Feed was a pivotal innovation that aggregated friends' updates into a single stream, revolutionizing content consumption on the platform and setting a standard for social media engagement.
- **Facebook Messenger:** Launched in 2011, Messenger facilitated direct and group messaging within the Facebook ecosystem, further embedding the platform into users' daily communication habits and challenging traditional SMS and email.
- **Instagram and WhatsApp acquisitions:** Zuckerberg's strategic acquisitions of Instagram in 2012 and WhatsApp in 2014 significantly expanded Facebook's digital footprint, diversifying its offerings and cementing its status as a global communication titan. These platforms, under Facebook's stewardship, have introduced innovations in photo sharing, ephemeral content (Stories), and encrypted messaging, influencing social media trends and user interactions.

Satya Nadella

Satya Nadella, appointed as the CEO of Microsoft in 2014, represents a unique kind of disruptor—one who transformed an already giant tech company from the inside out. He was born on August 19, 1967, in Hyderabad, India. Nadella's journey to the pinnacle of the tech industry is a narrative of vision, resilience, and strategic innovation. His leadership has not only revitalized Microsoft but also repositioned it as a leader in cloud computing, AI, and enterprise technology, affecting millions of users and businesses worldwide.

Redefining Microsoft's Path

Before becoming CEO, Nadella held various roles within Microsoft, giving him deep insights into the company's operations, culture, and potential areas for growth. His tenure as the executive vice president of the Cloud and Enterprise group was particularly notable, during which he led the transformation of the company's cloud infrastructure and services. Nadella's ascendancy to CEO came at a critical juncture when Microsoft faced intense competition and a need to pivot from its traditional software-centric business model.

Key Achievements

- **Azure cloud platform:** Under Nadella's leadership, Microsoft aggressively expanded its Azure cloud platform, making it the backbone of the company's growth strategy. Azure's comprehensive offerings in cloud services and AI have positioned Microsoft as a formidable competitor to Amazon Web Services and have been crucial in the digital transformation of businesses around the globe.
- **Office 365 and Microsoft 365:** Nadella spearheaded the shift of Microsoft's flagship Office suite to a cloud-based subscription service, Office 365, thereby ensuring its relevance in a changing tech landscape. This move not only boosted revenue but also enhanced productivity and collaboration for users, further extending with the introduction of Microsoft 365, which integrated Office suite with AI and cloud services.
- **LinkedIn acquisition:** The acquisition of LinkedIn for $26.2 billion in 2016 marked a strategic expansion of Microsoft's portfolio into professional networking and social media. This move has created synergies between Microsoft's cloud, AI, and productivity tools and LinkedIn's vast professional network, offering unique opportunities for professional growth, recruitment, and business development.
- **Quantum computing initiative:** Nadella has been instrumental in positioning Microsoft at the forefront of quantum computing research. By investing in cutting-edge technology that promises to revolutionize computing power and efficiency, Nadella is leading Microsoft into a future where quantum computing could solve complex problems beyond the reach of current classical computers.
- **Artificial intelligence and ethics:** Under Nadella's direction, Microsoft has not only advanced in AI technology but has also been a vocal advocate for ethical principles in AI development and usage. This commitment is embodied in the establishment of Microsoft's AI and Ethics in Engineering and Research (AETHER) Committee, ensuring that AI technologies are developed and deployed responsibly.

Jack Ma

Jack Ma, the cofounder of Alibaba Group, is a disruptor whose influence extends far beyond the confines of e-commerce. He was born on September 10, 1964, in Hangzhou, Zhejiang, China. Ma's journey from an English teacher to one of the most prominent figures in the global digital economy exemplifies the transformative power of entrepreneurial vision and persistence in the face of adversity.

The Emergence of a Visionary

Jack Ma's foray into the digital world began in the early 1990s when he was introduced to the Internet during a trip to the United States. Recognizing the potential of the Internet to connect businesses worldwide, he launched China Pages, one of China's first online directories, in 1995. However, it was the founding of Alibaba in 1999, from his apartment in Hangzhou, that marked the inception of his disruptive legacy. Alibaba started as a B2B marketplace connecting Chinese manufacturers with overseas buyers, a novel concept that would revolutionize global trade.

Key Achievements

- **Alibaba.com:** Ma's initial platform laid the groundwork for what would become a global e-commerce titan. Alibaba.com democratized access to global markets for small and medium-sized enterprises (SMEs) in China, breaking down barriers that once favored large corporations.
- **Taobao and Tmall:** In response to the entry of eBay into China, Ma launched Taobao, a consumer-to-consumer (C2C) platform, in 2003. Its success, bolstered by a focus on user experience and free listings, led to the creation of Tmall, a business-to-consumer (B2C) platform catering to higher-end brands. Together, Taobao and Tmall redefined retail in China, fostering an ecosystem that supports a wide range of businesses from start-ups to global brands.
- **Alipay:** Recognizing the lack of trust in online transactions and the underdeveloped banking infrastructure in China, Ma introduced Alipay in 2004. This digital payment platform facilitated secure online transactions, accelerating the adoption of e-commerce by instilling trust among consumers and merchants alike. Alipay's success has since positioned it as a cornerstone of the digital economy in China and beyond.

- **Singles' Day:** In 2009, Alibaba transformed Singles' Day, a celebration for single people in China, into the world's largest online shopping event. The annual November 11 sale has shattered sales records year after year, highlighting the immense scale of China's e-commerce market and Ma's genius in marketing and customer engagement.

Jensen Huang

Jensen Huang, cofounder and CEO of NVIDIA Corporation, is a prime example of a modern disruptor whose innovative vision and leadership have significantly shaped the landscape of computing, artificial intelligence, and graphics technology. He was born on February 17, 1963, in Taipei, Taiwan. Huang's journey from an immigrant student to a pioneering technologist illustrates the transformative power of perseverance, foresight, and technical expertise.

The Path to Disruption

Huang's disruptive path began with his education in the United States, where he earned a bachelor's degree in electrical engineering from Oregon State University and a master's degree from Stanford University. His early career included roles at LSI Logic and Advanced Micro Devices (AMD), where he honed his skills in semiconductor design and technology.

In 1993, recognizing the potential for graphics processing units (GPUs) to revolutionize computing beyond just gaming, Huang cofounded NVIDIA. Under his leadership, NVIDIA has evolved from a graphics card manufacturer to a global leader in AI computing, influencing various industries from entertainment to autonomous driving.

Key Achievements

- **GeForce GPUs:** NVIDIA's GeForce line of GPUs, introduced in 1999, set new standards for graphics performance in gaming and professional applications. The GeForce series became synonymous with high-quality, immersive graphics, driving advancements in visual computing.
- **CUDA (Compute Unified Device Architecture):** Launched in 2006, CUDA transformed GPUs into powerful parallel processors, enabling researchers and developers to leverage the immense computing power of NVIDIA GPUs for complex scientific, engineering, and AI applications. This innovation opened new possibilities in fields such as deep learning, data analytics, and scientific simulations.

- **NVIDIA DRIVE:** NVIDIA's DRIVE platform is a comprehensive suite of hardware and software solutions for autonomous vehicles. By integrating AI and high-performance computing, NVIDIA DRIVE aims to accelerate the development and deployment of self-driving cars, reshaping the future of transportation.
- **DGX systems:** NVIDIA DGX systems, designed for AI research and enterprise applications, provide unprecedented computational power for deep learning and other forms of AI development. These systems have become essential tools for organizations seeking to harness the potential of AI in various domains, from health care to finance.
- **NVIDIA Omniverse:** Introduced in 2020, Omniverse is a platform for real-time collaboration and simulation, enabling creators, designers, and engineers to work together seamlessly in a shared virtual environment. Omniverse leverages NVIDIA's advancements in AI, rendering, and simulation to facilitate the creation of complex 3D content and digital twins.

Mary Barra

Mary Barra, born on December 24, 1961, in Waterford, Michigan, is a trailblazer in the automotive industry and a paragon of transformative leadership. As the first female CEO of General Motors (GM), Barra has not only shattered the glass ceiling in a traditionally male-dominated industry but has also driven significant innovation and strategic shifts within one of the world's largest and most influential automakers.

Path to Leadership

Barra's journey to the top of GM is a testament to her deep-rooted connection to the company and her extensive expertise. She began her career with GM in 1980 as a co-op student, inspecting fender panels at a Pontiac plant to help pay for her college tuition at General Motors Institute (now Kettering University). After earning her bachelor's degree in electrical engineering, she went on to receive an MBA from Stanford Graduate School of Business, which was sponsored by GM.

Over the years, Barra held numerous roles within the company, from managing plants to leading global product development, purchasing, and supply chain operations. Her diverse experiences and deep understanding of GM's operations and culture positioned her uniquely for the role of CEO, which she assumed in January 2014.

Key Achievements

As CEO, Mary Barra has been instrumental in steering GM through a period of profound change and disruption. Her leadership has focused on several key areas:

- **Electric vehicles (EVs):** Under Barra's guidance, GM has committed to an ambitious vision of an all-electric future. She has overseen the launch of the Chevrolet Bolt, one of the first affordable long-range electric vehicles, and announced plans to release 30 new electric vehicles globally by 2025. Barra's strategic focus on EVs aims to position GM as a leader in the electric mobility revolution, reducing the company's carbon footprint and addressing climate change.

- **Autonomous driving technology:** Barra has championed GM's advancements in autonomous driving through its subsidiary, Cruise. By acquiring and investing in Cruise, GM is at the forefront of developing self-driving technology, with the goal of creating safer, more efficient transportation solutions. The company's commitment to autonomous vehicles is evident in its ongoing testing and planned commercial deployment of self-driving cars.

- **Innovation and R&D:** Barra has significantly increased GM's investment in research and development, focusing on cutting-edge technologies such as battery development, connectivity, and advanced driver-assistance systems (ADAS). These investments are critical to maintaining GM's competitive edge and ensuring the company's future growth and sustainability.

- **Corporate Culture and Leadership:** Barra has also worked to transform GM's corporate culture, emphasizing accountability, transparency, and a customer-centric approach. She has led efforts to streamline operations, reduce bureaucracy, and foster a more agile and innovative environment within the company. Her leadership style, characterized by openness and a focus on teamwork, has earned her respect and admiration both within GM and across the industry.

- **Environmental and Social Responsibility:** Recognizing the importance of corporate social responsibility, Barra has committed GM to sustainability goals, including a pledge to achieve carbon neutrality by 2040. She has also been an advocate for diversity and inclusion, promoting initiatives to ensure that GM's workforce reflects the diversity of its customer base.

Marie Curie

Marie Curie was a pioneering physicist and chemist whose groundbreaking research on radioactivity revolutionized science and medicine. Curie was born on November 7, 1867, in Warsaw, Poland. Her relentless pursuit of knowledge and remarkable achievements have left an indelible mark on the scientific community.

Marie Curie, born Maria Sklodowska, showed an early aptitude for science. Despite facing significant obstacles due to her gender and limited access to education in Poland, she excelled academically and eventually moved to Paris to continue her studies at the University of Paris (Sorbonne). There, she earned degrees in physics and mathematics, setting the stage for her future scientific endeavors.

Key Achievements

Marie Curie's work spanned a number of achievements. Some of the most profound ones are highlighted as follows:

- **Radioactivity:** Curie's most notable contribution to science was her extensive research on radioactivity, a term she coined. Working alongside her husband, Pierre Curie, she conducted experiments that led to the discovery of two new elements, polonium (named after her native Poland) and radium. Their meticulous work on isolating radioactive isotopes laid the foundation for understanding atomic structure and the behavior of radioactive materials.
- **Nobel Prizes:** Marie Curie's achievements were recognized with the Nobel Prize in Physics in 1903, shared with Pierre Curie and Henri Becquerel, for their collective work on radioactivity. In 1911, she was awarded the Nobel Prize in Chemistry for her discovery of radium and polonium and her investigation of their properties. Curie remains the only person to have won Nobel Prizes in two different scientific fields.
- **X-ray machines:** During World War I, Curie applied her scientific expertise to practical use by developing mobile X-ray units, known as "Little Curies," to assist battlefield surgeons. These units provided life-saving diagnostics for wounded soldiers and marked a significant advancement in medical technology. Her efforts in this area earned her the recognition and gratitude of many.

Marie Curie's work has had a profound and lasting impact on various scientific fields and medical practices:

- Her research on radioactivity paved the way for the development of radiation therapy, a crucial treatment for cancer and other diseases. The discovery of radium, in particular, revolutionized the treatment of tumors and contributed significantly to the field of oncology.
- Curie's work provided critical insights into the nature of atoms and the behavior of radioactive elements, influencing the development of nuclear physics and chemistry. Her pioneering research has inspired countless scientists and led to further discoveries in atomic theory and quantum mechanics.
- As the first woman to win a Nobel Prize and the first female professor at the University of Paris, Curie broke numerous barriers for women in science. Her perseverance, intellectual rigor, and groundbreaking achievements continue to inspire and empower generations of female scientists worldwide.

Take the Future Readiness Score at www.iankhan.com/frs or scan the QR Code

Notes

Chapter 1

1. Harari, Yuval N. *Sapiens: A Brief History of Humankind.* New York: Harper, 2015.
2. Diamond, Jared M. *Guns, Germs, and Steel: The Fates of Human Societies.* New York: Norton, 2005.
3. Hawking, Stephen. "We are all now connected by the Internet, like neurons in a giant brain," as quoted in Socratic Method, accessed July 15, 2024, Socratic Method (The Socratic Method).

Chapter 2

1. Aslan-Seyhan, Irem. "The Early History of the Pulleys and Crany Systems." *Foundations of Science* 29(12).
2. "Wheel." *Britannica.* https://www.britannica.com/technology/wheel.

Chapter 4

1. Gates, Bill. *The Road Ahead.* New York:Viking Penguin, 1995.
2. Ng, Andrew. "Why AI Is the New Electricity." Stanford Graduate School of Business.https://www.gsb.stanford.edu/insights/andrew-ng-why-ai-new-electricity.
3. Ledford, Heidi, and Ewen Callaway. "Pioneers of Revolutionary CRISPR Gene Editing Win Chemistry Nobel." Nature News, October 7, 2020.https://www.nature.com/articles/d41586-020-02765-9.

4. Topol, Eric. "Redefining the Future of Healthcare." Frontiers, June 12, 2024. https://forum.frontiersin.org/2024-eric-topol.
5. Coelho, Paulo. *The Alchemist*. London, England: Thorsons, 1995.

Chapter 5

1. Jobs, Steve. Stanford commencement speech, June 2005.
2. Schwab, Klaus. *The Fourth Industrial Revolution*. Crown Currency, 2016.
3. Nadella, Satya. Email to employees on first day as CEO. https://news.microsoft.com/2014/02/04/satya-nadella-email-to-employees-on-first-day-as-ceo.
4. Wolcott, Robert C., and Kaihan Krippendorff. *Proximity: How Coming Breakthroughs in Just-in-Time Transform Business, Society, and Daily Life*. New York: Columbia Business School Publishing, 2024.

Chapter 6

1. Gallo, Carmine. *The Innovation Secrets of Steve Jobs: Insanely Different Principles for Breakthrough Success*. New York: McGraw-Hill, 2010.
2. Gates, Bill. "Remarks of Bill Gates, Harvard Commencement 2007." *Harvard Gazette*, June 7, 2007. https://news.harvard.edu/gates-commencement-2007.
3. Williamson, John N. *The Leader-Manager*. New York: John Wiley and Sons, 1986.
4. Watson, James D. Foreword to *Discovering the Brain*, by Sandra Ackerman, iii. Washington, DC: National Academies Press, 1992.
5. Dijkstra, Edsger W. "The Humble Programmer." Communications of the ACM 15, no. 10 (1972): 859–866.
6. Eisenhower, Dwight D. "In preparing for battle, I have always found that plans are useless, but planning is indispensable." In *Six Crises*, Richard Nixon, 253. New York: Doubleday, 1962. Also reported in *The New York Times*, November 15, 1957.

Chapter 7

1. Gulli, Chiara, Bernd Heid, Jesse Noffsinger, Maurits Waardenburg, and Markus Wilthaner. "Global Energy Perspective 2023: Hydrogen Outlook." McKinsey & Company, Oil & Gas.https://www.mckinsey.com/industries/oil-and-gas/our-insights/global-energy-perspective-2023-hydrogen-outlook.

Chapter 9

1. Branson, Richard. "Space is Virgin territory. We are going to democratize space travel so that it's affordable and open to all." Quoted in Virgin Galactic, "Our Mission," accessed July 11, 2024. https://www.virgingalactic.com/our-mission.

2. Musk, Elon, quoted in Chris Anderson, "Elon Musk's Vision for Space Travel," Yahoo News, accessed July 12, 2024, https://uk.news.yahoo.com/elon-musk-reveals-what-life-on-mars-will-be-like-for-first-settlers-145000047.html.

3. Bezos, Jeff. Quoted in "Jeff Bezos: 'We Have to Go to Space to Save Earth,'" Dom Galeon. Futurism. Updated November 6, 2017. https://futurism.com/jeff-bezos-space-save-earth.

4. Clark, Stephen, "SpaceX Starship Lands for the First Time after Test Launch." *Spaceflight Now*, May 5, 2021.

5. Spair, Rick, "The New Space Race: How Private Companies Are Leading the Charge to the Stars." *Rick Spair DX*, April 15, 2024.

6. Tsiolkovsky, Konstantin. "The earth is the cradle of humanity, but mankind cannot stay in the cradle forever." In Robert Godwin, *The Rocket and the Reich: Peenemünde and the Coming of the Ballistic Missile Era*. Burlington: Apogee Books, 1999.

7. "The Human Brain in Space: Euphoria and the 'Overview Effect' Experienced by Astronauts." *Universe Today*.

8. Armstrong, Neil, quoted in remarks at the Apollo 11 30th Anniversary Press Conference, Kennedy Space Center, July 16, 1999.

9. In *Cosmos*, 1980. Quoted in Robert Lea, "Are We Really Made of 'Star Stuff?'" http://Space.com. Accessed July 11, 2024. www.space.com.

Chapter 10

1. Carlson, Kara. "At SXSW, Mark Zuckerberg Says Metaverse Is 'Holy Grail' of Social Experience." *Austin American Statesman*, March 16, 2022. https://www.statesman.com/story/business/2022/03/16/sxsw-facebooks-mark-zuckerberg-says-metaverse-future-internet/7051230001.

2. Ashton, Kevin. "Kevin Ashton Describes 'the Internet of Things.'" *Smithsonian Magazine*, January 2015. https://www.smithsonianmag.com/innovation/kevin-ashton-describes-the-internet-of-things-180953749.

3. "Aircraft Maintenance Planing." GE Aerospace. https://www.geaerospace.com/systems/saas/maintenance-insight.

4. Pichai, Sundar. "Connectivity Is a Human Right." Interview by Archana Sohmshetty. *Stanford Graduate School of Business*, February 11, 2022. https://www.gsb.stanford.edu/alumni/lifelong-learning/view-from-the-top/sundar-pichai.

Chapter 11

1. United Nations, Department of Economic and Social Affairs, Population Division, *World Urbanization Prospects: The 2018 Revision, Highlights*. New York: United Nations, 2018. https://population.un.org/wup/Publications/Files/WUP2018-Highlights.pdf.

2. "Barcelona Smart City - About Smart Cities." About Smart Cities. Accessed July 12, 2024. https://www.aboutsmartcities.com/barcelona-smart-city.

Chapter 12

1. Galeon, Dom. "Bill Gates: 'We Have to Go to Space to Save Earth.'" *Technology Review*, February 14, 2021. https://www.technologyreview.com/2021/02/14/1018296/bill-gates-climate-change-beef-trees-microsoft.

Chapter 13

1. "Perspectives from the Global Entertainment & Media Outlook 2024–2028: Seizing Growth Opportunities in a Dynamic Ecosystem." https://www.pwc.com/gx/en/industries/tmt/media/outlook/insights-and-perspectives.html.
2. Caldwell, J.H. "A Moving Target: Refocusing Risk and Resiliency amidst Continued Uncertainty." Deloitte Insights, February 1, 2021. https://www2.deloitte.com/us/en/insights/industry/financial-services/global-risk-management-survey-financial-services.html.
3. "The Data-Driven Enterprise of 2025." McKinsey Digital, January 2022. https://mck.co/4cVEK7E.
4. Goasduff, Laurence. "Gartner Survey Finds 72% of Data & Analytics Leaders Are Leading or Heavily Involved in Digital Transformation Initiatives." Gartner Press Release, May 5, 2021. https://www.gartner.com/en/newsroom/press-releases/2021-05-05-gartner-finds-72-percent-of-data-and-analytics-leaders-are-leading-or-heavily-involved-in-digital-transformation-initiatives.
5. "Worldwide Digital Transformation Spending Forecast to Continue Its Double-Digit Growth Trajectory, According to IDC Spending Guide." IDC Research, November 1, 2023. https://www.idc.com/getdoc.jsp?containerId=prUS51352323.

Chapter 14

1. "Losing from Day One: Why Even Successful Transformations Fall Short." McKinsey & Company, December 7, 2021. https://www.mckinsey.com/capabilities/people-and-organizational-performance/our-insights/successful-transformations/.
2. Reichheld, Fred, Darci Darnell, and Maureen Burns. "Net Promoter 3.0: A Better System for Understanding the Real Value of Happy Customers." *Harvard Business Review*, November-December 2021. https://hbr.org/2021/11/net-promoter-3-0.
3. Choney, Suzanne. "Satya Nadella: Why Businesses Should Embrace Digital Transformation, Not Only to Survive – But Also to Thrive." Microsoft News Center Staff. https://news.microsoft.com/features/satya-nadella-why-businesses-should-embrace-digital-transformation-not-only-to-survive-but-also-to-thrive.
4. Delfino, Devon, and Dan Shepard. "Percentage of Businesses That Fail—and How to Boost Chances of Success." Lendingtree, April 8, 2024. https://www.lendingtree.com/business/small/failure-rate/.

Chapter 15

1. Margolis, Sheila. "Definitions of Work Engagement by Academics." *Engage. Retain. Prosper*, April 9, 2016. https://engageretainprosper.com/definitions-of-engagement-at-work-by-academics.
2. Gallup. "State of the American Workplace." Gallup, accessed July 15, 2024. https://www.gallup.com/workplace/236927/state-american-workplace-report-2017.aspx.
3. Forbes Communications Council. "Here's Why Customer Retention Is So Important for ROI, Customer Loyalty, and Growth." Forbes. Accessed July 15, 2024. https://www.forbes.com/sites/forbescommunicationscouncil/2023/09/06/heres-why-customer-retention-is-so-important-for-roi-customer-loyalty-and-growth.
4. Matchable. "Corporate Volunteering Statistics (+ What They Mean for the Future of Volunteering)." Accessed July 17, 2024. https://www.wearematchable.com/blog/corporate-volunteering-statistics.
5. Business Insider. "The Truth About Google's Famous '20% Time' Policy." Accessed July 17, 2024. https://www.businessinsider.in/The-truth-about-Googles-famous-20-time-policy/articleshow/46962732.cms.
6. Sparrow Connected. "Transform Your Retention Rates with Strategic Communication." Accessed July 17, 2024. https://www.sparrowconnected.com/blog/transform-your-retention-rates-with-strategic-communication.
7. Buckingham, Marcus, and Ashley Goodall. "Reinventing Performance Management." *Harvard Business Review*, April 2015. https://hbr.org/2015/04/reinventing-performance-management.
8. Eventbrite. "Millennials: Fueling the Experience Economy." *Eventbrite Blog*, June 16, 2017. Accessed July 17, 2024. https://www.eventbrite.com/blog/academy/millennials-fueling-experience-economy.

Chapter 17

1. "Safe Enough to Try: An Interview with Zappos CEO Tony Hsieh." McKinsey & Company, accessed July 12, 2024. https://www.mckinsey.com/business-functions/strategy-and-corporate-finance/our-insights/safe-enough-to-try-an-interview-with-zappos-ceo-tony-hsieh.
2. American Psychological Association. "Work and Well-Being Survey," APA, accessed July 12, 2024. https://www.apa.org/news/press/releases/2012/03/well-being.
3. "Workplace Wellness: Johnson & Johnson's Healthiest Employees Goal," Johnson & Johnson, accessed July 12, 2024. https://www.jnj.com/workplace-wellness-johnson-johnsons-healthiest-employees-goal.
4. Rocío Lorenzo et al. "How Diverse Leadership Teams Boost Innovation," Boston Consulting Group, January 23, 2018. Accessed July 12, 2024. https://www.bcg.com/publications/2018/how-diverse-leadership-teams-boost-innovation.

Chapter 19

1. i4cp, Institute for Corporate Productivity. https://www.i4cp.com.
2. Kane, Gerald C., Doug Palmer, Anh Nguyen Phillips, David Kiron, and Natasha Buckley. "Accelerating Digital Innovation Inside and Out." Deloitte Insights, June 4, 2019. https://www2.deloitte.com/us/en/insights/focus/digital-maturity/digital-innovation-ecosystems-organizational-agility.html.
3. "The Bottled Frappuccino." Starbucks. https://archive.starbucks.com/record/the-bottled-frappuccino.
4. "Samsung Electronics Announces New Advanced Semiconductor Fab Site in Taylor, Texas." Samsung Local News, November 23, 2021. https://semiconductor.samsung.com/us/sas/local-news/samsung-electronics-announces-new-advanced-semiconductor-fab-site-in-taylor-texas.
5. Brandenburger, Adam, and Barry Nalebuff. "The Rules of Co-opetition." Harvard Business Review, January-February 2021. https://hbr.org/2021/01/the-rules-of-co-opetition.
6. "Enhance the Value of Your Supplier Relationships." Supply Chain Management Review, March-April 2019. https://www.scmr.com/article/enhance_the_value_of_your_supplier_relationships.
7. "PwC Pulse Survey: Executive Views on Business in 2022." PwC. https://www.pwc.com/us/en/library/pulse-survey/executive-views-2022.html.
8. "How Real-Time Collaboration Software Can Increase Productivity by 30%." Team at Slack, September 2, 2021. https://slack.com/blog/collaboration/increase-productivity-by-30.
9. "Gartner Survey Reveals a 44% Rise in Workers' Use of Collaboration Tools Since 2019." Garner Press Release, August 25, 2021. https://www.gartner.com/en/newsroom/press-releases/2021-08-23-gartner-survey-reveals-44-percent-rise-in-workers-use-of-collaboration-tools-since-2019.
10. Tavares, Frank. "Quantum Supremacy Achieved by NASA and Google." SciTechDaily, October 23, 2019. https://scitechdaily.com/quantum-supremacy-achieved-by-nasa-and-google.
11. "Argo AI and Ford to Launch Self-Driving Vehicles on Lyft Network by End of 2021." Ford Newsroom, July 21, 2021. https://media.ford.com/content/fordmedia/fna/us/en/news/2021/07/21/argo-ai-ford-lyft-network.html.

Chapter 20

1. Kay, Alan. "The Best Way to Predict the Future Is to Invent It." Stanford Engineering 1, no. 1 (Fall 1982).

Acknowledgments

I owe a lot of people. Thank you to my commissioning editor at Wiley Publishing, Victoria Savanh, who believed in the Future Readiness Score and its potential. Thanks also to everyone on the Wiley team who has made the project possible including Trinity Crompton, Sangeetha Suresh, Purvi Patel, and Kim Wimpsett.

Thanks to my speaker bureau partners, whose support is relentless in helping me reach audiences worldwide.

Aurum Bureau – Gabriela

Big Speak – Amy Eddy

Crown Speakers – Koby Fleck

Dynamic Speakers – Jay Klahn

Leading Authorities – Mike Penny

Speaking.com – Mike Frick

Thinking Heads – Paula Bautista and Ben Myatt

Washington Speaking Bureau – Monica, James, Kristine

Thanks to participants in my episodic series *The Futurist* for inspiring me to think big, some of whom include

AstonMartin Formula 1, Bluelake Minerals, BNP Paribas 3 Step IT, CGI, Dassault Systems, Einride, Freuds Communication, Kayrros, KPMG, London Business School, Lord Adair Turner, Massachusetts Institute of Technology, Mirros, MIT, Harvard, MSC Cruises, NetApp, North Carolina SweetPotato Commission, Papercup, Phinia, Quantexa, Red Sea Global, DSM Firmenich, Sapien, BitTensor, and others.

About the Author

IAN KHAN IS a theoretical futurist and future readiness researcher specializing in emerging technologies. His expertise spans digital transformation, algorithms, robotics, automation, generative AI, blockchain, cybersecurity, and sustainability.

Ian is the creator of the Future Readiness Score (FRS), a metric he developed after extensive observations across various industries. Recognizing the lack of a straightforward metric for assessing future readiness, Ian devised the FRS as a comprehensive framework. This tool helps organizations understand the state of disruption in their environment and identify critical areas that need attention to achieve a future-ready and "undisruptable" status.

A popular keynote speaker on emerging technologies, Ian addresses the intersection of technology, leadership, and society. His widely read books include *Metaverse For Dummies*, *The Quick Guide to Prompt Engineering*, and now *Undisrupted*.

Ian's passion for visual storytelling is evident in his production of several acclaimed business documentaries, available on Prime Video, Emirates Airlines, and leading streaming platforms. These include *Blockchain City*, *GX Now*, *The Future of Work*, and *The Bitcoin Dilemma*. He is also the creative director and host of *The Futurist*, an episodic series on Prime Video that delves into the impact of emerging technologies on business and the future.

Ian advises some of the world's top brands, Fortune 1000 companies, and governments on future readiness, guiding them to step confidently into a fully prepared future. His keynote engagements include prestigious clients such as McAfee, Nestle, BMO Bank of Montreal, Tigo, Intel, Swift, BOMA, University of Rochester, Microsoft, HID, NASSCOM, ServiceNow, and leading industry groups and associations. Ian is also a three-time TEDx speaker.

Learn more about Ian's work on his website at www.iankhan.com

Engage with Ian Khan

Whether you have read this book end to end or just gone through some of its chapters, I hope you have found some useful ideas that can help you become future ready.

Engage with me for leadership workshops, keynote speeches, breakouts, and other formats to change how you see future readiness.

Please send business inquiries to

contact@iankhan.com

or visit

www.Iankhan.com

Index